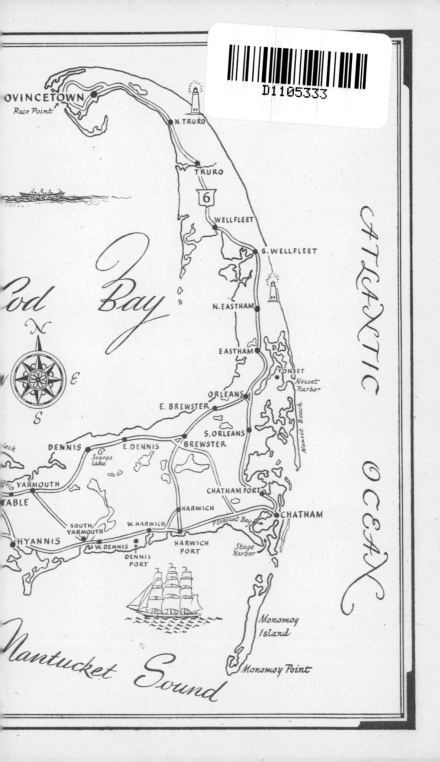

BLUE-WATER MEN

and

OTHER CAPE CODDERS

THE MACMILLAN COMPANY
NEW YORK · BOSTON · CHICAGO · DALLAS
ATLANTA · SAN FRANCISCO

MACMILLAN AND CO., Limited
LONDON · BOMBAY · CALCUTTA · MADRAS
MELBOURNE

THE MACMILLAN COMPANY
OF CANADA, Limited
TORONTO

Folk of Cape

CONGREGATIONAL CHURCH, WELLFLEET

BLUE-WATER MEN

and Other Cape Codders

by
Katharine Crosby

THE MACMILLAN COMPANY · NEW YORK

1946

PRINTED IN THE UNITED STATES OF AMERICA
BY J. J. LITTLE & IVES COMPANY, NEW YORK

TO BRUCE

CONTENTS

ILLUSTRATIONS

BLUE-WATER MEN
and
OTHER CAPE CODDERS

1. *To Begin with—*

THIS MIGHT possibly—just possibly—be the last book written about Cape Cod by a contemporary. That is, about the Cape in its prime, those seventy-odd years between the clipper ships and the automobiles which were its golden age of romance and adventure.

During the mid-twenties, when this era was nearing its end, I had a chance to explore the less well known parts of the Cape and to make friends with such of her people as God let me. For good and sufficient reasons your true Cape man or woman is not given to easy friendliness with off-Capers. But my affection for the place, along with a Cape name, made it possible to dig up stories and folklore which otherwise might not have got into print. The first Crosby of our line was a lay preacher in Eastham, where he begat thirteen children; this was back around 1640, and so I am ninth or tenth cousin to practically the entire native population.

I saw all the old blue-water men, the Great Captains of sail who had carried the flag across the blue waters of the Gulf Stream to the limits of the known world—saw them and got their stories and their pictures and the pictures of their ships. Only half a dozen of the hundreds who had gone from the Cape were left. The home-staying men and women of their day had their stories, too, and some of them were still to be found. But by now all the captains and many of the others will have sailed away over the horizon, taking their stories with them.

With the aid of my rusty shorthand I got pretty much what they said the way they said it. At the time I was helping Lyman Armes edit the *Cape Cod Magazine,* and most of the stories were published there; some appeared in the *Boston Transcript,* others I am only now getting round to writing. I am especially grateful to Arthur A. Williams of Holliston, Massachusetts, for his permission to use material from the *Cape Cod Magazine,* which he published.

Some places, like some people, are magnets for adventure. Cape Cod is one. About anything that could happen anywhere has happened here. There is a story of one sort or another for every grain of yellow sand on the sandy old paw. Take a place like this, all set for excitement, and give it a zestful, seagoing population, and you get a lively combination. Among its activities have been piracy, witchcraft, moon-cussing, bootlegging, bundling, fighting, and pioneering; and among those taking part have been Eskimos—though they moved away some time ago—Indians, Vikings, Pilgrims, Quakers, Hessians, and Portuguese, not to mention witches, mermaids, artists, and realtors. It was always the native of Pilgrim stock, however, who had most of the excitement, or who made it if it did not come naturally.

There is nothing formal about the Cape, and there will be no formality in this record of my explorations. Cape Cod's history has been written in other books. This is mostly the first-hand stuff I picked up during the year I drove some five thousand miles over its smooth highways and its sandy back roads in my little Ford roadster, Lizy

Jane—about the people, present and past, and their houses and their ships and their way of life.

We will ramble along from village to village and almost from house to house and poke off down side roads and probably get lost on most of them. In some of the older houses we will go up attic to see how they were put together, peek into their cupboards at their old pewter and glass, and maybe stop in the kitchen for a dish of huckleberry grunt or quahaug chowder or the kind of succotash the Pilgrim mothers really made. But most of the time we will just visit with the family.

Whatever I got of the humor, the sprawl, the doggone spunk of my Cape kinsfolk is here set down. If you sense some nostalgia between the lines it is because this is being written just around the corner from that other land's end, Cape Flattery—and it is a long way off in more than miles.

Whatever superficial changes the war and modernity may make in their living pattern, Cape Codders will never be like other people. They will always be able to get the point of view of the man—husband, he was, of one of the village librarians—who couldn't tell an autoful of tourists how to get to Chatham. It was not far—maybe fifteen or twenty miles—but he had never been there.

"You certainly haven't been round much," the driver said tartly.

"I've been in Singapore and Hong Kong and Archangel, places like that," the villager replied, "and four times across the continent. But," he explained, "I never had any business to Chat-ham."

They live along contentedly in their old gray-shingled farmhouses where maybe half a dozen generations of their family lived before them, and they make a comfortable living from their sandy acres and fishing and/or the summer visitors with which the Lord has blessed them in their later years. The year I was there they were getting a special kick out of life because a cloud of realtors had come down from Boston and settled over the whole Cape from the Canal to Provincetown. One came to feel a little sorry for the eager young realtors, who were dickering with men who had traded the pants off their customers all over the known world before they were born.

They did get a few tracts—at a price—and some of them put up incredible signs, like Rosie Grove, and Pink Geranium Park, and others promoted some swanky summer colonies; and the old *Cape Cod Magazine* was revived for the duration, which is where I came in. The boom petered out without making many major changes, and the "natives" had a lot of fun and made a little money— possibly more than anyone else.

Let's give the Cape a once-over before getting down to details.

Cape Cod starts from the Canal.

Don't let anyone from Plymouth or Marion or Wareham tell you he is from the Cape, because he is not. The Cape begins at the Canal and is hinged to the mainland by two bridges. You have to cross water to get to it. From each bridge a road goes to Provincetown, at the tip of the Cape. By the inside road, from Sandwich, the distance is about sixty-five miles; by the outside road, from Buzzards Bay, it is ninety-five.

The Cape is shaped like a right arm with a clenched fist. Falmouth is the pointed shoulder-blade, Chatham the sharp elbow, and Provincetown the hand. It is a county in itself—Barnstable County, pronounced "Bahnst'ble." This county is divided, New England style, into townships, usually spoken of as towns. There are fifteen of these towns, each with its own very individual character, its own government, its town meetings, and its ructions generally. Town government was born in Provincetown harbor and has been raised to a fine art in the Fifteen Towns.

So much for the political set-up. By nature all Cod is divided into two parts—Upper Cape from the Canal to the elbow, Lower Cape from Orleans on down to Provincetown. Wherever you may be, down-Cape is toward the tip and up-Cape is toward the Canal.

Most of the show places and the summer resorts are on the Upper Cape. Running along the north shore the King's Highway picks up the older and more beautiful villages like beads on a string. They have streets shaded with wineglass elms, and the larger and more dignified old houses. On the south shore the villages are more likely to be given over to summer visitors, because the water down there is warmer than along the north shore—and summer folk are notoriously tender.

The Lower Cape is different—oh, very different. Not so long ago it was an island, cut off at the elbow by Jeremiah's Gutter. It did not last long—one storm dug the gutter and the next one filled it up—but it still seems like an island, remote from up-Cape ways and remoter still in looks. It is wild and very wind-swept. Much of it is rolling moors with spreads of gorse; some of it is tumbled dunes with scrub pine and beach plum and coarse grass. Some of it is farming land, flat as Kansas.

All up its stormy Back Side runs thirty miles of pale gold beach, between the blue ocean and the golden dunes, the Wonder Strand of the Norsemen's sagas.

Because of the sparsely settled villages and the lack of architectural lure most motorists sweep on through to Provincetown, where there is more to see, or anyway more to look at. So the Lower Cape has remained pretty much as it always was. The magic is there, only most of it is off the highway on the crooked little back roads that make a network over the moors and through the scrubby woods.

It is very easy to get lost on these roads, or indeed anywhere in the county, for the way the Cape swings round to all points of the compass is confusing. My bump of location being in reverse, I was forever getting myself into a hopeless tangle; but I finally worked out a system which you may find useful. Stop the car and study the map to find out just where you are—if possible. Then carefully work out the direction that will take you to Falmouth, or Chatham or whatever, and when you are sure of the right road turn in the opposite direction. I did that lots of times, and always came out right. Seriously, it really is like that. Only on the back roads it is worse, because there you can't possibly find out where you are to start with. Just drive till you come to water, and pray it will be salt so that you can follow it to the next town, whatever that may be. Unfortunately there are an awful lot of ponds in most of the towns.

The Cape is an adventure in itself. It changes certain portions of its anatomy from year to year, and sometimes sensationally. Since the Pilgrims landed there, its forests of big trees have become barren moorlands; but that is a minor alteration. Take Monomoy, down off Chatham, for instance. One year it was a peninsula, the next an island; but, the last I heard, it was part of the mainland again. It is made of two capes that broke up and came aground here. Its lighthouse, which was built on the shore, was a mile inland, last time I saw it.

Cape lighthouses are fugitive things anyway, forever pursued by the sea and often overtaken, or left behind by the retreating waters like Monomoy's.

Some years there is a beach at the foot of the Clay Pounds in North Truro, some years there is not; it all depends. Then there is Chase Garden River in Yarmouth: back in 1007, when Thorvald, Leif Ericson's brother, explored the Cape, it was really a river; but now you can jump across it easily—you would take it for a drainage ditch.

The ocean shore (Back Side), remote and sheltered from observers by bluffs and dunes, was made for skulduggery, and pirates and wreckers and moon-cussers had their way with whatever came ashore by whatever means. Even the honest men of the Fifteen Towns—most of whom were on the whole a proper and God-fearing lot—saw no harm in taking what they could get after the fact. In a land of scarcity, which the Cape definitely was, wrecks were clear velvet. In many a small parlor you find the paneling from some ship's cabin, and some think the bowed-roof houses were framed from the ribs of stranded hulls. Certain it is that, between professionals and amateurs, nothing that came ashore was wasted.

During the Prohibition era the native abilities of that small cut of the earlier population would seem to have survived. With its desolate shores and many hidden coves and inlets, the Cape was a natural for landing contraband. A book could be written about bootlegging there. I was told that few of the native stock ever found their way to the county jail, where the "foreign element" figured largely. Anyhow it was not a pretty story, and Lizy Jane and I kept our eyes at home as ladies should. What we thought is nobody's business. Moon-cussing was good clean fun in comparison.

In the old days most of the wrecks were probably unprovoked, because they could easily have been. More good ships laid their bones on the shifting sands and shoals off the ragged elbow of the Cape than on all the rest of the Atlantic coast put together; and many another broke up off the long beaches from Nauset to Peakéd Hill Bar.

The sea made the Cape, and the Cape made the men and women who lived aboard it—made them tough and lean and wiry, put sand into their guts, and stood them on their own two feet in a world of rubber stamps. Above all, it put into them the secret of contentment, part of which is to be where you want to be and to know you are there.

If you look carefully at the villages you will notice that no two of them are alike. No two of them are at all alike. Each has its own way of building a house, and its own style of fencing in its dooryard. Each has its own character, its own personality. This is mostly the result of sand. Well into this century, each village was isolated from the others by long stretches of sandy roads. Until the railroad pushed its way through to Wellfleet and finally to Provincetown most travel was done by stagecoach. The lumbering four-horse coaches plowed along hub-deep from one end of the Cape to the other. It was a hard, slow trip, and no man in his senses made it unless he had to go. Even for a woman to hitch her horse to the democrat wagon and drive over to the village store two or three miles away took a good half-day. People did not move round much unless they had a good reason for doing so.

But don't imagine they stayed home. They went everywhere else, as occasion required, men and women alike, provided the women were married to sea captains. Anywhere they could go by water, they went. They could always go up to Boston by sailing packet; but they generally had in mind more distant ports than Boston.

One reason for the contentment which the people of these villages have in common may be that so many of the older people saw most of what the rest of the world had to offer and proved to their own complete satisfaction that it had nothing on the Cape. So they came home and settled down, convinced that they were lucky to be able to live in the best place there was to live. They passed this conviction on to their children, who have seen no reason to question its validity.

But it is not a negative or brooding contentment, for with it goes a dynamic quality of initiative and enterprise which they call "sprawl" hereabouts. "Sprawl," on the Cape, suggests a mixture of guts and git-up-and-git; and most Cape people have it.

The local attitude toward mainlanders is not one of easy and open-hearted hospitality. It is not just a British reserve handed down through the centuries, either, for it is not so noticeable in the Maritime Provinces, which are otherwise more British. During my year of exploring the Cape, I came to feel very much at home there. Each one of us has, I suppose, his own spiritual home, the one place in the world where he feels he really belongs. It may be half a world away from his birthplace and his background, but when he finds it he knows it as his. I felt that way about

Cape Cod, and still do. Besides the sort of accessibility that years of newspaper experience inevitably give one, I felt myself, not a sight-seer from Boston come to gape, but more than half native both by inheritance and by taste. I made many good friends, and we got down to first names, and they told me their family stories and showed me many a holy of holies that genuine outsiders would doubtless have missed. And yet the ice never quite went out. We never sat down in the kitchen for a cup of tea or took potluck at suppertime. I was always on probation. Some of this was probably my fault—some sort of lag in me. But much of it was this natural reserve of theirs.

For this I blame the novelists, who have invented a grotesque Cape "type." Readers everywhere have swallowed it, and they pour down the highways looking for the originals. If you and I had been sold to the world as quaint old oddities, as fair laughingstock, and summer visitors whom we regarded with more or less justice as certainly no more than our equals stared at us and tried to get us talking to hear how we sounded—we should have been put on the defensive too. It really is too bad, for Cape people have something we mainlanders need—they have a way of life that is healthful and satisfying and often beautiful. It is our loss if we don't go looking for the real values they can show us. You can get plenty of belly-laughs on the Cape; but most of them come from watching the summer folks, and not the winter residents.

A doctor went down-Cape looking for a likely spot to spend his declining years, and he learned quite a lot. He did not find the spot, for he came to the conclusion that people simply did not have declining years here. They stayed active and lively till they had about all they wanted, and then they just dried up and blew away—practically. He talked with a hale little woman in her middle eighties, trying to find out the secret of the prevailing longevity, and asked the obvious question:

"Do you suppose it's the good clean air down here?"

Aunt Tempy said it might be that, partly. "But mostly it's our contented hearts."

Of course there are other factors. One is the leisurely pace, the easy rhythm of living. Nobody drives himself or hustles. People are brisk, but relaxed. Then the sense of permanence, of belonging to the environment, of having deep roots, must have much to do with it. It eliminates a lot of restlessness and a deep unease. You need to live in the Far West to appreciate the difference.

In the West you build a house that will sell readily—in fact, the banks won't finance it for you if you don't. Or the home you buy must be one with a "good resale value." Then you decorate it according to the taste of the moment. It is all so transient, so restless. You no sooner get your roots in than you yank them up and move over to another part of town, or maybe another state altogether. Life is a series of rapid adjustments, and they can be mighty wearing as you get older.

On the Cape you are deep-rooted, or as the seagoing men call it, deep-anchored.

Another thing: most people are comfortably off, and don't have to worry much about money. They may not have as much as some of the city folks, then again they may have a good bit more—you can't always tell and you certainly won't be told. In one of the villages, I knew a middle-aged housewife with hair plastered severely to a knot at the back of her head and a calico apron over her neat gingham dress—her neighbors told me she played the stock market and paid an income tax on her winnings. I am sure she came through the panic all right, too, for Cape Codders don't take chances with the weather—if the glass is falling and it's smurrin' up for a storm, they run for port. Anyhow, most of them have enough for what they want, and taxes. And that is plenty good for the health.

A lot of their work is done in the open air; and it is wide-open air, keen and lively. In climate the Cape is better than most of New England, more equable, not quite so cold in winter, not nearly so hot in summer. But they have other things in their favor. They were not brought up on cigs and cokes, they come of sturdy, clean-living stock with a lot of sprawl and savvy. They have always had plenty to do and plenty of time to do it in.

2. *Sandwich Comes First*

WHATEVER DAY it may be anywhere else, it is always Sunday afternoon in Sandwich. Some sort of spell holds the little village to the quiet and peace of that day. On the main street, to be sure, there are the rival curiosity shops with their displays of Sandwich glass, and the old Inn where, in Daniel Webster's day at least, the hilarity was anything but Sundayish. Still it is a quiet, peaceful little place where you can sit and dream the time away if that is what you like. If you must have excitement it is only necessary to start a couple of glass experts—and that means practically anyone in town—discussing the authenticity of a couple of salt cellars: early Sandwich or late Woolworth?

Fortunately the down-Cape highway by-passes the village. Its curving, shaded roads converge about the placid little millpond whose mill was once the center af activity. If you prefer a fancy name you can call the pond Shawme Lake. The mill was made over into a tearoom some time ago. Rising above the elms, and reflected in the pond, is the white Congregational church, practically new, according to local ideas, since it was built in 1848. There is a great difference in New England spires. This is a Wren church, and Wren designs have a distinction all their own. There are two in the county, and you can compare them with some of the other older churches. This one is specially graceful. Along the roads are the elderly white houses with their lawns and trees and flowers. I say "elderly" because they don't call a house old here unless it has at least two centuries behind it. Most of these have only one or maybe one and one-half.

The first settlement made by Englishmen on Cape Cod was in Sandwich. A group of "undertakers"—definitely not to be confused with morticians—were given leave by the Plymouth authorities to "view and sit" here. They did so in 1637, if you can imagine those busy pioneers doing much sitting or viewing either. Next year Myles Standish and John Alden came down and fixed their boundaries for them, and then they organized a church for themselves. We would probably call their set-up communistic today: there were common lands where they could pasture their cattle or cut their firewood; each man owned his own place, of course, but permission from the town fathers was necessary before he could sell it, and if they thought his customer was not godly enough they could and would refuse; no outsider was allowed to settle in the town till he had the approval of the minister and church. They wanted to keep the town pure.

Twenty years later some Quakers, driven out of Plymouth and other towns, came to Sandwich and succeeded in establishing themselves there in spite of the authorities. If they had been then the quiet, law-abiding folk they are today, all would probably have gone well with them; but they were a young and argumentative group and aroused cruel opposition wherever they went. It was somewhat less cruel here than in most places, because quite a few people were ready to accept their teachings. In fact, two of the leading offenders had to be taken to Barnstable to be whipped because the Sandwich authorities refused to act. Still there was plenty of really outrageous persecution. It is a proof of the courage and persistence of the Friends that they succeeded in establishing their church and becoming respected citizens.

Some of their descendants still live in the town. Out on Quaker Meetinghouse Road their church stands on a knoll among tall pines. It is, I believe, the first Friends' meetinghouse to be built in America, and is still used for quarterly meetings, which Friends come from all over the country to attend. I sometimes wonder if something of the special graciousness and tranquillity of the lovely old town may not be due to the "inner light" of their triumphant faith. Maybe some of the business ability of the glass dealers may be traced back to them, too, for they were shrewd bargainers.

They held their first dangerous meetings in the Baker house out on the Valley Road. It is built on two levels, one story in front but two behind, where the land slopes down to the pond. Its typical Cape gable has a little window each side of the larger ones to light the cubbies where the children slept.

I was lucky in having for guide to the older houses the local historian, William Nye. He knew his town. Not only was he descended from one of the original "undertakers," but all his eighty years had been spent here, and he knew everyone. Whenever we came to a house that looked specially interesting Mr. Nye was sure to have friends who lived there and were more than delighted to show us how it looked inside.

Out on Quaker Meetinghouse Road is the Stephen Wing house, wide, white and two-storied, with some of its original small-paned windows still left. Stephen Wing was one of the original members of the Friends' Meeting, and he built the house in 1641. Its walls are a foot and a half thick, but whether they are filled with stone, brick, or beams is not known. It was solid enough to be used as a blockhouse when the off-Cape Indians threatened to make trouble.

There are several Wing houses in town, and all the Wings were Quakers. One of the houses, bought by a mainlander and altered, had been called haunted. But the sounds heard, though eerie enough for a ghost, were really echoes on the road outside—a queerly echoing road it is, but no harm ever comes of it. On the dining-room wall hung the original deed. The house was sold—sold, mind you, not built—to Daniel Wing in 1640. "It lieth between the land of John Shawson and William Newland," both its rolling wooded acreage with its hills and hollows and its little pond, basking serenely in the sun. No terror now of Indian war whoops on that echoing road beyond the lane, or of torment for religion's sake.

Often the land drops off abruptly from the roadside, and houses are built to follow it down. One of these, a Quaker house, has dear knows how many stories at the back, for the bottom is quite out of sight from the road. But you can see the land spreading away for miles and miles, with meadow and marsh and the blue of salty inlets trailing in from the Bay beyond.

If you have a chance to go to Sandwich, don't leave till you have taken a hike out across the marshes to the dunes and the sudden, breath-taking view of the Bay. The early settlers made great use of these marshes. The salt hay fed their cattle and thatched their roofs. Timbers for the early houses, supplies for the village, and materials for the glass factory used to be brought in on scows poled up the inlets at high tide through the marshes, then dragged overland by teams of oxen.

I found Quakers still living in the Holway house on the King's Highway near the East Sandwich station—Holways, too, descendants of an early owner, Barnabas Holway. It stood as stanch and foursquare as it did when it was built two hundred years before. The great kitchen, now the living room, had a wide-planked floor and generous fireplace and brick oven. Holways had lived in it more than a hundred years, and the same furniture had lived here with them, till some of it had come to seem almost human. You could reasonably imagine the tip table and the roundabout chair gossiping together at midnight—"What I could tell 'em if I'd a mind to!"

It was a picture-book house outside, with crimson ramblers rambling up the front and onto the roof and almost blocking the front door. Its blinds had weathered to a light and subtle green. They needed repainting to preserve them, but the owners couldn't have it done—for any painter would go mad trying to match the color.

Out in the yard was the boat shop, also built in 1720, where they used to make whaleboats for many a fine whaler to take on her long voyages. The planks in the attic floor were more than two feet wide.

To see a really old house—the oldest in town, it is, and maybe on the whole Cape—go look at the Saltbox-Roof House. You have to know where to look for it. First you go up the main street past the Daniel Webster Inn (hereinafter to be referred to as the Inn) till you come to School Street. Turn right on this and you will soon reach the end, where you will face the gray façade of what used to be Sandwich Academy. To the right of this is a narrow lane that runs along the shore of the millpond and stops short at the door of the House with the Saltbox Roof.

Old-fashioned wooden salt boxes were higher on one side than on the other, with a lid that made a long slope down to the low side. Old Cape houses frequently have this type of roof, often as the result of remodeling done long ago. The roof of a two-story house is extended down on one side over a lean-to addition to make a couple of extra rooms on the ground floor.

This particular house has not only such a roof but several rambling ells as well, which with their sagging roof lines and ancient shingles form about as picturesque a dwelling as could be found in the whole U.S.A.—I mean one fairly and honestly picturesque, not one just made to look that way.

Known also as the old Hoxie house (Hoxie is a Quaker name, too), it is jammed in between the pond and a hill. As you see it from the lane it is two stories high, with a very low story on the back or pond side. So the roof is short and steep on the shore side but takes a long, drooping slant toward the water, stopping just above the windows; according to tradition it was once thatched instead of shingled.

The name does not come from the builder but from a whaling captain, Abraham Hoxie, who bought the house only two or three generations ago. One thing he did was to tear down the old chimney, and a witness told me of finding a brick cut with the date 1637—at the time someone scrawled the figures in chalk on a beam in the attic as a memorandum. If the date is true the house must have been built by one of the original ten settlers the year they got there; but nothing else is known of its history until 1688, when the Reverend John Smith and his wife and their thirteen children moved out of it.

It must have been one of the nobler dwellings of its day, for it had two fine square rooms and two or three smaller ones besides a capacious woodshed across the back. The thickness of the walls suggests that it was built originally of hewn logs. These may have been used as protection against the Indians; or perhaps the early settlers did not have the means for sawing them into planks. The windows are recessed so deeply that the sills make seats in the thickness of the walls.

It is probable that the walls were not plastered inside originally, but the chinks between the logs were filled and smeared over with clay to keep out the wind and weather. The wide planks came later, too, because these first houses had for floors only the earth on which they stood, trodden down. Then around the outer edges of the room stretched the great sills; and chairs were so scarce and precious that they were reserved for grown-ups, while the children sat— still as little mice—on the sills or in the chimney corners. In those days the young uns were strictly to be seen and not heard.

Mr. Nye, who told me all this, said the smaller houses were very small indeed, with only one room. Against the back wall was the chimney, with a big fireplace. Unless the house was built up against a hill for warmth, the oven was on the outside; and it is hard to see how the women did their baking when it rained or there was deep snow. The little houses had few windows, and they were small. The roof was steep and thatched—a thatched roof had to be steep to shed the rain. There are little houses like these in the "pioneer village" at Salem.

Fireplaces used to be enormous. The biggest I heard of was eight feet wide, four feet deep, and five and one-half feet high. Children could sit in the chimney corner at night and look up at the stars. Candles were rarely needed for family industries because there was light enough from the flames of the great fire—a four-foot log so thick that it took a strong man to roll it into the house and get it onto the andirons would make quite a conflagration.

Mr. Nye's remark that one of the early ministers lived in an "unpartitioned barn" gives an idea of the simplicity of pioneer living, for the minister generally got the best there was.

Where there was an upstairs chamber, as in the Hoxie house, it was reached by a ladder. A rare luxury was the chicken-ladder stairway, which we stare at aghast today because it is so steep and difficult. So much depends on one's point of view!

The Hoxie house has suffered many changes in its three centuries, but the effect is still beautiful—maybe better than when it was younger. The ancient windows, so hard to wash because of the risk that they will fall out of their ancient muntins, remain. On one side of the larger windows are hinges where once hung the shutters—big wooden ones, and only one to a window.

The front door, with the steep little hill snuggling close up to its doorstone, has the remains of a pair of long blinds of a later period. Because they did not sufficiently screen the door from the morning sun, somebody planted a lilac bush and a strawberry tree alongside to give it more shade.

A jasmine vine runs up to the roof and has tried, as so many Cape vines do, to get away from the wind by working its way indoors. This one decorates the whole parlor wall.

The woodshed on the water side long ago was made into a living room with a fine view of sunsets across the pond. But the parlor, with its elderly if not really old finish, is more interesting. The low wainscot is hardly more than an exaggerated baseboard, and the low window seats are paneled. A summertree crosses the ceiling. The fireplace has been closed up but is probably still there; anyhow it has a good, simple mantel and the usual chimney cupboard with the usual store of Sandwich glass and other treasures. Such things do not sit round on mantels or whatnots; they are put away, and you don't get to see them unless you have a friend at court—maybe not then.

They used to call this house Fort Hoxie because, during the Civil War, the captain had a small cannon out front on the terrace and fired it for every one of the Union victories. One of the Hoxie men—in spite of being a Quaker, apparently—went off to war and fought at Gettysburg; and in the cupboard, along with the glass, are his knapsack and haversack. He was in the regiment commanded by Colonel Fletcher Webster, son of the immortal Daniel.

Joseph Jefferson, the actor, used to come often to Sandwich for the hunting, and he wanted to buy this house for a summer home. If his friend, President Cleveland, could have got the house near by he would probably have bought it; but the negotiations fell through, and they both went across to Buzzards Bay instead. Just as well, maybe—

they used to stick dormer windows on old houses those days, if they were unfortunate enough to have the money.

There were two women on the Cape whom I should have specially loved to know. One of them lived just beyond Chase Garden River in Yarmouth, and I shall tell you about her later. The other, who lived right here in East Sandwich, was a Hoxie—Aunt Marthy Hoxie. You can't miss her house because it is on the King's Highway, on the right as you drive down-Cape, across the street from a small white schoolhouse, and also because it has a bowed roof. It is one of the very sweetest little old houses to be seen in all New England, and that is saying a lot. It probably got that way from belonging to Aunt Marthy. Houses, like animals, often take on the characteristics of their owners.

Being a Hoxie of Sandwich, Aunt Marthy was of course a Friend. Early in her youth she had been betrothed to a Quaker minister, or elder, or whatever they were called in those days; but he died, and little Miss Hoxie remained true to his memory all her long life, alone here in her tiny house at peace with herself and the world. Her doors were never locked, for she had faith in people. And people kept faith with her. She had a lot of money, had little Aunt Marthy, and because there were no banks, or they were too far away, she kept it with her. A relative of hers told me she had known Aunt Marthy to have ten thousand dollars in gold stored away in a nail keg out in the woodshed.

Her thrift was as strong as her trustfulness. She owned some railroad stock, and every year she got passes to go up to Boston by train for the annual meeting of the stockholders. When the great day arrived the old lady would array herself in her best—in her silver-gray taffeta gown and her exquisite real-lace kerchief and her white satin bonnet—and board the train for Boston.

But when she arrived she didn't dare to venture out from the station into the terrible great city all alone—the very thought terrified her. "Thee wouldn't have me do *that!*" So she sat patiently in the waiting room of the old South Station till the afternoon train was ready to take her back home to Sandwich. Although she had not been able to attend the meeting she considered the day well spent, for hadn't she saved the passes from being wasted?

Her house had been restored when I saw it, but rather well. In the two small rooms downstairs the fireplaces had been opened up, and only necessary painting had been done. The tiny room upstairs was reached by one of those chicken-ladder stairways I have mentioned—short treads backed by boards slanting steeply up between narrow walls—no risers. If the look of age was gone from the house, I suppose that was unavoidable: summer folks must have white paint.

Back on the main street of the village, the rambling old inn is named for one of its favorite guests. Daniel Webster used to come to Sandwich for his fishing and gunning, and he had a special room—one with a sliding panel in the door that made it easier to pass in the drinks. The old statesman must have needed a bit of a lift after the trip down from Boston, concluded by an all-day ride on the stagecoach from Plymouth to Sandwich, terminus of the line. A whole day in the lumbering vehicle with its four horses, jolting and swaying through sand up to the' hubs even on the main highway, would tucker out the stoutest hunter.

Good sports they were in those days, Daniel and his friends. "Those days" were around 1820; and the inn was old even then, though not as an inn. It began life as a parsonage in 1694 and did not become a tavern for a hundred years after that—and quite a change it must have been.

The lakes and marshes of the Upper Cape were the sportsman's delight in fall and winter. With dog and gun he hiked along the winding roads through the scrubby pines, his whole body tingling in the sweet sharp air with its smell of pines and sea. Stretches of brown marsh, the great rounded waves of the dunes with V's of blue sea in the notches between them, and so inland to the ponds, sunk deep in the winter woods. Beneath the gray-black ice lurked plenty of gamy fish. The hunting was good, too, what with deer and quail and ducks, well worth the long hard trip, especially with the inn there to welcome the hunters at the end of the day. They would sit up late before the fire drinking their grog and swapping tall stories and great laughs.

In later years President Cleveland used to stay there, and his crony, Joe Jefferson, when they came for the hunting or fishing. Their stories were probably as good as anyone's. One summer Cleveland's son was born, over at Buzzards Bay, and a Sandwich man who used to fish with him, went over to congratulate him. On the way he met Jefferson, on the same errand, and the two went on together.

On the front porch of Gray Gables, the Cleveland summer home, they found the happy father talking with the doctor. When one of the guests asked one of the few questions you can ask about a baby, how much it weighed, Cleveland answered proudly:

"Fifteen pounds!"

"Mr. President, I must correct you," the doctor protested. "The baby weighed only ten pounds."

"I refuse to be corrected," retorted the President. "I weighed that child myself, on the same scales Mr. Jefferson and I use to weigh our fish!"

In my day one of the local celebrities was Dodge Macknight, whose water colors were hailed as revolutionary. He was a summer resident who made good. You would know his East Sandwich home by the high privet hedge along the front; but it took the right password to get into the big rose garden hidden away behind the house.

Nowadays traffic flows past the house endlessly, for it is on the main road; but Mr. Macknight told me of the earlier days when all day long you would see only an ox team or two plodding along through the sand.

Another famous townsman—a townsman by right of year-round living there—was Thornton Burgess. Burgess is a good Sandwich name, and I heard of two other wearers of it who got some measure of fame; and no doubt there have been more, even if their fame was not so wide as his. I never met him myself, but Lavinia Walsh, who was one of the *Cape Cod Magazine's* most treasured writers, contributed an article about him.

Mrs. Walsh describes Thornton Burgess's boyhood in the white-piazzaed house on Jarves Street, then proceeds to the Brier Patch—the only original immortal Brier Patch. First she tells how to find it.

"If you follow the main Cape road Capeward," she writes, "until you come to what is known as Spring Hill, and turn in at a wood road behind the property known as the William Chipman place and go on for a space through a green glory of entangled locust trees, elderberry bushes and budding goldenrods, with red and black masses of wild cherry overhanging a roadside growth of blackberry vines laden with shining black lusciousness, you will come to it presently, the Brier Patch.

"And perhaps you will think it looks like any other brier patch—but it doesn't! For right out before you, all in a twinkling, troop the little people of the Green Forest, and the Green Meadow—they may not all belong there but they have come just for you. And 'What a delightful gathering!' you'll say. Reddy Fox, and Jerry Muskrat, and the renowned Peter Rabbit; Johnny Chuck and Happy Jack; Bobby Coon, Chatterer the Red Squirrel, Sammy Jay, Bob White; and even Old Mother West Wind with the Merry Little Breezes, come from somewhere over behind the Bourne hills."

The second Burgess, a heroine in her day though her fame is local, figures in the historical museum. This square white building facing the village common has a special case for the souvenirs collected by Hannah Rebecca Burgess. Mrs. Burgess voyaged all over the world with her sea-captain husband. Like so many seagoing captains' wives, she studied navigation; but, unlike most of them, she went on and became master of sail. They were both young—still in their twenties—when they made their last voyage together. At Valparaiso Captain Burgess was taken ill and died. His valiant girl-widow took command of the ship and brought her back to her home port—Sagamore Harbor —and dropped anchor there for the last time. A painting of their bark *Speedwell* hangs on the wall near her collection.

While we are in the museum we might stop to look at

the old musket which made local history once on a time—
for it killed the last wolf to be seen in Sandwich. A big
gray fellow had strayed down onto the Cape in the days
before the Canal and was terrorizing the town. No one
was able to get it, though bounties were offered for its
head. One day it leaped out of the woods right into the
path of young George Braley's horses. Luckily he had his
gun, and he shot it, later collecting three bounties for it
from town, county, and state. It took a Swift to finish
the job. This was William Swift, horse trader and cattle
dealer, who bought the body and showed it all up and
down the Cape at a dime a head. His three younger
brothers were to go to Chicago and make a fortune in the
stockyards. Swift is a Quaker name.

The third Burgess put Sandwich on the map and kept it
there for forty years all by herself. I found her a person
worth traveling a long way to see, and a lot of people must
have felt the same way about her, for they used to come
from far and near, on foot and in buggies or democrat
wagons, even from a distance by bargeloads, to see the
miracles she wrought.

It is always interesting to find Cape men or women
in a difficult situation and watch their reactions. When
Mrs. Arabella Burgess was three years old she started tam-
ing animals. She had no children to play with, so she made
playmates of the small animals in the yard. Toads, at first
—she made clothes for them out of colored paper and
dressed them up, their little hands and feet sticking out in
the cunningest fashion.

"They liked it, too," she told me; "they would sit just
as still and let me fuss with them! And always in the
morning, when I came out to play, there they were wait-

ing for me. Of course I fed them, but I think they liked being petted, too, and played with."

Snakes were her next adventure, big black ones. They got so tame that they would climb into her lap and curl up. She took one in her apron to show her mother, but that long-suffering parent went for the fire tongs; so she kept them outdoors after that. Several years later she got interested in worms and caterpillars. Her interest was quite scientific, too.

"I wanted to find out whether, if I tamed a caterpillar before it went into its chrysalis, it would still be tame when it came out as a butterfly, in the spring," she explained. "So I got a beautiful green carrot worm and made friends with him. At first he would stick out his horns at me when I took him up; but I'd tap him on the back and he would take them in again. He always stuck them out if anyone else touched him. I fed him things I thought he liked, and made a little nest for him in a box. He would stay around with me during the day; but at night he always disappeared, and I never knew where he went.

"I told my father about him and asked him to be careful not to step on him when he went out to the woodpile. Every morning Father would come in and tell me that my caterpillar had come back to his box and was waiting for me; but one morning he came in very sad and told me my pet had hidden away under a chip near the woodpile and he had stepped on it. So I never found out whether the butterfly would have been tame."

When I knew her Mrs. Burgess was a spry little woman in her mid-eighties with lively blue eyes and rosy cheeks and fluffy white hair. Her house backed up to the pond, almost across the road from the church, and it had a little pier for rowboats. This pier was the scene of the oddest tea parties you could imagine, with guests ranging from Joseph Jefferson to Quinn the big eel.

When Mrs. Burgess was forty the doctor told her she ought to spend her days out of doors taking it easy. She had an active brain, and the idea of lying around all day doing nothing did not appeal to her—no Cape woman would feel right, holding her hands like that. She had to have something to take up her time. Sitting out on the little pier one day, bored almost to death, she thought she would see if she could tame an eel. There were plenty of eels in the water round the pier; but they were shy, and none of them would come near, even for the tempting tidbits she threw them. The best she could do that first year was to persuade one of them to stay a short distance off and take what she threw to him.

The second year one eel came so close that she could almost touch him. The third year—she had patience, that woman—he began eating out of her hand. From then on, it was easy.

"It proved eels have some way of talking," the old lady said, "for my eel must have told the others I was all right and had food for them. They came by the dozen after that, and got real tame. They would let me stroke them, and it wasn't long before I could take them out of the water and up into my lap. They were real clean and nice, too. People will go on thinking eels are slimy and disagreeable," she said indignantly; "but they aren't, not if you don't frighten them. They won't throw their slime unless you scare them. I learned how long to keep them out of water and used to feed them in my lap. They didn't seem to mind the air at all. It was different with fishes—I never tried to take them out of the water—it would have been bad for them."

When she had won the eels over, Mrs. Burgess went after the fishes. Among her friends were shiners, perch, and horned pout—these last used to stand up on their tails and stick their heads out of water to catch bits of food thrown them. Only the pickerel she would have none of: they were "vicious greedy things," and she always drove them away.

To call her guests to dinner Mrs. Burgess would put her hand into the water and wave her fingers back and forth. Immediately they would come swarming about her. The men over at Herring River gave her all the dried herrin' she wanted—which was lucky, for as time went on the demand grew.

Joseph Jefferson was a frequent guest. He used to sit beside her on the pier and try to figure out why it was that when she put her hand in the water and waved her fingers a few times the fish would come rushing from all over the pond. He decided they must catch vibrations through the water just as land creatures catch them through the air.

It was different with the turtles. They lived in the water too, but she had to use her voice to call them. She would call, "Come, come, come!" and a dozen little black heads would pop up out of the water and make for her as fast as their flippers could carry them. They came to know her voice, too—when she went out in the rowboat with a friend for a sunset row, or maybe across the pond to see a neighbor's garden, she had to talk in whispers if she didn't want little black heads to trail the boat.

For a number of years she kept the whole affair pretty much of a secret, because she didn't want to be "pestered." Then one day a newspaperman from Boston came along in a rowboat and stopped to watch her.

"Belle, what are you doing?" he demanded.

"Feeding the fishes."

"Well, it's lucky you weren't born when they were hanging witches," he said. "It's simply uncanny."

That next week the story came out in a Boston paper, and then people began coming. Several times a day she would have to give up her work and go out and satisfy their curiosity. They had come so far she hadn't the heart to refuse. She kept it up for forty years. Then the pier blew down in a storm; and it had become such a chore for her that she gave it up. When I knew her she had a room full of birds and a parrot named Pollarundum and a pet hen whose life she had saved as a chicken, but she had no fish.

Everybody had told me she was a wonderful woman, with a strange power over animals. What was it in her that gave the shy under-water creatures confidence in her? Was it just the result of her patience and her quiet, unfrightening ways? Or were they more intelligent than we realize and able to recognize her friendliness? When I asked her what it was, she thought a minute.

"Well, of course I always fed them, and treated them kindly. But"—she hesitated—"I really think, if you're going to do it properly, you've got to *like* them!"

Of course what really made Sandwich famous these later years was glass. The site of the glassworks, picturesque ruins of mellowed old brick, is over near the depot. Its fame did not really begin till the glassworks were gone.

While they were operating—1825 to 1888—they were an industrial concern turning out things for the most part that everyday people used every day and could buy for fifteen cents and up. To be sure, they were doing things with glass that had not been done before, in America anyhow, and developing secret processes and formulae; but nobody got excited about it. Only after the factory went out of business and the secrets were lost did the glassware become of interest to collectors and the name Sandwich a word to conjure with.

It was in 1824 that Deming Jarves (pronounced with two syllables) came down from Boston for the hunting. He was agent for a glass company in Boston and was ambitious to set up for himself. There was a lot of sand lying around, as there is anywhere on the Cape, but he noticed too the abundance of firewood for the furnaces. At that time the town was covered with a white-pine forest. So he bought some wood lots and built his factory —at first with only one small furnace and employing only seventy men. But eventually the Boston and Sandwich Glass Company, as it was legally known, had four large furnaces and had five hundred men and boys on its pay roll. As the total population of the town is about fifteen hundred, this was big business. Everyone, even the ministers, worked there. A good gaffer was highly respected. Between the glassworks and the saltworks which preceded them as an industry the forests vanished; but it may have been a good investment at that.

The glassworks were run with much dignity. No smoking was allowed, and the language of the workmen had to be attuned to the ears of the two clergymen who worked there weekdays—they always carried their Bibles with them, I suppose to keep the laity from forgetting their high calling.

Not being a native Sandwicher, I am not an authority on glass. So I quote from a series of articles by Lavinia Walsh, who lives in Sandwich and knows her glass (the series appeared in the *Cape Cod Magazine*).

"The Boston and Sandwich Glass Company made the first pressed glass in America," she writes. "They also used some compound in mixing their metal which brought a silvery sheen that was never equaled in any other factory. Another particularly distinctive achievement was their colored glass. It is undisputed that their Golden Ruby, Sapphire Blue, Purple, Jade Green, and Opalescent, which were made from secret formulae, were never equaled."

Of the lace glass, originated here between 1840 and 1850 and never made anywhere else, she says: "This lace glass is superior to any pressed glass ever made, not only in the excellence of the quality of the metal but also in the marvelous construction of the molds. The designs were of extreme fineness and very beautiful, giving the pattern a frosted appearance. These lace articles are easily the aristocracy of the glass kingdom." However: "Golden Ruby Glass! Those are the magic words when glass is mentioned in Sandwich. And why? . . . Because the perfection to which ruby glass attained in the Sandwich Factory has never been excelled before or since." She tells of an old German alchemist who discovered that glass could be given a crimson color by means of gold. "The Sandwich ruby glass is like solidified flame. It has the indescribable color of a red-and-gold sunset. There is an elusiveness of tone in its living red that not even the opal glass of Sandwich with its lovely changing colors possesses."

Mrs. Walsh's articles ran through all the summer issues of one year from June to the middle of September, and anyone specially interested in the glass will find an old file of the magazines worth digging up, though by now they may be pretty hard to come by.

A woman is given much of the credit for starting the furor for Sandwich glass. Appropriately enough I found her, Mrs. Hazel Blake French, living not only on Jarves Street but in the house which Deming Jarves had built for a wedding present for his son. She was making jewelry, using bits of the semiprecious glass instead of jewels and designing the settings with Cape motifs. On my little finger is one of her rings—a square-cut "jewel" of ruby glass in a silver setting of wild grapes.

In a sunny front window she had a colorful display of her work which had traveled to New York and other cities for exhibition by arts-and-crafts societies. She knew her glass, and she had developed an original idea into an original career—Cape style. The exhibitions of her work had called attention to the beauty of Sandwich glass, and certainly helped start the vogue for collecting it. Rings, bracelets, necklaces, pendants, the unimaginable richness of the colors given a halo of romance by their origin, and by the themes of their settings—sea gulls, fishes, seaweed, rope, bayberries, wild grapes, pines, even whales.

Her career goes back to her childhood, when she had a passion for color and used to go prowling into the cellars of the factory ruins, looking for bits of glass. Not broken dishes—no, indeed—but bits that had never seen a mold: dripped or spilled or slopped many years before and left there for a little girl to pick up and hoard as treasure. She must have been courageous, for the cavernous passages were deep underground, dark and dank and gloomy—hazardous, too, with tottery masonry and treacherous pitfalls, terrifying to a small person down there all by herself among the shadows. Again and again she went, for there all about on the earthen floor, flung around the base of the great stack, even covered over by earth and to be found only by digging, lay her treasure—secret treasure, to make it still more alluring, for she told no one.

Of course only a child would have thought of those useless and forgotten blobs of color and light, often dulled with dampness and dirt, as treasure; but, picked up and rubbed clean on her pinafore, they were rubies and emeralds and opals and sapphires and everything else she could find in the rainbow. What took her back time after time was her insatiable ambition to find all the colors there were. Every time she found a different red or a new opalescent piece, she added it rapturously to her trove.

As she grew older her interest waned, and she put her collection away and forgot it; but, loving color and jewels, she went to art school and specialized in jewelry designing, using the ordinary semiprecious stones like the rest of her class.

One day during summer vacation when she was walking along past the old factory some sparks of color in a refuse heap caught her eye, and she discovered several scraps of glass. Then the big idea was born: Have them cut like jewels, and set them! She picked out a few of her best specimens and sent them to a lapidary for cutting. She had a lot of grief before a way was found to do the work safely—the glass often was flawed and would fly to pieces when cut; but finally methods were worked out, and she was on her way—and so was Sandwich.

It says a lot for the Cape as a whole that it is not anti-climax after Sandwich. Most of it is anything but that. The other towns are nothing like Sandwich, or like one another, for that matter. Each one is unique, when you come to know it.

3. *Falmouth and Her Whalers*

SOMEHOW, in spite of being a neck-and-neck competitor with Hyannis for business leadership on the Cape, Falmouth has managed to keep a good share of her native charms. She has a Main Street and, like her rival, a "Queen's Buyway"—relic of the boom year. She has also on her outskirts a star collection of 1880–1900 cottages. But, in spite of all the summerites can do to mar her trusting beauty, she remains a really lovely village.

Not that I want to idealize the town. I heard the winter life spoken of quite disparagingly by some of the younger fry. Also she had her racial problem, somewhat of her own making—if an outsider may offer an opinion. Her politics were no sweeter than those of any other New England town although, since she got a town manager, they may have settled down. Anyway, Falmouth is a fine-looking old town.

If you come to Falmouth last, having gone down-Cape on the inside and come back up the outside, you will be struck by the style of the houses grouped around the village green. They are a lordlier sort than those of the other villages, more like those of Salem and Newburyport, though less grand, because here on the Cape people never had anything like the wealth of the old North Shore worthies. However, Falmouth was a prosperous town, and these houses show it.

The little heart-shaped park was not meant for anything so frivolous as a village green when it was set aside long ago. Indeed it was to be something much more important—a "Meeting-House lot and Training ground forever." The Meetinghouse was built square in the middle of the lot, with the whipping post—secondary instrument of correction—off in one corner.

What remains of the whipping post can be seen in the historical society near by; but there is no record of its ever being used. The story that has been told of the flogging of a Quaker at the post during the height of the persecution is highly improbable, as most of early Falmouth sympathized with the Quakers.

Since the middle of the last century the Church has faced the green (of course there are other churches, but in Falmouth "the Church" means the venerable First Congregational Church of Falmouth). The town fathers decided then to move the Church off the green, and they had to cut down two of the elms to let it through. In their place are two saplings planted after the moving, which are already sizable trees. The Church is a good example of the early New England type, with a graceful white spire pointing toward heaven. A Paul Revere bell in the steeple carries the cheery inscription:

> The living to the church I call;
> Unto the grave I summon all.

Falmouth was a great whaling town in the early and middle 1800's. A friend took me round to meet some of her fellow townsmen, and several of them turned out to be retired whalers. One had been born at sea on a whaler and became a mate when he grew up. He knew the business and was quite scornful of a whaling picture being played at that time—"Down to the Sea in Ships." The cast thought they had had a tough time out on location, but he called it "pink-tea whaling."

Over in Teaticket, in a little house across the road from the post office, lived a retired whaler who was still going strong at the age of eighty-five. He had a peddler's cart and made the circuit with it down to Provincetown and back—the "little trip round the Horn," he called it. One of the local philanthropists used to give him cigars "to keep his nose warm" on the cruise.

Falmouth was and no doubt still is a great town for octogenarians. They had an exclusive little organization called the Eighty Club, but quite a good proportion of its thirty-odd members had run over into the nineties. Oddly enough, all but one of the members at that time were men, though the one woman was the oldest of the lot, being ninety-five.

I met a man in Falmouth who had been round the world four times. He was a second mate, which struck me as a distinction in a world I found largely populated with captains. It seemed that a second mate was something like a sergeant in the army. The captain of a vessel gave the orders, the first mate passed them along, and the second mate saw they got done. This meant, he explained, that you had to know how to swear. Another man told me that this chap was "the best second mate his captain ever had—knew his Bible back'ards and for'ards."

Captains were czars on their ships and were strong for etiquette. One Falmouth captain took his brother on a voyage. First day out, brother went up onto the quarter-deck to complain about something, but was ordered off.

"Brothers no longer!" the captain said. It was he who commanded a coastwise vessel during the Civil War and did a lot of sailing up and down the coast. "I never turned out for anything but a lumber schooner," he used to say. A lumber schooner is a mean thing to ram, for it doesn't sink and whatever happens, happens to the rammer.

One captain they told me about was a tyrant at sea, but a charming man ashore. Like most captains, he left his authority on shipboard. He drew a sharp line between what could be said and done on ship and ashore. "That's all right offshore, but on land we talk differently," he would say. His wife used to sail with him quite often, and she kept him toned down. She was so popular that their ship used to be greeted with cheers when it made port. When she went to sea, being afloat was like being in Falmouth. Some men would not ship unless they were sure she was going along, the captain drove them so hard trying to make time and get back home.

Another woman, a Mrs. Davis, used to ship regularly with her husband, and her four children were all born at sea. For all she was a quiet little woman with a soft voice, she had a strong personality and was queen of her ship. She wrote some mighty interesting letters home. The log of one of the captains, Silas Jones, was published in the local paper. He must have been a good mixer, for he got along with all kinds of people—dined the missionaries and wined the native kings.

There is a lot to Falmouth besides the main village. It includes the other Falmouths—East and West and North, and Falmouth Heights; then there are the innumerable resort villages along its deeply indented coast. The township, as I have said, is the pointed shoulder blade of the

Cape, jutting out between Vineyard Sound and Buzzards Bay. It is not one of the smaller towns, and yet it was a surprise to find a fourteen-thousand-acre ranch in the middle of it. Standing with your back to the pond—Coonamesset Lake—and looking out over the level fields, you would think you were in Kansas or any of the pancake states. The lake—if we must call it that—is an extra. It is the Cape's way of signing off.

"You might think you were somewhere west of Wichita," it says, "but you are not. You're in little old Cape Cod. If you don't believe it, look at me."

You can get lost in the town's tortuous network of back roads almost anywhere, as I discovered one day when Lizy Jane and I were out looking for the Rainbow Roof House over near West Falmouth. I had an artist friend along to make us some pictures and wanted to impress her with our Cape savvy. We got there eventually, but came to have a solid respect for the possibilities of Falmouth topography.

This was open heath country, the rolling hills becoming dunes as we neared the shore. It was a surprise to find these moorlands so far up-Cape, especially off here on the "summerfied" south side. A winding lane guarded by stone walls and further sheltered by the low hills took us to the house, and then slipped on past it across the heath and out through a gap in the dunes to the beach.

Roses loved that house—white moons over the side door, pink ramblers mantling the front entry. Ancient rose vines almost hid the front of the house, several feet thick on its walls, making a forest of roses outside the attic windows. Woodbine and wisteria covered the old stone wall, and an old-time perennial garden on the south side blazed with blue larkspur, orange lilies, and purple monkshood. The summer air was sweet with the roses and new-mown hay and the sea. The quail bobwhiting to the wind was one with the heath rolling wide to the dunes and the sea.

It was an old, old house, probably built about 1685 by a Quaker named Bowerman. The ninth generation of Bowerman descendants was living there, and all of them had been members of the Society of Friends. In the older days the house was a sort of halfway station for the Nantucket members of the sect, who used to stay here overnight to break the long journey to Sandwich, where the quarterly meetings were held. From here in West Falmouth they would go on by chaise or horseback through the woods to Sandwich. Our hostess had been Virtue Bowerman before her marriage.

What made this house memorable in my experience was not its setting or its history but its attic. You can live on the Cape quite a while without ever getting to see an attic, and a tourist or summer visitor stands almost no show at all of ever climbing the steep little stairs that lead to most of these glorified old clutter-holes. Therefore attics have more lure for outsiders than almost anything else. Tourists dream of them, and hard-boiled antiquers drool when one is mentioned. To the owners they are likely to be simply an unfinished part of the house where they put things that are too good to throw away, and where their ancestors did the same thing for quite a spell.

Of course after a few generations things pile up. The Cape housewife is a tidy soul as well as a thrifty one, and she never lets the clutter get ahead of her. I never saw an attic, however ancient, which was untidy. But once in a while the attic gets really too full, and then somebody does something drastic. Artists in Provincetown in the early days used to furnish their studios with antiques from the town dump. Even the thriftiest would rather, I fancy, chuck the stuff away than give any antiquer the satisfaction of having bought it. Of course there are exceptions; but they generally know the market price, which is what the antiquer secretly thinks it is worth. I know one man with a two-hundred-year-old attic who stood his wheelbarrow under the window and dumped the surplus stuff into it. He was mildly regretful afterward, when his wife got home; but there was quite a lot left when I saw it.

Collecting attics is a grand hobby. You don't take them away, of course—just enjoy them and keep their memory warm. Pleasant and inexpensive, it takes up no room in your house, and is not too easy. Of all the attics I was privileged to see, the attic of attics was in this Rainbow Roof House on the Falmouth moors.

There are half a dozen of these bowed-roof houses on the Cape. Nobody seems to know just how they happened to be built with a curve instead of straight. The usual theory is that seagoing men liked the feeling of strength that a curving rafter gave them, reminding them of the stout hulls of their ships, in reverse. Another theory is that they were built with ship's timbers salvaged from wrecks. Whatever the explanation, they give a house a distinction, and a specially nice attic like no other attic in the world. Arching beams leap into the shadows and recall the nave of a Gothic cathedral; and because the houses are old the beams and rafters and the wide boards that run from ridge to eaves have darkened to a rich umber with golden lights.

Downstairs the house was rather disappointing to me— the rooms showed the changing taste of many periods, not only early American but early Victorian and middle and late as well, from old pine to golden oak and white enamel. As a record of the evolution of furniture it was priceless, and made one realize the absurdity of a "period room," meaning arrested development. A house that is lived in is constantly having its furnishings changed, added to, and eliminated as needs and tastes change. Such an evolution is common in old houses on the Cape, and it is very precious, so full of meaning and vitality. This house was a lovely rambling old thing with charmingly haphazard entries and stairways and cupboards, but I was looking for something more.

Just then our hostess opened a narrow door and revealed a steep little chicken-ladder staircase rising from my very feet.

"You might like to see the attic," she said.

I might, indeed.

The first thing that struck me when I put my head above the floor was the chimney. Instead of being orthodox brick like other Cape chimneys it was built of fieldstone, an irregular mass, straight on one side but swinging out on the other to take in a small fireplace, its jagged bulk effective against the shadows. The stone hearth was cluttered with the sort of things it should have been cluttered with: three-legged iron pots, a Dutch oven, a proper old kettle, and so on. They had not been put there to look period, but because they belonged there.

The women of the family used to do their spinning up here in the attic, and no doubt it was handy to cook themselves a meal here sometimes. Up in the throat of the chimney stretched an iron rod called a trammel bar, and on it hung the hooks and trammels that held the kettles over the fire. This goes back before the days of the

swinging crane and marks an early step in the evolution
of the fireplace. Anyhow the kettles had a good right to
be there.

On the beams rested old pewter coffeepots and other
odds and ends of tableware set up there to be out of the
way. Stuck away under the eaves and in the corners, and
indeed practically everywhere, was the accumulated clutter of nine generations of active living. Unlike most of our
houses today, it had never been a house where people just
stayed between one place and another place; it was a home
where they were born and lived and died, where they
laughed and wept and worked—yes, and prayed.

Back under the eaves, among the cobblers' benches and
boxes and trunks, I counted six spinning wheels, some for
wool, some for flax. No doubt each bride who came into
the family brought her own wheel. There again was a case
of evolution: some of the wheels were large, and some
were small; but they had so many variations that you could
really have arranged them by age according to the im-
provements. Chairs were there, too—ladder-backs and
Windsors and Hitchcocks. The battered high chair showed
what that house must have known about children. The
original stout splint seat had long been worn out by the
succession of squirming infants, and its hard-wood replace-
ment had lost two coats of paint and was worn smooth
and thin by still later generations.

On a four-poster bed was a hatbox with a picture of a
beaver on it. This had belonged to one of the great-
grandfathers; and a dignified figure he must have been with
his fine hat, his long-tailed coat, and his stock and dickey.
No doubt he carried a cane, if that was not against the
Quaker custom, and wore glove-fitting trousers.

In those days the Friends considered music a frivolous waste of time, if not downright ungodly. When Great-Grandfather heard his son whistling he ordered him, "Stop that heathenish music!" And Great-Grandmother Huldy felt the same way exactly—when a wandering fiddler came down the lane she waved him away excitedly: "Go away! Go away! We don't buy music here!"

But they had their worldly clothes, some of which were put away in chest drawers in that attic. There was another hatbox with Castle Garden on it; and very carefully laid away in a drawer was a little wedding gown of gold-colored taffeta.

The owner of the little gown had a lovely name: Chloe Wing Swift. She was eighteen in the 1830's when she came here as a bride in the golden frock with the huge sleeves and billowing skirt, wearing over it a silken cape and a small bonnet. The artist just had to get the gown into a picture of the attic; so I squeezed myself into it and posed in the ladder-back chair while she sketched the dress and drew in the kind of face she thought went with it; and I here and now set down for the record that a ladder-back is no kind of chair to pose in. Chloe must have been a tiny thing: I am small, but the dress would not fasten up the back, and the sleeves were tight around the armscye. Downstairs we saw a silhouette of Chloe—the artist must have gone psychic, for she had done a surprisingly good likeness. My hostess told us Chloe was a sweet and gentle little person. She lived only seven years after her marriage, but had three children in that time.

It must have been a great day when the Friends arrived for their quarterly meetings. The women of the family made elaborate preparations with cooking and baking and brewing, and the best dishes and silver were brought out. Among the women who stayed there overnight was Great-Aunt Charity Chase. She was a famous preacher in her day, for the gentle Friends were ahead of the rest of the churches in believing that, in religion at least, women equaled men.

Of course a house as old as this was bound to have some interesting papers. One of these was "An Invoice of Sundrys which my Desire Allen had from us her parents when she removed from us." It shows what a well found bride was likely to have:

A Bed and Bedstead & Cord, one pillow
4 Sheets and one old one for a head Cloth
5 Laced Pillowbeers 4 Towels one Table cloth
2 Bolster cases one Cotton & Linen
6 pewter plates 2 pewter Dishes one Bason
one pewter Cup 4 porringers w Small ones
2 Cheny plates 6 hard metal Spoons 6 pewter ones
2 Earthen Basons 2 Earthen plates a Looking Glass
A New warming pan 6 New Black Chairs a Round Table
one Square Ditto A pair of New Tongs
A Tramel one tub one Meal Trough one Small
Kettle one Broad Cloth Coat for to Dispose of to purchase
Iron ware with A case of Draws 3 Knives & forks
3 good Coverlids.

If this book was arranged strictly according to the road map it would begin with Bourne instead of Sandwich and Falmouth. Bourne runs across the head of the Cape from bay to bay, and so geographically it does come first. But the Canal split the town in two and left it straddling the waterway like Siamese twins with a couple of bridges for ligaments between them; and its personality suffered. Most of its villages are summerish anyway. For residents in up-Cape towns it was a favorite summer evening sport to drive up to Bourne and park alongside the Canal, where they could see the New York boat go through, all lighted up, her band playing and everyone on deck waving. The cars would blow their horns, and we all felt very gay and excited. So it was in the simple twenties, when it did not take much to make us happy.

Over on the Shore Road somebody discovered the hearthstone and cellar walls of the original trading post for this region; and a good copy of the little building with its steep thatched roof and tiny diamond-paned windows has been built there. The Pilgrims used to bring their furs to the post to barter with the Indians for corn, or with the Dutch traders from New Amsterdam for whatever they had. There is a park here now, and it is quite a rendezvous for tourists. I should like to see a reproduction of an entire village of those early days somewhere on the Upper Cape, like the one in Salem, for the vivid picture it would give of what the first settlers were up against.

Like Falmouth, Bourne is a master place to get lost in once you leave the main roads. A geologist wanted to take a look at the boulders of Bourne one day, and promised me a story about them; so I went along. Most of the time we did not know where we were going; and when we got back we didn't know where we had been except in a general—very general—way. If your car has not been painted recently and is good at climbing trees, the wood roads are quite all right, especially after you get out of them.

All the boulders on the Cape are said to be immigrants—there is not a native boulder in the county. The nearest ledge they could have broken off from is five miles inland from Bourne; it therefore has the lion's share of them. But Barnstable is a close second, to judge by her stone walls.

Our immediate objective was Great Rock, on Great Rock Road a mile southeast of Bourne village. We found it all right. It stood eleven feet above the ground and reached down out of sight like an iceberg; and the geologist figured it must weigh about four hundred tons. At the ground level it was chipped by the many brush fires that must have burned around it through the centuries.

Many thousands of years ago all New England was covered by a great ice sheet, or glacier, which moved down slowly from the north and picked up large blocks of rock which it carried for many miles. When the ice finally melted it dropped the boulders in Bourne and other places far from their parent ledges. (Great Rock must have traveled at least five miles, and perhaps twenty, before being dumped here; and of course the rocks beyond it on the Cape traveled much more than that.) As the ice sheet advanced it pushed up ridges of debris—clay, sand, gravel, and boulders—before it, forming the rugged hilly country of the Cape. There is no well defined drainage system, only a confused mass of hills with kettle holes (deep undrained depressions) between them holding small ponds. The backbone of the Cape was formed in this way—there is not a ledge anywhere beyond the Canal.

Instead of turning back from Great Rock we went ahead, winding this way and that over the branching roads, up hill and down dale, through wild interesting country. The road to the boulder had been rough but passable for any careful driver; beyond it there was just a network of rough, narrow little cart tracks squirming along through the scrub pines; and we were lucky indeed not to meet another car on them. We held in general to the southeast, and wriggled up and down and round about over the helter-skelter little hills, dumped down without rhyme or reason and fuzzed over with scrubby pitch pines.

When our cart track came out suddenly onto a main road we spied a branch road off to the left and took it, to see what became of it. First it took us through the Hole in the Wall (a narrow notch between the hills), then out on top of a high hill with a fine wide view. Driving through the Hole we met another car with some men in it who obviously were not sight seeing; the geologist had had some experience with moonshiners in the South, and so we carefully looked the other way. It was wild enough country for anything. It would be fine for hiking, but I would advise a compass.

4. *Mashpee, the Indians' Town*

To GET a real thrill out of life, try riding along a modern Cape highway with two Indian chieftains beside you. The chiefs with whom I did this were perfectly authentic too, even if their Wampanoag blood was mixed with alien corpuscles and they knew little or nothing of the Wampanoag language. One of them was Chief Red Jacket, and the other was Chief Morning Star; and they were taking me round to see the sights of Mashpee.

Now Mashpee is the smallest township in the county in population, and most folks miss it entirely. I had driven through the village twice without seeing it—and I was looking for it, too. The township is tucked in between Falmouth and Barnstable with a bit of frontage on Vineyard Sound. It belongs to the Indians, or to what remains of them. Few white people live within its borders, but most of the cranberry bogs which give employment to the townsfolk are owned by absentee whites. There has not been a full-blooded Indian in Mashpee for over a hundred years. During the Revolution a camp of Hessian prisoners was located there; and so there is a strain of Hessian blood along with some Portuguese (both white and "black") and more than a strain of Negro. But their set-up is like that of the rest of the Fifteen Towns, with a town hall and a public library and a couple of churches besides a school—which is doing well, with the entire population only about four hundred.

The two chiefs were taking me to the old church built
in 1684: a bare little building on a side road without steeple
or tower but well kept up and shining with white paint.
It was rarely used, and its narrow old box pews and small-
paned windows had an unlived-in-look. Around the
church in the sparse grass beneath the scrub pines clustered
the gravestones of departed Wampanoags. It went back
to the days of John Eliot, apostle to the Indians; he found
the local dialect too much for him, and it was Richard
Bourne that got the township set apart for the Wampanoags.

The saintly Bourne not only got the Indians some land
they could call their own; gentle and tolerant and wise, he
won their confidence and taught them. Generations later,
I was told, an Indian medicine man made some return to
one of the Bourne family by healing a little boy whom the
white doctor had failed to save. Their town became a
refuge for Quakers driven from neighboring towns.

Once there were eight or ten tribes of Indians on the
Cape, and they were a fine friendly cooperative lot. Without them the Pilgrims probably would not have survived.
The Indians not only supplied the white men with food
but taught them to farm and to fish and helped them adapt
themselves to their new and difficult environment.

Always when the Indians had the white men in their
power they were kind and helpful: when the whites were
wrecked, the red men fed and sheltered them; when
danger threatened, they would walk many miles through
the forests to warn them. One fine sachem, Iyanough, for
whom Hyannis and Wianno are named, was respected
even by the white men; but his death and the eventual
wiping out of the race from the lower Cape are laid by

some writers to the severities of Myles Standish, who had an idea still somewhat prevalent, that war is the only way to peace. One likes to forget the treatment they got from the men they had helped, the men who are our own fore-bears.

Across the country there are many different types of Indians. Only from the Middle West to the Cascade Range do you find the horse Indians, with finely developed bodies. In the Far Northwest, between the Cascades and the sea, were the canoe Indians, with big arms and shoul-ders and spindly legs. Because they fished without farming they had a low living standard; but the Indians of Cape Cod could both farm and fish, and that combination makes for progress in the arts of peace, whether by reds or by whites.

Any man or woman in Mashpee who can claim descent from the Wampanoags is proud of the fact, and has a right to be. The two chiefs introduced me to a couple of sweet-faced old ladies in whom the Indian strain was strong: Mrs. Sarah Rockwell and Aunt Rhody Sturgiss. Mrs. Rockwell was the daughter of the beloved Parson Amos, who was not only an eloquent preacher but a sweet musician. Both women were fully conscious of the dignity of their race. They were indeed a splendid people, these early settlers of the Cape, and their chiefs were often men of character and ability. Only in one other place in Massachusetts is there even such a faded remnant of the native stock.

That summer the school children of Indian descent were giving a pageant in which they represented scenes from their ancestral life and history. Girls costumed as squaws tended papooses and ground the family corn. Boys rigged out for hunting practiced archery or told tales about the campfire. Though the rude tepee was made of burlap bags it gave more than a suggestion of the real thing, there in its natural setting. A rich mine of Indian lore must exist on the Cape. Either the older people have forgotten, or else the natural Indian taciturnity has combined with an ingrained and quite understandable distrust of white people to make it hard for them to tell what they may know. I found one could get much more from white men in the neighboring villages who had heard the tales as boys when they all played together.

Eben, the older of the two chieftains, was one of the most intriguing men I met on the Cape. A man in his middle sixties, gray-haired and stocky and with a touch of native dignity, it was hard to imagine him as a camp cook, which he was then; but it was still harder to see him as a dancer of fire dances and a rough rider with Buffalo Bill, which he had been. He had had still a third career, of which more anon, but his experience on the road was the most colorful.

When he was a young fellow, back in 1875, a man named Montana Charlie who had some sort of traveling Indian road show—very likely a medicine show—took Eben on tour for a winter and sent him up to Oldtown, Maine, to be taught the sort of things an Indian needed to know for atmosphere. War dances and fire dances are not in the tradition of his peaceable tribe; but he learned them, sporting a hatchet that was "painted up to look like a tomahawk." He joined another show after that and learned still more of the things a good Indian should know. Then Buffalo Bill heard about him and took him out on tour with his company of cowboys and Indians.

Now his troubles began. The Cape Indians were not horse Indians, so far as we know, but Buffalo Bill, being first of all a showman, expected his Indians to ride, wherever they came from—to him a noble red man sans horse was unthinkable. So Chief Red Jacket had to ride, whether or no. It was plain to me that he was never an enthusiastic horseman. He spoke very respectfully of Buffalo Bill, always as Mr. Cody, and still cherished his old outfit with the grand feather headdress, which he put on to have his picture taken. I must say he looked anything but convincing in the home-town setting of green grass and pitch pine; but that is how it is when a man tries to live up to what people expect of him.

When the troupe got to Boston he left it and spent several winters at Austin & Stone's glorified side-show museum. Much of the time he seems to have sat on the stage "taking care of Montana's exhibit of horns." He was vague about the details except that while he was there he went to cooking school and learned the profession at which he was working when I knew him. He was not an ordinary domestic or restaurant cook, mind you, but the kind that goes out with state foresters or with hunting or fishing parties. This was more in keeping with his racial memories—forest and stream and campfire—and he seemed happy.

Between jobs he was practicing a side line he liked best of all; and that was basket-making.

He would probably have given his whole time to the baskets if he could have made them pay, for he was proud of his skill in this lost art of his tribe. His father had taught him the art of making the "old antique baskets" that had come down from father to son through no one knows how many generations. Eben taught a few of the younger Indians his craft, but he was not optimistic about their carrying it on.

"None of them has time now to make baskets. They get an automobile, and away they go. I tell them, if they don't own a house or even a shingle, they have to have an automobile. They say," he quoted wryly, "the truth is not to be told on all occasions. They don't know how often I keep still. . . . Now there's only a few of us left, and they will go marry outsiders."

Eben had the distinction of making a fish basket which was unique. Experts believed he was the only man in the world who knew how to make it. It was a small pear-shaped affair with an opening at the smaller end and a long handle of peculiar workmanship which went over the shoulder knapsack-fashion. He made it from narrow strips of the white oak which he gathered in the woods but which are gone now along with his secret. He made smaller, square baskets for berries or eggs, which he told me were of different workmanship from baskets made by other Indians. He had none to show me because the "museum in Cambridge"—I suppose he meant Harvard—had bought up all he made; but I found a man in one of the Falmouth villages who had a small private collection, of which he was rightfully proud. Eben's baskets are collectors' items now.

Still to be found through the woods were paths made by the early Indians. There used to be many of them. At an intersection on the road across Mashpee between Waquoit and Cotuit, I came upon an "Indian tavern"—one of those piles of brush about four feet high often found at the V of a forking trail. Maybe they were formed by one Indian after another depositing a twig to show which road he was taking; but the white men call them Indian taverns. The Indians themselves are mum about the piles; but the white men who know them best say that even nowadays every time an Indian passes one he adds a twig and makes a wish. Certainly somebody is adding twigs, for the piles are growing in size.

The Money Hole is something else again. That is a hole with a pine tree growing up in the middle of it, on a trail not far from Popponesset Beach, which is on the Mashpee shore. According to local tradition Indians were digging there once for some unknown reason when they saw a strange light and fled. They never went back to finish the job, and it is said they don't like to go by there after dark to this day. It happened long enough ago for a good-sized tree to grow up in the hole. Of course a favorite theory is pirate gold.

Few of the Mashpee Indian legends have come down to us. One is about a girl named Ahsoo, ugly of face but so beautiful of voice that even the fishes in the sea fell in love with her. One big trout was so eager to get nearer to her that he gouged out Cotuit River in his efforts. He failed, and Ahsoo died of a broken heart. (Stories like this in which animals and humans are regarded as equals are common among the canoe Indians of the Northwest, too.)

Another legend concerned the Indian giant Maushop, who used to wade across to Martha's Vineyard at low tide without getting his knees wet. He smoked a pipe with pokeweed in it; and when you find yourself in a smother of fog it is more than likely the smoke from his pipe.

They say he used to curl up on the Cape with his head at Truro and his feet tucked in at Falmouth. He liked it because it was soft and sandy; but one morning he found his moccasins all full of sand, and it made him so mad he snatched them off and flung them into the water of the South Sea, there they are to this day. One of them is named Nantucket, and the other is Martha's Vineyard.

That's all I've been able to find out about Maushop, and I am not too sure about that.

5. *Old High Barnstable*

ONE SWEET spring morning my little car and I went moseying along through the ways and byways of Barnstable village—Old High Barnstable, the shire town of Barnstable County. If you don't know the Cape in April you don't know the Cape, and you don't know April. Without getting lyrical about it, let me remind you that the Mayflowers are out amongst the pine needles, perfuming the woods and fairly carpeting them. Also the woods are flushed with the red buds of the maples and the clear yellow-green buds of the willows.

As for the color of the water lapping the golden beaches —imagine a diamond the color of a zircon, or a zircon with the sparkle and life of a diamond. That is how any one of the four seas looks on a lively spring morning.

Then there is the air, so sweet and winy, and the bird songs lilting down from the wineglass elms—Excuse me, I'm just on the ragged edge. We don't have spring in the Far Northwest, just months named April and May— though, to be quite fair, we don't have spring thaws, either.

Barnstable is one of the loveliest towns in all America any time of year, though April puts her at her best. Her grace is spiritual as well as physical. One of the two oldest towns on the Cape, she has aged with distinction. Part of her quality is due to the kind of men who founded her,

59

part of it to her having the county courthouse—we won't say anything about the county jail.

There was a time, old residents tell you—back in the eighties, say—when practically all the men of substance who shaped the affairs of the county lived within a mile of the courthouse. This affected the physical aspect of the town. The massive granite courthouse with its ancient cannon and its shadowing elms is impressive; but so are the houses. These beautifully proportioned old dwellings were built in an era when taste was really good. They are larger and more dignified than those of most other towns, and have a character of their own. Falmouth has fine dignified old houses, too, but those of Barnstable are different.

Besides the small, very old, houses the village has a number of these others, large and substantial, built something more than a century ago, at both ends of town. When the "new" courthouse was to be built, each end of town hoped to get it; so the rival factions put up fine houses to accommodate the crowds of guests who would come in while court was sitting. Gorhams headed the east faction, and Lothrops the west. The Lothrops won, but the town is richer for the rivalry.

There is a story about those cannon on the courthouse lawn. When I was there Alfred Crocker was the clerk of court and had been for thirty years. His long association with legal minds made him explicit about details, but did not prevent him from telling a good story. He told me how the cannon got there—and he knew, because he put them there himself.

Their story began back in 1812, while we were at war with England. His grandfather, Loring Crocker, lived in Barnstable and owned the saltworks, which were a major industry along the bay shore. Brewster, the second town east, had been threatened by the British ships which were harrying the coast: her saltworks would be destroyed if she did not raise $4,000 to save them. That was a lot of money, but the town raised it.

When the British came to Barnstable they saw a bigger and more prosperous-looking community; so they raised the price of salvation to $6,000. But they did not know the Crockers of Barnstable. Loring said they would fight first. That very afternoon he sent a couple of teams of heavy horses pounding off on the long trip to Boston after cannon. They brought back four, and he set them up on the Common Fields where the saltworks were. He put a guard there with a gun and orders to fire if the British attempted to come ashore, and another guard in the church steeple to ring the church bell if he heard the shot. The enemy did not like the look of things, so they up-anchored and sailed away.

Some years ago Alfred Crocker found these two cannon —one buried in the sand—and set them up where they are now.

The minute you get into one of the older houses, you become involved in the lively story of the town. For instance there is the Sturgis library. It stands well back from the road with a great tree in front to soften its square white austerity. Its doorway is off-center, with two windows on one side and one on the other; but the design is good, and you don't miss anything. In our local architecture we get along beautifully—and "beautifully" is the word—without symmetry. We leave that for more regimented souls.

Along in the middle 1600's this house was built as a

parsonage for a beloved clergyman, the Reverend John Lothrop. He was one of the most highly educated and enlightened men who came to New England in those early days. Back in England he and many of his parishioners had been thrown into prison for their more liberal theology. While he was there his wife died, leaving him with six small children to think about while he was finishing his sentence. When he got out he and a group of his followers came to the new world to found a parish in the wilderness where they would be free to worship as they liked.

It was because of his vision and tolerance that Barnstable treated the Quakers more kindly—or maybe we should say less harshly—than the other towns. Indeed the influence of his fine intelligent mind is still felt in the character of the village.

To the west of his house and on the same side of the road stands Gray Shingles, called the oldest house in the village and supposed to have been built the year after the settlement of the town and used as a tavern. Two-storied in front and one behind, it has the saltbox roof that so often resulted when more room was needed on the ground floor and the roof was brought down to cover the addition. A series of typically Capy little ells added still more room from time to time, no doubt little houses moved up and fastened onto it. This house was unspoiled by any attempts at restoration but looked very stanch and strong.

Over in the center of the village, on the corner of Bow Lane and the King's Highway—there's an address for you! —stands the Crocker house, the largest in town. It was built in 1790 by Deacon Timothy Phinney, who built and sold many of the larger houses. This one was bought by young David Crocker for his bride. His portrait shows a dream of manly beauty with a mouth that was the masculine version of a cupid's bow. It is hard to imagine a man like that being high sheriff, but he was. Succeeding generations kept building onto the house till they got to the barn and had to stop. Behind the house, back along Bow Lane, roamed an old-fashioned garden with a box hedge that must have been pretty ancient. Some venerable elms shaded it, and it was all very casual and lovely in the spring sunshine.

One could afford to build well in the seventeenth century. Kittredge says a one-story frame house could be built then for about $25. He describes a two-story one that was built in 1642, its frame of oak and with a stone chimney, which cost only $100. Of course they did not look then as they do today, for their roofs were thatched with sedge grass from the marshes and their walls of hewn logs were chinked with clay. At first, too, their floors were just the packed earth, for sawing boards was a long hard job and one they no doubt put off till more essential things were done.

Those first settlers had so many things to get done before they could be even safe, let alone comfortable, and they nearly all had to be done at once.

Conspicuous in the village was the Blue-Blind House. This has been a landmark for generations—you always directed strangers "so many doors from the Blue-Blind House." I don't know what would happen if anyone were to change those faded old blue shutters to the orthodox green—you simply could not find a thing in town! Fortunately one of its later owners said something in his will about keeping them blue. It is a very dignified house with a chimney at each end—which is an unusual arrangement here—and symmetrically placed windows.

Next door to the Blue-Blind House—see how easy it is to use the name!—stood the old Amos Otis place. It was not so typical of Barnstable as the larger houses, but was much more typical of the Cape as a whole. It dated back to 1745, about the time when the Cape-type house was being developed into what we now have. Its front wall was clapboarded and painted white, but its end walls were shingled and gray with age. Its roof ran down to a low lean-to ell in the back, giving it one of the most graceful roof lines I've seen, and it still had its big central chimney. There lived James Otis, the famous orator of pre-Revolutionary days. He represented the liberal wing of thought as opposed to the Tory, which was pretty prevalent in the old town.

Over on one corner of Bow Lane was a "high single" house. Near there folks walking to church on a Sunday used to stop by a rock to put on their shoes and stockings before they went into the Lord's house. Centerville communicants came from so far they had to wait over for the afternoon service, and they spent the time visiting in this house. It used to get so crowded that the children would have to be shooed out into the yard to play "to keep its sides from bursting out."

One could go on forever telling tales of Barnstable dwellings. The one which impressed me most was the Gorham house over Cummaquid way, which means East Barnstable. A big gray-shingled house, it had a small entry in the middle and rooms on either side. At the back the kitchen, originally longer than now, had the two typical small rooms at each end. Its fireplace was built to hold five-foot logs—fortunately the Cape was well timbered in those days—but now held the kitchen range, with room to spare. The walls were covered with feathered sheathing.

Across the back of the kitchen had once been a lean-to shed with a small diamond-shaped window. That little window—prepare for a shock!—was used by master or mistress of the house as a peephole. Through it they kept watch over their Negro slaves to make sure they were working as they should, out in the meadows back of the house. Oh yes, there were lots of slaves on the Cape before the Civil War and half of them were owned in this one town, at that time I suppose the most prosperous. The Gorhams must have been kind to their colored folk, for there is a story of one slave whose dying wish was that he might be buried at his msitress' feet. Another slave-owner seems to have lacked a proper sense of humor, though, for in his will he solemnly asked that his slaves be sold and the proceeds used to buy Bibles for "each of my said wives and my grandchildren."

Fireplaces in the two front rooms of the Gorham house of course had paneled mantels—the one in the dining room was recessed and quite stately. What stories must have been told by the men of that pioneering family as they sat at ease in their roundabout chairs, smoking and drinking their rum! John Gorham, who built the house in 1690, was lieutenant colonel in the Indian wars and second in command of the whaleboat fleet. The "old French wars" and the Indian fighting made wonderful fireside tales, especially for youngsters sitting still as mice in the chimney corner.

But it was not its fireplace or its wainscots or its paneling, or even its history, which made this house unique among those I had seen. It was the way it was built. Exposed in the rooms are the timbers of its framing—in the best room the cornice and summerbeam (summertree, it is sometimes called) are carved, but in the others they were left rough-hewn. Sill and plate and gunstock post were all heavy and massive beyond belief. The best room had low window seats and inside shutters, a rare feature in Cape houses. I thought the shelf above the fireplace had been added to the paneling, though it was so well done you could not be quite sure. Also I suspect the roof was once of the salt-box type, from the way a back room upstairs was timbered. But the house had been remarkably untroubled by the generations sheltered within it, and showed little sign of age. It should be good for centuries more.

One could write a book about the houses of this one town alone—I have not even mentioned the old stagecoach tavern, opposite the library, or the Cobb-Shaw house next door—both those names roost in my family tree—but one must stop somewhere.

As a rule you did not find the retired sea captains living in the older houses. This was probably because they came home from the sea pretty well feathered and eager to build themselves new and up-to-the-minute homes. But that did not mean they weren't interesting. You might know the house of Captain Ansel D. Lothrop, for instance, by the big wrought-iron knocker on the door. The captain picked it up in Malta. They were tearing down an old house, and he salvaged the knocker. Later he had it silvered and hung it on his front door, and when you went to call most of High Barnstable could hear you knocking.

He was having his four o'clock coffee when I banged on his door that afternoon. The coffee was a relic of the time when a day was divided into watches and you ate accordingly. This time was not so far past for him as it was for most of the retired shipmasters, for Captain Lothrop, though he was eighty-two, saw service at sea in World War Number One, not to mention fifty years of it before that. He had followed the sea for the best part of his life, and had his papers for steam as well as sail.

He filled his chummy little pipe and sat down with me in the sitting room bay window to tell me of the days gone by. But his eyes kept straying out to the fields and woods. Only the day before he had had one of the battles of his career out there—"Fire got away from me and took to the woods," he explained briefly. His face and hands were somewhat scorched—but that was nothing. "I enjoyed it!" said the captain. He was living very much in the present, and went back to the past with an effort.

"Yes, I've been round the world," he admitted. "How many times? Let me see . . . clean round, not part way and back . . ." He paused to sort out his voyages. So many had been nearly around. "Three," he decided, "all the way around." Oh yes, in a square-rigger, of course. "All the Barnstable boys went in them. Too lazy to go in coasters. Our men all went off deep water. I can remember over a hundred shipmasters I used to know here in Barnstable. Now I'm the only one left."

He fetched paintings of two of his ships, the *Agenor* and the *Conqueror*—six years he commanded the former, ten years the latter. The pictures were done by a Chinese artist out in Hong Kong. But his first voyage, made when he was sixteen, was on the *Belle Creole* out of Boston. Was he homesick that first night? Homesick? No, didn't have time to be.

"Too busy shoveling snow. Left Boston in a no'therly

wind and snowstorm. When we got to Shanghai it was like being back on the Cape—eight Cape Cod boys came aboard from other ships anchored there. We had a lot of boys from round home on our ship, too, and the officers. Captain Allen was from Yarmouth, First Mate Nelson Hallett from Centerville, Second Mate Samuel Thatcher from Yarmouth. Seven boys in the crew were from round here —four from Barnstable, two from Yarmouth and one from Orleans. It was a first trip for most of us, too. Once, out in Shanghai, that was in 1863, we had thirty-four Cape Cod boys from the different ships. One of them was Captain Gustavus Crowell of Harwich, then first mate of the *Wild Rover,* and another was Captain Mark Hall of Dennis."

For five years, during the Civil War and after, he stayed in Shanghai, "because the *Alabama* was there." Running down to Singapore and Penang with coolies—"not much romance in that," he said. Carried coolies south in winter and freighted sugar north in summer—carry coolies down, bring back sugar. Routine stuff.

Not much of a talker was the captain. Fragments out of a lively past were told in the fewest possible words. Out in a typhoon a couple of times. "Typhoon" is the Chinese word, "hurricane" the Spanish, "cyclone" the English. Once was out in the South Indian Ocean. Running in a heavy gale, a wave came over astern. He and the mate were standing by the after cabin. The wave took him to the main hatch, eighty feet forrard of where he had been. The mate? Never saw him again.—So much for that story.

Lost a ship once. On a reef in the Java Sea. Got eleven feet of water in her in twenty minutes. Yes, they got ashore all right.—And so much for that story.

THE CHURCH AND MILLPOND, SANDWICH

AUNT MARTHA HOXIE HOUSE, SANDWICH

FISHING BOATS, WOODS HOLE

THE GREAT MARSHES, BARNSTABLE

No, he never got piled up on Cape Cod; but came near it once. Saw Cape Cod Light—summer folks call it High-land Light—through a smother of snow, off the jib boom. Came about almighty quick. Close shave. Close as he wanted.—And so much for that.

The other typhoon? That was his second voyage in the *Endeavor*. In the China Sea. "Worst one I was ever out in." What happened? "Nothing."

In 1912, after half a century at sea, Captain Lothrop decided to settle down ashore. But when the World War came he answered the call, though he was over seventy, and saw two or three more years of active service before he finally retired. Asked if he didn't hanker sometimes for the sea, he looked out over his tidy acres and his garden, and shook his head.

"I wouldn't want to go to sea again now, the way things are," he said. "Take a man who had been to sea in a sail-ing vessel, and they don't set good. If a sailor comes up to you and tells you to go to the devil you can go or not as you like, but there isn't anything you can do to him."

He went on, "A captain used to be king of his ship. His word was law. But now it is different. If he has to be out on the bridge in the middle of the night and wants a cup of coffee, he's either got to make it himself or else pay the cook overtime to make it for him. No, with things the way they are, I'd rather be ashore."

It occurred to me the cook's point of view might be in-teresting, too, but I saw no way to get it.

It isn't always spring and summer on the Cape, though off-Capers are likely to think of it that way. Great winds sweep the sandy old arm from shoulder to fist in winter, and blizzards bury it deep in snow. It claims a somewhat milder climate than the rest of Massachusetts; but, even leaving out hurricanes, it has its bad moments.

Alfred Crocker told me about a storm he had good cause to remember. It happened some years before he became clerk of court, in fact back in the days when he was a mail clerk on the train that ran from Boston down-Cape to Wellfleet. The train stopped there because the railroad did—it had not been put through to Provincetown yet.

"It was a December night in 1872, and snowing hard," the story starts. "We were three hours late leaving Boston, and four hours later we had only got as far as Holbrook, twenty miles out. We should have been in Wellfleet by then, but it was snowing harder and beginning to drift."

It was way past suppertime, and the passengers were getting hungry. But the train carried no diner on the short run, and the little twenty-five ton engine was too busy nosing through the drifts to stop anywhere for refreshments. Young Crocker was hungry, too, so he set out to see what he could do. In the express car he found a barrel of crackers, a fifty-pound box of sausages and a lot of empty cartons. These were all being shipped to some consignee; but this was an emergency with all those hungry folks back in the day coaches, not to mention himself.

His car was heated by a coal stove, so he dusted off the coal shovel and used it for a skillet to fry the sausages. The empty boxes made individual service possible, and the crackers completed the banquet.

Anyone who slept that night slept sitting up. When they got to a station a few would get off, but there were still plenty left. The snow kept falling, and the wind blew it into drifts. The little engine made heavy weather of it. She wasn't rigged with a plow, just had a couple of

dickeyboards stuck on her cowcatcher. They left Boston
on Thursday evening. Next forenoon, Friday, they got
into Sandwich, ordinarily a two-hour run from Boston.
There a kindly expressman named Boyden brought two
milk cans of coffee and a stack of sandwiches to the passengers, of whom by now there were about forty.

So far progress had been rapid compared with what
was to come. You get the big winds down Cape. Big
winds mean big drifts. The train made Hyannis that evening after seventeen miles of plugging with two engines,
one at each end, one burning coal, the other burning wood.
At ten o'clock that night they set out again for the long
push down-Cape, but part way across from Hyannis they
stuck—and stuck good and hard. By this time the snow
was so deep that from a little distance all you could see of
the train was the bell-mouth of the smokestack. The wind
blew the snow in faster than the crew could shovel it out,
so there was no use shoveling.

Next morning—it is Saturday now—a train came down
from Hyannis. This added a third engine, and enabled
them to get through to Yarmouth. There they got a plow
made out of a flatcar loaded with steel rails to hold it
down on the tracks, and went on. That night they got to
Orleans, just round the elbow of the Cape. There still remained the worst of the run down the forearm where the
weather is always specially virile.

All next day—Sunday—they were ramming the great
drifts. They would push ahead a few feet and stick, then
they would back up and get momentum for another push,
which would give them a few feet more. It must have been
anything but soothing for the passengers. By ten o'clock
that night they made Eastham, three miles beyond Orleans.

This was a great occasion. Everybody piled out of the train and trudged through the snow to the village inn. The innkeeper had killed a couple of hogs the day before, and they got busy and fried all the lean meat on both of them.

"The landlady stood on one side of the kitchen stove and I stood on the other," Mr. Crocker said, "and we fried chops for our crowd till midnight. I was what somebody called the 'decaterer.'"

Monday noon, with half a dozen passengers left aboard, the train crawled into Wellfleet. They had been a jolly crowd, taking the whole experience as a lark. Mr. Crocker wondered how many of them were still living. A few months later the tracks were extended to Provincetown, but that day everyone was perfectly willing to stop in Wellfleet.

Mr. Crocker said they met the up-Cape train in Holbrook, much belated. On it was a wedding party returning to Boston from Centerville. The colored caterer who had gone down to serve the wedding feast fed them the ice cream and cake that were left over. They got into Boston in the small hours of the morning to find the ground deep with snow and no cabs or horsecars—the horses were all sick with epizootic. Boston's "big fire" came along during that epidemic, and got its head start because so many of the firehorses were sick.

6. *Hyannis and Round About*

BARNSTABLE TOWNSHIP crosses the Cape, facing the Bay on the north and Nantucket Sound on the south. Scattered over it are some two score ponds and a dozen villages. Out in the grandiloquent west many if not most of them would be called lakes and cities, but here even the larger ones are likely to be simply ponds and villages. In this township rises the loftiest eminence anywhere east of the Canal. Shoot Flying Hill, elevation 210 feet. If you don't think that is high, you should see the rest of the town. It got its name from a way the Indians had of shooting the wild fowl as they flew from the Great Marshes to Wequaket for a drink of fresh water. They shot the birds in flight.

The Great Marshes stretch between Shoot Flying and the Bay. The Pilgrims, who used to come there from Plymouth to cut hay, called them the Hay Grounds. Sandy Neck, a long skinny arm of sand dunes and scrub pines, shelters Barnstable Harbor from the sea. This neck is a natural way station for migratory birds, and hundreds of varieties stop off there on their way north or south, besides a big colony of night herons that nest among the pines.

Largest and most important of the villages in a business way is Hyannis, the shopping center for the whole mid-Cape region. The *Cape Cod Magazine* office was there, on the main street, but I was in it only once. I worked out of

Centerville, a small village three or four miles west along the Sound. It had less historic interest than some of the villages, but it made a good center from which to radiate —and my job involved radiating.

Its chief virtue, though, was that I could stay in the home of one of my tenth cousins, Evelyn Crosby. She was of both Pilgrim (Mayflower) and Puritan stock, and she knew most of what was to be known about that part of the country. She lived in a big three-story house that her grandparents had kept as an inn. But, except for me and an old dog and an occasional tourist, she lived there alone. An attractive young woman, she was a college graduate but Cape to her pretty fingertips. I don't recall ever seeing her hurried, though she had plenty to do. She ran the big house single-handed, tended a growing real estate business, and with the help of the village constable looked after the cranberry bogs without which no home on the Cape is quite complete. The constable, Mr. West, is a shining example of what years do to a man in that county—Evelyn writes me he is ninety-three, and thinks nothing of taking a five-mile hike from West Barnstable to Centerville. I thought of him as quite an old man twenty years ago, but it was my error.

Off to one side of the house and well back from the road stood the big barn, flanked on one side by the house and on the other by the cranberry hall. In the old days that barn had sheltered the twenty horses of the two stage-coaches which broke their up-Cape or down-Cape run here, as well as the carriage and saddle horses of lone travelers. But that year my little roadster was the only occupant except a couple of chickens.

One of the chickens was a rooster, kept as company

for the hen. As near as I could make out my cousin didn't want another hen because she didn't want another rooster, for she was a strict believer in monogamy. One day we drove over to Brewster to see a modern poultry plant run by a woman with its batteries of pedigreed birds. They compared notes on their way of doing things, and I don't know which was more scandalized.

The cranberry house had once been a public meeting place known as Liberty Hall, and it stood across the road from the inn. But it had outlived that stage of usefulness and had been moved over near the barn. There Evelyn and the old constable used to toil for hours on end. The cranberries would be put through the separator, then into a big trough where they would be screened, and then run into barrels and boxes for the city markets. Today the separator is run by electricity, but then it was done by hand. I've known her to stay out there most of a long winter night with the temperature outside down around zero trying to keep enough fire going in the railroad stove to save the berries from freezing—and apparently quite indifferent as to whether she herself froze or not.

There was a cranberry growers' association which would have handled the whole process for her, but like so many Capers she was independent and liked to handle her own crop. Now, owing to labor difficulties—which probably means the constable has retired—she writes me she is selling the crop "on the bog."

Most evenings we sat in front of the fire in her living room and talked about the Cape she knew so well. Alfred Crocker, the venerable clerk of court, lived across the road and sometimes he would come over and yarn with us. He came of distinguished pioneer stock and not only knew the stories but knew how to tell them. He was one of the best mid-Cape raconteurs. It was very cosy those long fall evenings sitting there by the fire while the winds, gathering their forces for winter, rattled the windows.

The house was not old enough to have a fireplace, and it was too old for a Franklin stove. So it had the less usual in-between type which they call a fireframe. It is so much less common than either of the others that you might like to know about it. An iron frame the size and shape of a fireplace opening, adorned with an oval brass placque and a brass ball on each corner, is set up against the face of the chimney. It projects several inches into the room, and under the shallow hood thus formed an opening into the chimney lets the smoke up the flue. The andirons stand in a bed of ashes on a brick hearth—a bed that may be five or six inches thick and that holds the heat a long time—and the fire is laid between a forestick and a backlog. It seemed to chilly little me that the forestick shut off a lot of the heat; but that may have been imagination. The fireframe is so shallow that the body of the fire comes partly out into the room, but the draft is good and the smoke always goes up the flue instead of into your face as you might expect and as it doubtless would anywhere else but on the Cape.

I got my meals in Hyannis or wherever I happened to be, but one stormy night Evelyn asked me out to the big old kitchen to have some quahaug chowder with her. (You want to forget how that word is spelled and pronounce it "kohog.") If you live outside the quahaug belt you might like to try it over on your clams. There really is little difference; the quahaug is a hard-shelled clam. They are both bi-valves.

Here is the recipe for quahaug chowder, Crosby style: Try out in a kettle a quarter of a pound of salt pork, add one pint of water and cook half a dozen potatoes diced fine, six smallish onions chopped fine and a pint of quahaugs also chopped fine, adding their liquor. Cook slowly half an hour or till done, stirring to keep from sticking. Then add a pint of rich milk that has been heated to avoid curdling and crumble in saltines or plain crackers for thickening, add a piece of butter the size of an egg, salt and pepper to taste. This is delicious fresh, and still better when heated over next day.

Some of the stories, told in the give-and-take of casual talk there by the fire, I took down in shorthand, but others had to be stored in my memory till I could get to my typer. I don't remember who told which, all I'm reasonably sure of is that they are true because they would be. They reflected the spicier lingo of an earlier day, the folk speech of the Cape as it is seldom heard nowadays, and also the folk wit of which traces are still found.

There was a snatch of the lingo in the remark of the old woman who had three husbands but each one died quicker 'n the one before him. When someone asked her what she did to them she sighed, "Godfrey domino, somepin the matter with 'em when I get 'em."

Then there was the sorrowful tale of Old Lady Bowen. Seems she was the proud possessor of one of the first union suits in town—those long-sleeved, long-legged ones which succeeded the undervest-and-drawers outfits. She was feeling pretty cocky in her new fangled running gear till the March thaw set in, with the roads a mixture of ice and slush. She slipped on a piece of ice and sat down kerplunk in the slush.

" 'Tain't right!" she cried, " 'tain't right! 'Tarnal union suit—wet your pants and change your shirt!"

Or take the tale of Bill versus Uncle Jabez. It happened back in the days when rum was the national beverage and a thirsty man who was poor in this world's goods had to use his wits. Fortunately Bill had his share for use in emergencies, for it was always low tide in his old leather wallet. Uncle Jabez ran the tavern in this town where hard likker had to be paid for with hard cash, and Bill's credit rating was none too good—in fact I gathered it was no good.

One day Bill took his gallon jug to a spring and filled it half full of nice cold water and fetched it over to the tavern. Wallet conspicuous in one hand, and jug in the other, he approached Uncle Jabez.

"Jabe," he says, "I've got a gang of men working for me over on the marsh gettin' hay. It's pretty hot, and they're thirsty. I want to get this jug filled up to carry over to them."

Jabe sees the wallet and he takes the jug. "It's half full now," he says, hefting it.

"Yeah, but I want a couple quarts more," says Bill.

Jabez takes the jug into the taproom and brings it back full. But Bill has put his wallet back into his pants pocket.

"My wife musta took the money, I thought sure I had some," he says, "I'll come round this afternoon and pay you."

"No you wunt," says Uncle Jabez, "you'll pay me now or you don't get the rum."

Bill heaves a sigh and says, "All right, take out the two quarts you put in and gimme back the jug. The boys 'll have to git along with what I got."

Jabe took the jug back into the taproom and poured two quarts back into the barrel, but it wasn't the same stuff he had poured out a few minutes before, also what he left in the jug was not the same. It was now half-and-half, which is all you need for a perfectly good drink. Bill took his jug and went home owing no man anything.

But Bill was not the only nimble-witted man in town. There was a carpenter who was hired to fix the church spire—I think it was the West Barnstable church, but am not sure. Anyhow he agreed to do the work for fifty dollars, but soon saw the job was going to be worth more than that. The church deacons held him to his price, and he couldn't get another shilling out of them. He finished the job, but when it was done he left the staging up.

"I'll take it down for another fifty," he said.

"We'll take it down ourselves," said the deacons.

"No you wunt," said he. "That there stagin's held by one nail," he said, "just one nail, and if you was to pull it first it would be sure death to you." So he got the other fifty and no hard feelings.

There were many tales of the sea captains who once lived round about. Most of them weren't whalers, either —there was a social distinction between whalers and merchantmen, not to mention captains of fishermen and packets. Merchantmen were the aristocracy of the sea.

One story concerned a captain who finished his last voyage in a barrel of oil. How and why he met his end remained an unsolved mystery, though people had their little theories. It was known that on the previous voyage one of the crew from his own home town did not come back, and nobody knew what had happened to him—he just wasn't there. The very next voyage it was the captain himself who failed to come back, or rather who came back in the barrel of oil, which was practically the same as far as he was concerned. Now at home that captain was an angel of light—even his wife said so. But get him out on blue water, walking his own quarter deck, and he became a holy terror. Just how bad he was nobody felt free to say, and of course that made it seem all the worse. And his death remained a mystery, and a mystery it is to this day.

Whichever one it was told me that story wouldn't mention his name or even tell the town he came from—merely said it was not more than fifty miles from Hyannis.

Now, that is an odd thing about the Cape. Things like that are strictly hush-hush. During the mid-twenties, when I was there, a considerable effort was being made to persuade the village papers all up and down to publish the names of those who had come to trial during the court session in Barnstable. But if the names were those of hometown or even home-county boys, not a single name would any of them print. In vain it was pointed out that the papers would be doing the public a service, because the notoriety would act as a crime deterrent.

"We're all more or less related here on the Cape," they explained, "and you never know what the repercussions might be." And they were right, too—with ten or fifteen thousand cousins more or less removed but all within easy driving distance you really do have to be careful.

Bundling was another thing you could never pin down to cases. It had been common in Civil War days. Evelyn told me her mother said she often heard it mentioned when she was a girl, though it was not done among the "better" families. It must have been a hangover from the previous century when it was common all over New England. I ran across an old "Bundling Song" at the Antiquarian Library in Worcester one day—not all of it is quotable even in these easy days, but this much will give an idea of how the custom was regarded by the soberer members of the community:

> Since bundling very much abounds,
> In many parts of country towns,
> No doubt but some will spurn my song,
> And say I'd better hold my tongue;
> But none I'm sure will take offence,
> Or deem my song impertinence,
> But only those who guilty be,
> And plainly here their picture see,
> And let it be in common fame,
> Held up to view a noted shame.
> Young miss if this your practice be,
> I'll teach you now yourself to see:
> You plead you're honest, modest too,
> But such a plea will never do;
> For how can modesty consist,
> With shameful practice such as this?

This song is credited with doing much to abolish the custom. But no doubt it had plenty of justification in fact. If your boy friend came from so far away that he couldn't get back the same night, or a storm came up, and the fire was out in the fore room, and even the kitchen was cold, and all the beds but yours were full—you couldn't ask him to sleep on the floor; now, could you? If your mother was the careful kind she tied your night rail round your feet or else wound you up in a sort of cocoon with a sheet, and anyhow you had a good chance to talk things over.

Scrabbling for a living was hard work before the summer folks began to come. But even so there were those who got by with a minimum of effort and a maximum of enjoyment. Of such were the residents of Happy Hollow, over back of the "new" hotel in Hyannis. Now Hyannis as I knew it was the most nearly conventional, not to say rotarian, settlement on the Cape, a busy shopping center for summer folks and tourists, quite lacking in anything that could be called atmosphere. With its main street and its little "shoppes" filled with souvenirs it was the last place you would expect to pick up a tale like that of Happy Hollow.

But it was a straight story. I got it from the local doctor, who had lived in Hyannis all his life and knew whereof he spoke. As we scuffed along through the dust of the little roads winding through patches of grass and scrub pines, past a couple of little old gray-shingled shacks that were all that was left of its wild and wicked past, the doctor told me about the people who had lived there so merrily. He explained how Gentle Annie got her name, and how much of a witch Zibe's wife really was—"She looked like one, anyway, and she told fortunes, and used to go barefoot in the snow"—and about Black Jane, who wasn't black but her husband was—and all the rest of the lively crew who kept the good citizens of Hyannis both worried and amused. In the bright sunshine of this warm June day it was hard to credit the old goings-on, when Zeke and Charlie played the fiddle and the bass viol and Three-Fingered Ruth made merry with Zibe and Gentle Annie and the rest.

Some of the stories were sketched in lightly. Like the one about Black Jane, who was "helping out" in an uptown family and drank the stove blacking because she had a thirst, and she had seen her employer putting alcohol into it. Nothing happened, she just got well lit.

Like several of her neighbors Three-Fingered Ruth was a successful beggar. She used to go round to back doors with a bag and collect from the kind-hearted. The doctor remembered seeing as a boy two of the "elect ladies" of the town slipping away from the hovel of Zibe's wife where they had been to have their fortunes told. They caught him watching, and warned him never to tell anyone he had seen them. It must have made an impression, because even after all these years he refused to give me their names.

Tamsey Ann was another of the celebrities, and so was Becky of the many husbands—these were of assorted colors and the ensuing families were red, white, brown and yellow. It was Becky, I think, who was responsible for the naming of Happy Hollow. She had come from another town, where the small boys "plagued the life out of her." When someone asked her how she liked it here she cried, "Oh, I am so happy!" And Happy Hollow it became.

But the King of Happy Hollow was none of all these. He stood alone, and there was none like him—and never will there be while time lasts. His name was Barney Gould.

Barney had been gone for twenty years; but mention his name to anyone, and the stories began to gush. Everybody on the Cape knew him; and many at a distance also, for he was a great traveler and famous in his day. It was a long day, for he lived to the usual ripe old age.

Barney and his wife, Gentle Annie, lived a life of connubial bliss interrupted only by the beatings she gave him when her patience wore thin—that was why they called her "Gentle" Annie. On the whole things went pretty well with them. Annie wasn't much of a housekeeper, by Cape standards or any other, but then she didn't have much of a house to keep. She wasn't much of a cook either, but Barney was a good provider—and he provided the food ready cooked. Like Three-Fingered Ruth he went round to the village doors with his roomy bag and always brought it back well filled. As one of the few of his old neighbors still left in the Hollow remarked, "Folks was good to the poor them days."

The Gould homestead had one room, and in that room the master and the mistress ate, drank, slept and danced. With the fiddler in good fettle and the neighbors all in and plenty of rum in the brown jug, you could hear Happy Hollow for miles. Good folks shivered in their beds at the sounds of unrighteous mirth, but next day they filled the yawning bags with food and forgiveness. "Folks was good to the poor them days."

Barney came of old Cape stock, belonged to a respectable family, of whom all but him had trod the paths of conventional living. But Barney had his own ideas, and he followed them to the joyous end. He had a passion for walking and contrived to make what living he and Gentle Annie needed by walking. With an old pushcart he went round doing errands for the townsfolk. He would walk to Falmouth, a score of sandy miles, for a dime. Anything for an excuse to walk.

Once he felt an urge to go to Philadelphia—why, no one can remember. But he did not walk—to satisfy his thirst for adventure he had himself boxed and sent by express.

Some boys nailed him in with a food supply and got him aboard the train. He must have arrived, for he got back.

But mostly he walked. One day he heard the captain of a fast clipper bragging about his vessel's speed. Barney jeered. He'd bet he could walk to Frisco faster 'n the captain could get there in that there vessel o' hisn going down round the Horn. The insulted captain took him up. The story goes, and there is no one to deny it, that when the ship sailed into San Francisco Bay our Barney was waiting on the dock to collect his bet.

When he got home he had great tales to tell of his trip. He had walked most of the way, but there were lifts on prairie schooners going west to Californy that helped. (He was probably the original hitchhiker.) But at that it was bad enough "what with Injuns that fit like wildcats and kep' a feller on the jump, and deserts and all."

When he got home he was pretty short of cash, so he let it be known that he would walk fifty miles round the old pavilion at twenty-five cents a throw. Some of his many friends got out printed fliers to advertise his stunt, and a crowd turned out to cheer him on his way. But some small boys got there ahead of him. They pulled up all the croquet wickets in town and planted them firmly in his path. They knew his eyesight was none too good, and counted on fireworks. They got them. Every time Barney tripped on a wicket he let out language that was purple-ripe. The customers felt they had their money's worth long before he finished his course and let him have the gate money—all of eight dollars.

So Barney Gould made fun and folklore for his town until he died. Happy Hollow passed with him, and the place where one would hesitate to venture after dark became just a harmless stretch of grass and scrub pine "down back of the new hotel."

Zibe's wife was not the only witch around. Long after the days of witchcraft passed—I'm inclined to think it was not altogether a "delusion" either—witches abounded on the Cape. Sea captains were terribly plagued by them, according to hints I heard dropped—you never could get the details. People don't like to talk about them. But I did hear about one witch right there in Barnstable who was quite all right daytimes—sober, industrious sort of woman, you'd say to look at her. But at night she changed herself into a cat and went yowling at the moon. Certainly that is no way for a good church member to behave.

Along the south shore of the township are a lot of summer colonies. One is pretty much like another, so far as I could see. Of course some were swankier, or older, or more gardened, but they could have been practically anywhere as well as here. The more modern cottages did try to capture something of the local feeling, and were at any rate less ornate than the older ones. But city folks seem to lack whatever it takes to be themselves. While some of their communities are quite attractive, they reflect their creators—there is none of the effortless flavor of the old-time villages. More than just age makes the difference.

Osterville I found different, though. The name would be Oysterville if it hadn't lost the "y" through years of hard use. Over across the bridge from it is the swanky resort of Oyster Harbors, with its clubhouse, its golf links and its yachting. Osterville is still quite largely native, and the point of special interest is the boatyard where they build the Crosby cat.

There are, of course, cats and cats, but the Crosby cat is in a class by herself. This is not family pride, it is solid fact. Anyone will tell you she is different. Naturally she isn't a feline, but a boat, a catboat—in fact, *the* catboat. Anyone will tell you that, too.

A little lane led down to the sea, and the shore was littered with all sorts of shops and sheds and lofts up and down for half a mile. Tied up at the small piers or moored offshore were a dozen boats of assorted styles. Close in was a 39-foot yawl just being finished off, her mahogany cabin polished, her galley ready for the dishes, everything shipshape. On the ways, ready for launching, was a cruising cat, twenty-six feet over all, one of a stock model. Small Marconi-rigged knockabouts with their high triangular sails of the Junior Wianno class, and larger knockabouts, not to mention yawls, launches and wee skiffs for tenders, lay at their moorings.

Members of the family disagreed about how long the Crosbys had been building boats—first at Centerville and then at Osterville. But it looked as if six generations of the family, all in one line, had been on the job. No wonder they could build a good cat.

The first boat-minded Crosby, of course a descendant of the prolific Thomas of Eastham, was named Jesse. He was born the same year as George Washington, and fought in the Revolution. When he came home he went to building vessels in Centerville. His son and grandson carried on the work. According to tradition—there seem to be no records—Jesse had a son Daniel who built vessels; and Daniel had a son Andrew who built ships. Andrew's two sons, Horace and Worthington, built cats. Horace was the originator and designer of the Crosby catboat, and his son, Manley Crosby, was the designer when I was there.

No one seemed to know just when the first catboat was launched, but it was about the middle of the last century, perhaps as early as 1845. Up to then the Cape fishermen always used a kind of boat that came from Long Island, long and narrow and pointed at both ends, with a yawl rig—it sounded to me like a variant of the pinky. The fishermen liked them because they rode high when the rollers went under them, and so were able to come in safely over the bar. Also they were speedy and could be raced out to the grounds in the morning and home again at night.

But Horace Crosby had a notion he could improve on them. He had gone into the business at the mature age of ten, and at fifteen he knew as much about shipbuilding as anyone. His descendants told me they were sure he could have made his discovery as early as 1840, whether he actually did or not. No one knows how he happened to get the idea, but he figured that a boat with a square stern and a single mast stepped well forward, and carrying a single sail with a boom and gaff, would make a good fishing craft.

The fishermen themselves did not think so—in fact they laughed at him and his fool notion, and predicted early and immediate trouble for all concerned. They told him that instead of her riding over the rollers the rollers would ride over the boat, fill the cockpit and sink her. Also she would be too slow. But Horace and his brother Worthington refused to listen to them, they kept right on working.

Now those were the days when interest in spiritualism

was rife and table-tipping was done in the best families. There has always been a mystic strain in the Cape psyche, and it crops out in surprising ways. As one of the Crosby men told me the story, the two brothers were laying the keel of their first cat when they got stuck trying to figure out the mathematics for the knees. While one of the boys— I forget which—went off to "ask the table" for the answer the other one kept on working with paper and pencil. When the table-tipper returned with the answer, it was the same one his brother had just arrived at with his figuring. Which may prove something—but I'm not sure just what.

A different version is given in the little Barnstable guide-book. According to that the boys' mother, Tirzah Crosby, was a spiritualist medium, and whenever the boys got stuck with a problem of construction they would go to her. She would get in touch with her husband, Andrew, and he always gave them the right answer.

Anyway, they went ahead and finished the boat and launched her, christening her *Eva*—whether for the first woman or for a girl friend history does not say. One fine morning young Horace went aboard and raised her new white sail and paid out the sheet to catch the breeze. You can imagine the jeers that greeted the new rig when he and *Eva* joined the fishing fleet. But he said nothing—just kept on going. Raced them out to the fishing ground, and got there first—a good long first. Raced them home again at night, and beat them again. Everyone was watching to see what she would do when she reached the bar— waiting to see the rollers take her and carry her down. But they didn't. She rode them like a duck—rode them higher than all the rest!

She got her name that first trip. A man on shore watching the fleet way she whipped round the bends in the channel yelled out—"Quick as a cat, b'gosh!" and so a cat she became. It is too bad no one knows where little *Eva's* bones are laid. The first of all the cats to ply the four seas of Cape Cod has long since gone the way of all boats—even the Crosby cats are not immortal.

Present members of the firm have no way of even guessing the number of boats that have been built in their yard. One of them told me of walking along the shore with his grandfather and seeing an old hulk rotting in the sand.

"One of our boats," said the old man, "we built her back in so-and-so."

But no records were kept, and only now and then would a bit of data like that come to light. Although they built several different types of craft, it is the cat which made them famous. They were called "thirty-year boats" in the fishing service, which gives a boat the hardest kind of wear. But the type has changed a lot since the time they were built for fishing rather than pleasure as they are now. Then they had no comforts, let alone luxuries, and no other power than the wind.

They were built of native oak and cedar, cut right here on the Cape—which was once forested, remember—and hewn and sawed by hand. Now they are built of mahogany and cypress brought from half around the world. On the grass near one of the shops they showed me a pile of spruce logs shipped here in the rough with their bark still on, from Hudson Bay and slowly seasoning to be used for masts and spars. The little cat is still an able boat, though her lines have changed and she has a cabin with engine and galley.

I got most of my story from "Uncle Billy" Crosby, who

had retired after fifty-four years of boatbuilding but was still one of the busiest men in the yard. Four younger Crosbys—sons and grandsons of the two men who invented the cat—were carrying on. They were building—among other types—a racing craft they had developed for children.

This brings me to one quite intriguing feature of summer life on the south shore—the mosquito fleet. In Cotuit, just west of Osterville, the children had come into their own with a yacht club that was all theirs. If you are under fourteen you belong to the junior section, and over fourteen to the senior. You can't become a racing skipper till you are at least ten, but you can ship as crew before that and learn how to handle a boat in the queen of all sports. Of course it is taken for granted you can swim, because the chances are you will have to. Often each child in the family—boys and girls alike—owns a boat, not to mention father and mother and possibly grandfather. Practically everybody in Cotuit races, except the family cat.

The junior club had been going on for years with its own officers and treasury—they were making both ends meet handsomely with annual dues of twenty-five cents— yes, cents. Nobody had any authority over it just because he was grown up. If that isn't an ideal arrangement from a young person's point of view, what is? Their boats were fourteen-footers, centerboard skiffs with lapstreaked sides and bottoms flat as a flounder. Cat-rigged, the one sail had a gaff so steep it looked like a leg-o'-mutton rig. Speedy little craft when they are right side up. But nobody seemed to mind if they went over now and then—it was all in the day's race. They go over easy but they don't sink, they just flop over and lie there. You climb up on the side and sit tight till the race is over and somebody has time to bother with you. The water is warm.

The beauty of it is, nobody worries. I mean nobody. If a mother said, "Be careful, darling" to her offspring they would look at her with amazement. On a racing afternoon I met a Cotuit mother heading her car for Hyannis. Oh, yes, her children were going to race, Betty and Joe were out in their boats. Too bad she couldn't be there to race her own boat, it was such a good wind. Perfectly matter-of-fact about it.

Of course these youngsters are getting things pretty easy compared with the boys of a generation or so back who went to sea in earnest and learned their ropes the hard way at the business end of a belaying pin. But they are getting a taste of what the place can give in the way of freedom and self-reliance.

7. Captains Contented

THERE IS no better way to spend a gray wintry afternoon when the wind is backening round and the glass is falling and it is smurrin' up for a storm than beside some old-time skipper's fireside listening to his stories. Certainly the cities I have known had little to offer in comparison when it comes to real entertainment.

Admittedly the "fireside" has lost some of its glamor with the years, for in most of the houses the fireplace in the settin' room has long been bricked up, very likely with its crane and andirons inside, and a sheet-iron stove piped into it. But the stories, whether told by deep-water men or by coastwise skippers, are as good as they ever were, and there is little to choose between them for excitement. For even the shorter voyages had a good range to them, coast-wise sailing taking in the Labrador at one end and the West Indies at the other, and their yarns were good enough for anyone.

Such a man was one of my mid-Cape friends. He had a long white beard and wore a long black cape, a sort of opera cloak, fastened with safety pins. Rain or shine he carried an umbrella; and if you asked him why, when the sun was shining, he told you it was to keep the wind off. In spite of his eighty-odd years he still went out in his dory spearing eels for a living. His eccentric style of dress amused the summer folks, but the chances are that he could cut circles round most of them, mentally or physically. He dressed the way he did because he wanted to, and that is reason enough for anybody, specially in Barnstable county.

When I went to see him he was living in half of his ancestral home, a small gray-shingled half-house with red door and trim. It had been a full-sized house when it was built, 193 years before; but when two brothers inherited it they could not get along together—or more likely their wives couldn't. So they did what was common enough in those parts, cut it in two and moved half of it across the road. In the captain's half the mantels and corner posts, not to mention the paneled wainscot in the fore room, were good as ever.

The captain went to sea about as soon as he could crawl, for his father was a captain; and his mother went along. When he was thirteen they decided the time had come for him to earn his own living. Vocational training in those days was simple. If you were going to follow the sea you began, as a rule, in the ship's galley. So his mother kept him home with her for three or four months and taught him to cook.

"But cooking at home with plenty of everything to do with, and on a ship where there were just four shifts for dinner and you had to use what you had, was two different things," he reminded me. "When they asked me if I could cook I said I could, but they was to remember that it said in the Bible—'If thou eatest any deadly thing it shall not harm thee.' Not one of that crew is living today," he said pensively. But really, as this was back in '54, the mortality could not reasonably be all laid to his cooking.

The four shifts of food? Well, for dinner the first day he would give them salt beef, the second day fishballs, the third baked beans, and the fourth potato bargain. This last is a true Cape dish, and is also called "sailor's hurry." It is a one-dish meal—and I got the recipe, not from the captain, who had probably forgotten it, but from Mrs. Amy L. Handy, who was the Magazine's culinary authority. She said she found the same dish in Paris disguised as Pomme de Terre Anna. She wrote:

On Cape Cod we make ours by slicing eight raw potatoes quite thin and leaving them in water while we try out on an iron frying pan some thin slices of salt pork, eight slices two by four inches—fry slowly and do not brown. Put in part of the potatoes and slice an onion over them, a little salt and pepper, then another layer of potatoes, onion and seasoning; repeat, using four onions in all. There is usually enough water to cook them, but it may be necessary to add a little. Cover the pan and cook slowly. Stir occasionally and at the last take off the cover so the potatoes will be free of water when done. Some Cape cooks don't stir the mixture but run a knife under it occasionally to keep it from catching on—it gets crusty and brown, and when turned upside down the slices of onion and potato are unbroken.

Getting back to the little lad in the ship's galley—on the fifth day he began all over again with salt beef. At supper there was often a kind of turn-over, really a fried mince pie. Or perhaps cold beef sliced and spread thick with mustard "to warm up their stomachs." Always, too, hot biscuits.

But of course he didn't cook very long, just while he was small. Later voyages he shipped before the mast. Having a cheerful way of looking at things, he was happy at his work, whatever it might be.

"I thought it was fine not having any responsibility and just having to obey orders," he chuckled; "if I was told to go aloft I went aloft, and that was all there was to it. I used to feel sorry for the officers, with so much more care on their shoulders. But when I got to be an officer," said the captain, "I was sorry for the men because they had to go aloft and I didn't."

The captain must have been born lucky, for he commanded six ships of varying rigs and tonnage, was out in all weathers and had his bad hours, but not only did he never lose a ship, but "I never cost my owners a cent for repairs from accident!"

The merchant captains had a social standing above that of both whaling and coasting captains. They were business men and traders, representing their owners in the great ports of the world, as well as officers. In Hyannis lived one of the most typical men of his class—Captain Howard C. Allyn, one of the Great Captains, and a man of the world in very truth.

A vigorous upstanding man I found Captain Allyn, not looking within twenty years of his age and with the blue seagoing eyes I soon learned to associate with blue-water men. (Every single one I met had them; and I don't believe in coincidences.) For thirty-five years he followed the sea and most of that time he was on blue water; so he had a right to them.

"Square-riggers always," he said brusquely, "I wouldn't command any other kind of vessel. When the last square-rigger to leave the port of Boston sailed out of the harbor I was on her quarter-deck. She was lost in a hurricane in the Gulf of Mexico, and I never went to sea again."

Few of even the veteran shipmasters of his day saw the

world as he did. This was partly because he made so many and such long voyages but also because he was the type of man to see and understand more than most. A great reader and a student of men and affairs, I found him tops in a class that was in itself outstanding.

When he was fifteen, which was during the Civil War, young Howard Allyn left his little home on the Barnstable plains and shipped as sailor on a coasting vessel. The sea was in his blood and he never had to learn to be a sailor like most of the boys, did not have to serve the usual apprenticeship in the galley of a coaster or a fisherman, feeding the crew while he learned his ropes and how to box the compass. Ten years later, at twenty-five, he had his own ship, was captain of *Importer,* sister of *Reporter* and *Exporter* of a once famous fleet.

His route would seem staggering to a seaman today. San Francisco was his home port. From there he carried wheat down round Cape Horn and up to the British Islands. The next leg of his trip was down round the Cape of Good Hope and up to Hong Kong. There he loaded coolies for the West Coast—and so back home. It took a bit over a year.

"The last load of coolies ever brought into this country was in my ship," he recalled. "They were brought over to work on the new Northern Pacific Railroad, which was being built then, but along in the eighties the government passed the Exclusion Act."

The seven long round-the-world voyages on *Importer* were by no means the only ones he made. When I asked if he could remember how many times he had been round the world he answered, "God, no!" so sincerely I knew it was no use pressing the question.

Always his wife went with him. She made the ship their home all those years, they had no other. She was a good musician, and there was always a piano in the cabin along with the captain's books. He had a thousand of them in his library, and that little cabin was a cultured home. In port they were entertained by the best society the place afforded. He was the only shipmaster ever made a member of the exclusive Hong Kong Club.

It was there in Hong Kong, by the way, that he found the famous Black Watch Regiment—it had been sent out to quell the Sepoy rebellion. They had a wonderful band (probably still have, for it was part of the regimental tradition), and the Captain invited it aboard ship and entertained it royally. They gave a concert, with Mrs. Allyn at the piano. Afterward he stood treat. In the cargo were several barrels of beer he had brought along to sell as a bit of speculation. "But after that party there wasn't any left to sell." When they went ashore for dinner or the theater they always wore full evening dress. "Silk hat and patent leather shoes, too," said the captain, chuckling over past grandeurs.

"It was a lovely life, that of a captain on a big square-rigged ship," he said, "a lovely life. For days on end there was little or nothing to do, just sit back and enjoy life. I got a taste for good reading when I was a boy at home. The boys in our neighborhood had a magazine club, and we used to get the best there was. So when I went to sea I made a practice of reading so much every day, and reading it thoroughly. There was all the time in the world, and nothing to distract my attention. Nowadays there is so much going on I only have time to browse, not to

read as I used to. The books? Oh, history, travel, philosophy, poetry—pretty much everything. Spencer's *Synthetic
Philosophy*, Plato, the Koran, Confucius, the Bible, ancient
history, Byron, travels of the Jesuit priests, explorations—
everything. I can't imagine a nicer kind of life than we
lived aboard our ships, Mrs. Allyn and I, on those long
voyages."

Of course there were storms, he admitted, and hours of
danger. But until the end—the very end—his ships rode
safely through and came rolling back to the home port.

That end came one October day in 1898. The good ship
Titan, last of her type as I said to sail from Boston, had
grown old in long and arduous service. She had been everywhere, carried every sort of cargo, weathered every variety
of storm and sea. But her old bones creaked, and her stout
sides were waxing feeble. She was not the ship she had
been—all right in ordinary weather or even in bad weather
under ordinary conditions, but not a ship for emergencies.

They had been getting a load of phosphates from a rock
off to the south of Porto Rico and were half full when
Titan sprang a leak. With a different cargo she might have
done better, but this phosphate stuff is heavy as lead and
it was loaded low in her hull, a mean cargo in any weather.
The captain decided to stop loading and head for port;
so they made sail and started.

October is the hurricane season in the West Indies, and
a regular typhoon struck the poor old *Titan*. It lasted for
days, driving her helpless before it, stripping her of masts
and rigging, and leaving her finally a wallowing, water-
logged hulk that was sinking every moment lower among
the seas that washed over her. Down in the cabin were

the captain's wife and their son, so he had more than his crew and his ship to think about in those terrible days and even more terrible nights.

For three nights he sent up rockets in the hope that some steamer might see them and come to his aid in spite of the mountainous waves. But not till the middle of the third night did they see an answering rocket. And then it was not the hoped-for steamer but just another sailing vessel, a Norwegian bark. She stood by them nobly, though, and her men must have worked like heroes in the hours that followed. The seas were still running hurricane-high, and the two vessels could not approach each other closely enough to take off *Titan's* crew directly. A small boat had to be lowered in the bark's lee as she lay headed up into the wind, and a rope from this little craft was made fast to *Titan*.

Overside went the captain's wife—over the rail and down the rope and into the water, and then she was pulled up into the tossing boat—and overside went the crew, one by one. Three times the boat had to row back to its mother ship with its load before all the men were off; the captain last, of course. It was two o'clock in the morning when he reached the Norwegian's deck.

They stood by till daylight, waiting to see the end of the once beautiful *Titan*. But they were never to see her final plunge, for when dawn came there was only an empty sea. She stayed afloat to the last possible hour, long enough to save her people, and then she went down.

Mrs. Allyn was done with the sea; and you can't blame her. The captain couldn't make up his mind to ship without her, though he had many opportunities, so they came to Hyannis and settled there. He went into the express

CRANBERRY BOG, YARMOUTH

THE KING'S HIGHWAY, YARMOUTH PORT

CATBOAT, BASS RIVER

STETSON HOUSE, SOUTH YARMOUTH

business, and made a success of it. It is always interesting to see the way Cape people adapt themselves to circumstances and like it. They seem to make their lives from the inside out, and it gives them a sort of stability—not to say durability—that may have something to do with their good long lives.

8. *The Wonder-working Woman of Yarmouth*

THE FEW SUMMER sojourners who stay on into October
are richly rewarded. All summer the scenery has been a
conservative blue and green, much trimmed with flowers
but still on the whole what you might call pretty. Now
it is something else again, for it simply goes mad. Not
only are our flowers brighter than those inland, but the
famous autumn foliage of New England also attains a
sharper intensity, a greater glory of color.

Sometimes the flaring sweeps of it are almost blinding.
Take those places out on the marshes where there are
masses of beach plums. Back in May we thought those
bushes lovely beyond words in their creamy fluff of bloom,
but now, seen across a sweep of rich gold meadow grass,
broad splashes of orange and vermilion, with a green-black
pine in the offing for accent, they leave you gasping.

In the woods, as if the trees did not have color enough
of their own, the woodbine turns light red and flames up
the trunks till it seems the woods must be on fire.

Fortunately there are stretches of pines which relieve
the eye for a bit till a turn in the road brings a new
outburst of color. The black road, wet and shining from
a passing shower, reflects the color in a different key.
The ponds near by give it still another variation. Then in
the afterglow of an autumn sunset the red trees intensify
the green fields to a vivid jade, keen and sharp as a knife.

Sometimes all this is combined with the cream of the long beaches and their ruching of white surf, and the turquoise or sapphire of the sea beyond.

I used to wonder what our Pilgrim ancestors thought, that first autumn of theirs in this new world to which they had come. Were they shocked at so abandoned a display of color, or did they realize that beauty is after all a manifestation of God? Certainly there is no record of their passing any sumptuary laws against it.

This fits practically the whole Cape, but I remember it specially driving along from Barnstable over into Yarmouth, the next town to the east, or maybe I should say down-Cape. But Yarmouth was lovely any time of year. To me the village of Yarmouth Port seemed loveliest of all. Its main street was the highway, but entering it was like driving down the aisle of a Gothic cathedral. The ancient elms planted close along the sides of the road interlaced their graceful branches high above the traffic, and cast green shadows down upon us. Through the verdant arch would dart a splash of orange—an oriole going home to his dangling nest; hang-birds take to elms for their building sites. Just back of the trees, their front doors almost flush with the sidewalks, is a string of the little half-houses characteristic of this village.

I stopped off in the Port one afternoon to get a story about the little half-houses; but I seem not to have written it, for even the notes have disappeared. But I recall the houses were built about a decade before the Revolution— say around the 1760's. Most of them were clapboarded on the front, with lovely velvety old gray shingles on the ends. Out of the broad gently sloping roofs stuck the big chimneys. Over them flickered the light and shadows from the elms. One thing to remember next Thanksgiving is that most of these trees were spared in the hurricanes.

There is not much about Yarmouth in my notes and clippings. I can't imagine why, for it is next door to Barnstable and you have to go through it to get down-Cape, as it straddles the biceps of the old arm just as the towns each side of it do. Perhaps there were no blue-water men left there from whom I might get a story, nor any special story-teller to give me copy. I was always going somewhere, and usually trying to make a deadline. On newspapers you don't try to make a deadline, you make it; but a magazine gives you a bit more leeway, so I hurried—but not too much.

For my one Yarmouth story I am indebted to a Dennis man. Stephen Hall, of whom there is to be more later, gave Lyman Armes and me some priceless copy; the magazine owed him more than we could ever sufficiently thank him for. That is why I know so much more about Dennis than about Yarmouth. But one day Steve said he wanted me to meet the Bray boys and find out from them about a remarkable woman who used to be a neighbor of theirs—Aunt Sophie Ann. He said they knew most of what there was to be known about her, but not all, for no one could know that. He was right, for she and her kind are a mystery to the wisest of our day.

A few decades earlier she would no doubt have been called a witch. That word was a sort of cover-all for any woman who had or claimed to have occult powers; we dub them psychic or parapsychic, and think we've settled them. Those are fancy words, and Stuart Chase would probably class them as blab-blab.

Back in Old Testament times Aunt Sophie Ann would

no doubt have qualified as a prophetess, an inspired woman. In the early days of the Christian era she might have been canonized, for her works were good. In this more matter-of-fact era we do not try to classify such a person, if we are wise; we call her an Unknown, and let it go at that. She was either a hang-over from the past with qualities slowly being lost to the human race, or a forecast of what mankind might be if it were to develop its latent abilities. Back in the Sandwich chapter I mentioned my regret at being too late to meet two women. Aunt Marthy Hoxie was one, Aunt Sophie Ann Kelley Chase was the other. My regret at not being able to know them is profound.

Stephen Hall took me first to meet the Bray boys, who lived on a small farm near the site of the Bray boatyard on the Yarmouth shore and near Aunt Sophie's old home. The two middle-aged men had known her well and respected her highly. The very suggestion of calling her a witch enraged them, and when they told you about her you understood their feeling. She had been dead only eight years, so her memory was still fresh with them.

Yarmouth has a short waterfront on the Bay, and Aunt Sophie's home was at the eastern end of it, near the mouth of Chase Garden River. To get there you follow a road leading down toward the shore from the highway, just up-Cape from the Brays' farm. A mile in from the highway it forks to the left, becomes a sandy cart track with high ridges of turf. It looked too much for Lizy Jane to navigate, so we abandoned ship and went the rest of the way afoot. A nice walk, for the little road wound intriguingly through the pines before it came out to broad marshes. On the left was a sheltered hollow with a long-neglected orchard cowering away from the winds. On the right a knoll was overgrown with brush, and a clump of ancient lilacs and locusts stood there as if they were trying to shield the old house behind them.

It must have been a fine house in its day, two stories, with a big central chimney and a four-sided roof, and a doorway that must have been dignified when it was there. Now the shingles were black with age, a great hole gaped in the roof, and the door was gone.

As happens with so many old New England houses left untenanted, marauding seekers for antiques had probably gutted it. Windows, doors, mantels, wainscoting, all interior finish, were gone. It was just a shell of a house.

We went inside and climbed an uncertain stairway to the attic, where the hole in the roof let in the daylight. We poked our heads through the hole and had a lovely view of the marshes and dunes and the sea, and the windings of the little river, which has so much more history than I knew about then. All I knew about the river at the time was that rumrunners were supposed to be using it to land their stuff from the sea, but you heard that sort of story almost anywhere along the shore, for the whole Cape was a natural for bootleggers. The river mouth was once a good harbor, before it silted up and became useless. The Brays' boatyard was on this side, and also the town landing and the wharves. Of all the buildings that once made this a lively settlement, only this rickety old house remained.

Steve wanted me to notice the way the house was built. Up here in the attic the white-pine beams were all hand-hewn with an ax, for the ax-marks showed clear with no sign of sawing. The construction interested Steve particularly, for he knew about old houses. Each side of the chimney was a king-post with five beams mortised into its top from its half of the four-sided roof. All five were fastened with wooden pegs.

"A watchmaker's job," he said reverently.

Aunt Sophie lived there in that old house all by herself for many years before her death, which was in her mid-eighties. She had no children, although she was herself the seventh daughter of a seventh son. That numerical fact is supposed to explain her powers, but even if it is anything more than a coincidence it explains nothing.

When she was a little girl, according to the local legend, Sophie Ann really had to quit going to school because she knew her lessons without studying them and soon learned all there was in the books, while her fellow pupils were still plodding through the early pages. When she grew up it was said she knew all the secrets of Masonry without ever being told them. She knew things without having to learn them.

Sitting in her old Boston rocker in the kitchen of this house, she would close her eyes and take long journeys. When she opened her eyes again she would tell you things that surprised you.

"I've known her to go to Greenland, and Iceland, and the Labrador," one of the Brays told me, "and not be gone fifteen minutes. She could tell you all about it, too."

There would be no fooling about a trip like that, for Cape men knew such places better than they knew their own county.

"I thought maybe she was some sort of a spiritualist," Mr. Bray confessed, "but I never knew of her going into a trance." He added something that is still Greek to me; I report it just on the chance that it may have meaning for someone else: "She said there wasn't anything to the story about the Old Man of the Mountain, he was just a crooked old tree."

Aunt Sophie had the power to heal people, and they came from miles around. The Brays told me one story about a man whose wife had been bedridden for years. Finally he put her, feather bed and all, into the back of his democrat wagon and drove down the rutted lane to Aunt Sophie's to ask her help. He took his wife and the feather bed in his arms and carried her into the house and laid her on the kitchen floor.

Aunt Sophie talked with the husband a bit, and then she turned to the woman and suggested she get up and walk round a little. She got up, and was able to walk from then on. Of course the woman may have been a neurotic, but even they are not too easily cured by any modern methods I know of. There were other stories, of lame folks who went there with their crutches and came away healed, leaving their crutches behind them. Of course you can explain that in various ways; but certainly she had something that people needed.

One time a husky chap, the village bully, boasted he could handle the old lady—she couldn't put anything over on him! The Brays chuckled at the memory of what happened to him. He had heard she could hold a man powerless in a chair without touching him—he just could not get up till she told him to. So he swaggered up to her and started "talking rough" to her. The little old lady laid one hand on his arm. He crumpled up and fell to the floor. She let him stay there till she was ready to have him get up, which was quite some time after he was ready to do it. He never bothered her again.

I surely would like to have met Aunt Sophie!

There isn't much in this book that I got from other books. Most of it came direct from people. But I ran across a book, not at all well known, which brings a very interesting piece of history right to the mouth of little Chase Garden River. It is called "Leif Eriksson, Discoverer of America," and was written by Edward F. Gray and published by the Oxford University Press (1930). According to the author, who seems to know his ground, it was into the mouth of this river—then a good harbor, remember—that Thorvald, brother of Leif, sailed with his crew in the year 1007. The Norsemen had made a settlement on the island now called Nomans Land (supposed to be a corruption of Northmen's or Norsemen's), which is just south of the Cape. On one of their trips along the coast they came to the Yarmouth shore where, according to the old saga, they landed and found some Eskimos asleep. They killed all but one of them, and he shot his arrow into Thorvald's stomach and killed him. Thorvald's men buried him there with a cross over him and named the place Crossness. "Ness" means cape or promontory.

There is a tendency to laugh off anything definite about the Norse discovery of this country, but the Oxford University Press did not acquire its reputation by publishing trivia. Anyhow it is a highly scholarly book by an Englishman who knows both the Cape and Iceland.

We cross the trail of the Northmen farther down-Cape. It is supposed the Eskimos preceded the Indians whom the Pilgrims found in possession of the coast when they arrived. The Indians are believed to have come from inland and to have driven the Eskimos on up the coast to Greenland, where they are today.

9. *Captain Hall and the Quivet Clippers*

MIDNIGHT and moonlight and a homesick boy clinging to a yard at the top of the tallest mast! The beautiful ship *Wild Hunter* rolled gracefully in the slow swell from the Atlantic but fifteen-year-old Tom Franklin Hall took no pleasure in the poetry of her motion. It did not bother him, for he had more than that to think about. He saw no good in her or any of her ways. A hell-ship she was, he thought angrily as he helped the other lads clew up the flapping sail below them. She was no better than a hell-ship.

Off her starboard quarter ran the low, white shore of Cape Cod—of Sandy Neck and the Dennis beaches and the almost meeting points, Sesuit and Quivet, with the little river between them shining faintly in the moonlight. On that river was his father's shipyard where the ship now rolling beneath his feet had been built and launched. A clipper she was, a thousand tons burden, and commanded by a Dennis man. She should have been like home to the lad aloft in the rigging. He had watched every plank and beam and nail go into place. Before that he had listened while his father discussed her lines and laid them down on the attic floor of the Sears house.

Instead young Hall looked longingly over to the passing shore and debated with himself the chances of making land if he jumped overboard, off his present perch, and swam for it. It looked a long way down to that moonlit, shining water, and he did not dare. But his throat ached with misery and his heart was heavy as a sounding lead, and he longed most ardently to be home with his mother and one of her good square meals.

It had been very different that morning, back in Boston. He had gone aboard as proud as a peacock to be starting out on his first voyage, bound for foreign ports, too—around the world before ever he saw Boston town again. Everything had been all right till he happened to catch sight of the chief mate wiping up the deck with a luckless sailor. Every day of his long voyage he was to see something of the sort and in time he would get used to it, but that time was still to come.

As a matter of fact, the mate never laid hands on Tom Hall, perhaps because he and the captain came from the same village, perhaps because the boy's father had so much to do with building the ship. But that first time it was a sorry sight. Supper made things worse. He was introduced to salt beef—it was more than salt, it was briny, a hunk of it served in a dishpan and you helped yourself with your sheath knife and ate it in your hands with some hardtack. Used to good cooking and a table with china and fine linen, the boy could not stomach this new fare, especially after what he had witnessed on deck, so he went supperless to bed.

Hardly had he fallen asleep, or so it seemed, when he was roughly wakened and ordered aloft to furl the main skysail. No wonder, as he swayed above the clumsy flapping canvas, up there in the moonlight, that he thought about that swim ashore.

But he did not jump. Still hungry, he finished his job and came down the shrouds the way he went up and turned in to sleep. Next day things looked better. There was another boy on board whom he liked, and they became chums. Salt beef became a thing that could be swallowed if you got hungry enough, and he did.

Things were better still when they reached the blue water of the warm Gulf Stream and the weather became soft and balmy. The *Wild Hunter* was no longer to be thought of as a hell-ship, she was his home.

A year before the mast, seeing the great sights of the world, down around the Horn and up to Frisco, over to Singapore and a good bit of India, down again and around Good Hope and up along to England, with holds full of rice. Then back to Boston, and so home once more to East Dennis.

He told me all this himself, as we sat on the lawn of his East Dennis home—Captain Thomas Franklin Hall, known locally as Thomas Franklin, because there are so many Halls in Dennis you use both first names as a rule. He was a fine-looking man in his middle eighties when I knew him, but his memories were so vivid you seemed to be living them with him as he talked. His father was Captain Christopher Hall, who financed the Shiverick yards at Quivet. In the captain's parlor hung portraits of his father and mother, and a fine-looking couple they must have been in their day.

So young Tom had grown up among ships and talk of ships, and he had made several trips on small coasting vessels, too, and of course had long since learned his ropes. Besides, the sea was in his blood. Once his homesickness was over he was all right again.

Speaking of the cruelties and hardships one associates with those great ships, the captain said, "There was some cruelty, but not so much as folks are saying. That mate on the *Wild Hunter* was a brute, and the deck was stained with blood, I might say, every day of the voyage. But on most of the ships it was different. Of course there had to be discipline and the captain and the mates had to get it the best way they could, for often they had hard men to deal with and they couldn't stop in mid-ocean and put them ashore."

It was a great occasion when they spoke their first ship. When their captain hailed her she answered in her captain's booming voice:

"The *Bounding Billow*, Buenos Aires to Boston!"

Aboard her as mate was Samuel Harding, afterward Captain Samuel Harding of Chatham, whom we shall meet later.

When he came home from that first voyage young Hall's parents thought it would be good for him to stay ashore a year and get more schooling. He started going to a school in Middleboro, coming home week-ends, but his formal education stopped soon after it began—for about a month later he met the master of another Shiverick clipper, the beautiful swift *Belle of the West*, and he asked Tom to ship with him for another voyage round the world—not before the mast this time, but as third mate! This meant coming aft, and was a great step up for a sixteen-year-old lad.

"My heels didn't touch the ground for a week," he chuckled.

He was quite the biggest thing on the ship, for a while. Giving orders to men old enough to be his father, strutting around on the after deck, messing with the other mates—it was pretty fine, and soon made a man of the youngster.

Every ship, he explained, carried from four to six boys before the mast, and they had a cabin of their own on deck and were really apprentices, taken on to learn the work. Most of them eventually became captains, as he did.

"There wasn't anything to being captain," he said modestly. "Why, I remember the time when there was a captain living in every house in this village—all but one or two, anyhow. If a fellow kept away from the rum, there wasn't anything could stop him from getting to be master of a ship sooner or later."

That second voyage of his, on the *Belle of the West*, showed him Frisco again, Melbourne, Hong Kong, Manila, and brought him back to Boston with a load of sugar, tobacco and hemp. There the captain left the ship and got married. Another captain was appointed in his place and the newcomer promoted young Hall to the berth of second mate, and put a cousin of his, one of the Crowells, in as chief mate. All their baggage had gone aboard and they were ready to sail when the former captain changed his mind. He besought the owners to give him back his ship. His wife wanted to go to sea, and he would like to make another voyage with her aboard. The owners gave in to his plea, and the new captain went ashore in great wrath with his luggage, while the old one came aboard, with his bride.

Before they sailed the captain discharged the chief mate and put Hall in his place. So he set out on his third voyage, a boy of only eighteen, in this responsible position. If anything should happen to "the Old Man" he would be in sole charge of the ship.

And something did happen to him. They got to Calcutta, and there the captain was taken ill with some spinal trouble that kept him flat on his back for months. So the boy had to navigate the ship down around Good Hope and up to England, loading and discharging cargoes and attending to the many business details of the voyage. He was twenty by this time, however, and very much a man of the world. The voyage lasted two years and a half, and when he got home he laid off for a while to rest. He "had eaten too much curried rice in India" and was not feeling quite himself. The owners offered him command of the *Belle of the West* for another voyage, but he refused.

When he finally decided to go to sea again he went as master of the bark *Egypt*—took her out from Portland, Maine, with lumber to Montevideo and Buenos Aires, round the Horn to Callao, in Peru—but he had to leave her there and come home by land, for he felt too ill for further voyaging. That was the end of his going to sea. He went out to Omaha; but he always came home to Dennis for his summers.

In his leisure time the captain did a bit of writing. One article caused quite a bit of discussion, for it defended Captain Cook's claim to the discovery of the North Pole. Another, called "Ship-Building at East Dennis," is still in demand, for it is a vivid and beautifully written account of an almost forgotten epoch in Cape history.

The old shipyard would be quite forgotten, probably, were it not for a tablet marking its site for which Captain Thomas Franklin Hall wrote the inscription: "In commemoration of an industrial enterprise instituted by Christopher Hall, a shipowner and retired shipmaster, in co-operation with David, Asa and Paul Shiverick, shipbuilders; whereby eight sailing ships of approximately one thousand tons register each and four schooners of smaller size were built, with the after ends of their keels resting about fifty feet south southeast of this spot." There is more, and the names of the ships and schooners built there. The ships were *Revenue*, 1849–50; *Hippogriffe*, 1851–2; *Belle of the West*, 1852–3; *Kit Carson*, 1853–4; *Wild Hunter*, 1854–5; *Webfoot*, 1855–6; *Christopher Hall*, 1857–8; and *Ellen Sears*, 1862–3.

They named her *Belle of the West* when they built her and launched her from the Quivet Ways. She was a lovely thing, the *Belle*, and many a man has dreamed of her besides Captain Hall. Sixty years she had been gone, but there were still those who loved her and spoke of her with longing. A lovely thing, and ageless in the memories of her lovers.

So it is always with good ships. More feminine even than women, they hold men loyal through the years. And so it must have been with all the ships they built at Quivet, which is also East Dennis, in the days when ships were ships and men were the kind of men who could man and master them. They were not only built at East Dennis, they were captained by East Dennis men. None others were fit for ships like these, none others went with them as masters. Seven of the eight thousand-ton clippers were built in the fifties for the gold-rush trade, Frisco and other West Coast ports; and built for speed.

I was often told that no big ships had ever been built on Cape Cod. Schooners and small vessels of various types, yes, but square-rigged ships—oh, no! But over in Dennis I found men who saw these square-rigged clippers built right there in their own home town and later sailed off around the world aboard them.

Old Asa Shiverick started building vessels well up Sesuit

Creek—call it S'uet, please!—in 1820. There for nearly thirty years he built smaller vessels—schooners, brigs and sloop-rigged craft. He sent his boys to Boston to work in the shipyards and get new ideas, and one of them, David, studied drafting evenings after his long day's work —drafting and model-making, both. When the boys came back they used to draft the frames for the new vessels on the attic floor of the Russell A. Sears house—to this day you can see some of the marks they made.

But along came the discovery of gold in California, and that far-away event led to the prosperity of the tiny village of Quivet, such prosperity as it had never known, might never know again.

The old bluff-bowed hulls were strong and sturdy; they made able ships, but they took their time—and time was precious. Designers were being pushed for speedier lines. So the streamlined bow came into being, developed from model to model till there evolved a whippet-like ship, sharp-nosed, lean-flanked, with racing lines and vast stretches of canvas cunningly planned to catch the lightest whiff of air. She "clipped" the records around the Horn and everywhere else and she "clipped it" over the seven seas, and she won for herself and her class the name "clipper."

Three sons of old Asa Shiverick, young Asa and David and Paul, took to the shipbuilding trade. With the enthusiasm and energy of youth they were all for building clippers, but several things stood in their way. For one thing, their yard was too far up the creek to permit the launching of a large ship. The stream was winding and shallow. For another, it would take more capital to finance such an undertaking. The bill for their last ship, the *Ellen*

Sears, calls for $70,000, and that was a lot of money back in the early sixties.

But Captain Christopher Hall, of East Dennis, also had the vision, and he had the money needed to start work realizing it. His long knowledge of ships and the sea, as well as his financing, gave the Shivericks just the kind of backing they needed.

First they moved the shipyard down stream till they could lay their keels near where the monument now stands in their memory. It was not, perhaps, as far down as it should have been, but it did well enough. Twice a year, at high-course tides, they could get their ships afloat half an hour or so on a tide till gradually they worked them out to deeper water.

Farther down a dock was built out to give a sheltered harbor. At its base were two stores which were intended for cod and mackerel fishermen respectively but the whole village used them.

The first ship, which Christopher Hall owned himself, he named the *Revenue*. The others he named as they were finished—he would consult with the owners but usually ended up by finding just the right name for each of them himself. Captain Tom Franklin Hall had half-models of several of them and it was interesting to see the growth of the clipper idea as the hulls grew more and more pointed and even the sterns began to taper, too.

After the *Revenue* came the *Hippogriffe*, with her figurehead of a flying horse. Then the beautiful *Belle of the West*, with "a pretty woman" carved from pine by a Boston artist beneath her bowsprit. After her the *Kit Carson*, and the *Wild Hunter*—a fine name, that, Captain Hall!—which made a good trip to Frisco for a boat of her size, 108 days out. Following them came the largest of all, the *Webfoot*, 1,100 tons, and she gave the least trouble of all when it came to getting her out of the creek. Unfinished when Captain Hall died was the seventh, and so they named her for him *Christopher Hall*. After that no more ships were built for six years, then the Shivericks built an eighth, this time on their own account. They did well with her, selling her before she was even launched. The last of her line, they named her *Ellen Sears*.

Over in East Dennis I found a grandson of Asa Shiverick, Captain David Shiverick. He lived close to the scene of his family's shipyard and worked on some of the later boats with his uncles, and of course remembered a lot of details.

Captain David went to sea as a boy. First he was lucky enough to go to the old Paul Wing academy in Sandwich, where he studied trigonometry and navigation before attending the school of hard knocks aboard ship. Boys went out young in those days—ten-year-olds went as cooks aboard the packets—"If you could make flapjacks and eat 'em yourself that was all they asked about your cooking."

"On the ships," the captain explained, "there was a boys' room in the forr'd deckhouse, the starb'd corner aft. It had six bunks, and we used to sleep there when we weren't on watch. There was plenty for us to do. They always sent us aloft farthest of anybody, to handle the light sails."

As a boy he loved the launchings, for they were great occasions, "like a fair," he said, with crowds coming from far and near to see the new ship leave the ways. All the carpenters "under bottom" got a glass of grog, he recalled, and they needed it, for it was a tricky job to knock out the blocks from under and free the ship for the coast down into the water. One ship, but not one of these, "shot her blocks" and killed several men.

None of those present at the launching of the *Kit Carson* forgot the occasion, for they "stopped the ship" on the ways. She had been built to catch the high freight rates and they rushed her through in ninety days, which was fast going then. The usual crowd gathered to see her launched. Some of the blocks had been knocked out and the ship started, ever so slowly, to move down towards the water.

At that moment someone rushed up with a telegram—the "freights were off." And so was the launching. They held her there where she was, and kept her till spring, when she was finally launched.

None of the ships were rigged here at Quivet, but in Boston. The first two were given jury-rigs and sailed there, but the later ones were towed, sometimes by the Province-town steamer. Captain Shiverick remembered vividly what happened one time when they towed a new ship out to the end of the dock to wait there for the steamer to come along and take her in tow. But the steamer was late, and the ship was restless.

"Oh, that was a pretty night—full moon, high water—a pretty night," he said. She was waiting there at the end of the dock when along came a little wind—just a little waft o' wind from the south, but she was off with it, half a mile out in no time, all by herself. The carpenters were all on board, of course, and the captain, but there was nothing they could do. She just stayed out there and drifted round till the steamer came along and "took her."

Another Shiverick lived near by—Oren, son and grandson of the shipbuilders. He was born just too late to work in the family yards, but his love for ships found expression in building ship-models and painting pictures of ships, though he was by trade a carpenter. When we went to see him he was working on the model of a Mackay ship, *Sovereign of the Seas*. While it was not a meticulous scale model it was a "fine sailorman's model" and one which "worked." Model-makers and collectors will know what that word means!

Many a time as he painstakingly attached some standing part of rope, rove it in shipshape fashion through its proper blocks and watched it do its work before it found its correct belaying-point, he must have felt in imagination the thrills of action on the high seas.

When we saw it the little ship was heeled down as if to the breeze that came in through an open window, the light of a kerosene lamp making shadows on her sails. Mr. Shiverick moved the lamp, holding it so we could see how he had "gone below." Sure enough, all the cabins were completely furnished, even to the tell-tale or compass over the captain's berth. The saloon was paneled in satin-wood and rosewood, and red-plush chairs stood around the table. The cabins had sliding doors. In the galley stood the range with its rail about the top. In the forward deck-house was the carpenter shop with its bench. On deck were a windlass that worked, fife rack, duplex pumps, capstan, binnacle and so on. Of course all the rigging would "run."

Mr. Shiverick had lately taken to painting ship pictures. He had not painted for more than fifty years, but finding a roll of canvas in the attic one day started him out again. His pictures were all of ships in action—one was *Raven* racing *Sea Witch* to Frisco, others were of *Staghound* and

Flying Cloud—none that I recall of his own family's. But it was clear enough that ships get into the bloodstream and stay there. One of his cousins had a boatyard up Plymouth way, still in the Shiverick tradition.

Much of this is quoted from an article which Frederick Hopkins, a ship-model expert, wrote for the magazine. He loved ships and made exquisitely perfect models of them, spending months in patient research into their minutest details. He became much interested in the Shiverick yard, and turned over to me the notes he had gathered on the six ships built there. They are too long to give in full here, but I shall attempt a summary.

The first of the eight full-rigged ships built here in Quivet was little *Revenue*, only 546 tons. (Tonnage is given in old measurement.) She was launched in 1850. Two years later *Hippogriffe*, slightly larger, with a tonnage of 678 tons, came down the ways. In spite of her small size she went everywhere—first voyage out of Boston to Frisco round the Horn, back to Callao, then to Calcutta, and so home to Boston. On one voyage to China she hit an uncharted rock in the China Sea, but she managed to work clear and made Hong Kong. In drydock there they found she still had a chunk of the rock rammed into a hole so big that if the rock had dropped out she would have foundered. The ledge she hit was later charted and named for her—Hippogriffe Rock.

Third was the pride of the fleet, the beautiful *Belle of the West*. Here is the description of her given in the notes: "Extreme clipper ship. . . . The small fore-rake of her stern, with a lively sheer of twenty-seven inches, and but slight flare of bows, gave her a most saucy and coquettish appearance, which was further enhanced by her graceful elliptical stern and handsome figurehead, a female image in flowing white garments fringed with gold. . . . Her run was long and clean. Authorities assert she was the sharpest ship they ever saw, and also the most beautiful." Boston and Frisco newspapers called her the handsomest ship that had ever appeared in those harbors, and one said: "Whatever bright-eyed little flirt she was named after need not be ashamed of her appearance." While she was never driven to any record voyages, she was never out-sailed at sea. She was 178 feet long and her tonnage was 936. Her time from Boston to Frisco on her maiden voyage was 132 days. She was later sold to the British and foundered in the Bay of Bengal in 1868, only fifteen years old.

The next ship to be launched from the Shiverick yards was *Kit Carson*, in 1854. She was larger in tonnage, rated 1,061, and was wrecked off Rio. *Wild Hunter* came along the following year, was the same length as *Belle of the West* but of heavier tonnage, 1,081. She was a fast ship, a sharp model carrying a great spread of canvas including three skys'ls. She made many of the ports we read of today in the papers—Frisco to Singapore, to Akyab, to Falmouth (England), Bremerhaven, Cardiff, Ceylon, Rangoon, Hong Kong, and back to Frisco. Off Formosa she hit a heavy squall and lost three men washed overboard, the jib-boom was carried away and her bowsprit sprung. She had a lot of tough luck and was finally rerigged as a bark. The *Boston Transcript* of June 27, 1882, carried this notice: "Fishing schooner *Colorado* of Gloucester has arrived at Halifax with crew of barque *Wild Hunter* from Boston to Revel, Russia, with cotton abandoned ninety miles off Halifax harbor, burning."

They built a ship a year at the yards for a while. In

1856 it was *Webfoot*, largest of them all—180 feet long, 1,091 tonnage. "A good sailor and a large carrier." She made five passages around the Horn to Frisco, her time varying from 110 to 152 days—on that long run she was kept 33 days off the Horn by heavy weather. Her run of 85 days from Calcutta to New York was exceptionally fast. She ran into a lot of bad weather during her thirty years of life. Her end came as she was leaving Puget Sound with a load of lumber for Callao. Off Cape Flattery she sprung a leak in a gale, then caught fire, was finally beached and abandoned, her hull breaking up.

Christopher Hall was last of the series, launched in 1858 and only 745 tons. After her, for whom I have no further data, came only *Ellen Sears*, a sort of postcript five years later, and I have nothing at all about her.

The length of their voyages presents a graphic picture of the way the world has shrunk in what is after all the lifetime of one man. But for men who loved the sea and their ships those long voyages were no punishment. One wonders if the pilots who take their winged ships over the same courses in a few hours get any comparable emotions.

I mentioned Captain Thomas Franklin Hall's article on shipbuilding. It was published in the Yarmouth Port *Register-Press*, and gives a vivid picture of life on a clipper. "The cabin of the *Belle of the West* was my home for four and a half years," he writes. "She at last became my sweetheart, my idol. She was a graven image before which for years I daily bowed and worshiped, and although she has been lying in her grave at the bottom of the Bay of Bengal for sixty years, I would delight, if it were possible, to erect a marble shaft over the spot where her sacred bones are resting."

He goes on to say: "The perilous task of doubling Cape Horn to westward, or 'running down the easting in the roaring forties' will hereafter gradually become a memory and a legend, to be known only in song and story. . . . In a brief quarter of a century the glory of sail has passed away. Sailing ships that at one time were the pride and wonder of their age have become a reverie and a dream. The sound of foaming waters tumbling beneath their advancing prows, the winds of the trades and westerlies, whistling and singing through their standing rigging, have died into the silence of eternity."

10. *Dennis Is a Storied Town*

GLANCED at casually as one drives along the King's Highway, there is nothing very impressive about the Dennises.
This is equally true on the other roads. North, East, South
and West Dennis, and Dennis proper, and Dennis Port,
not to mention Quivet and New Boston, differ among
themselves but offer the tourist nothing to rave over. We
are now almost, though not quite, out of the elm belt,
and there is nothing romantic to look at in the villages.
Those along the south shore are mostly summerfied, like
the rest that are strung all along from Hyannis to the
Harwiches like beads on a string. Maybe the older ones
were different once, but most of them have taken on the
same summer coloration. The warmer water of the South
Sea is responsible for this.

The township is long and narrow, wedged in between
Yarmouth on the west and Brewster and Orleans on the
east. It used to be part of Yarmouth but was set off from
it along the line of the old east and west parishes and the
new town named itself for its minister, one of the few
Cape towns not named nostalgically for some place in the
old country. It was a friendly divorce, with no bad feelings, quite unlike Brewster and Harwich next door whose
separation was still repercussing.

But when you get to know the northern Dennises they
turn out to be rich in interesting people and houses and

stories. What the magazine would have done for copy
without them I don't know. Just before the deadline you
were pretty sure to see either Lyman Armes's car or mine
parked in Steve Hall's dooryard getting one last story.
And it was likely to be a good one.

The house is in New Boston, and that is over beyond
Chase Garden River and down across New Boston River,
which is no longer a river, but a ditch you could jump
across with your feet tied. Going down-Cape there's a
road to the left and that is the one, and the house is at
the far side of the brook; but that is not so far. The house
is one of the very, very few Early American dwellings
left intact on the Cape—or, for that matter, anywhere else
in New England.

People call it the Howes-Hall house, and its chimney
brick bears the date, 1700. It was built by Prince Howes,
who was a grandson of that austere old governor of the
Plymouth colony, Thomas Prince. The Howes came to
Dennis in 1637, and are still there. The Halls, also of
course of Pilgrim stock, married into the family and
eventually took over the homestead.

Nothing has ever been done to modernize or change it.
The roof had been reshingled that summer, replacing what
looked like the original shingles, but its sag had never
been straightened. The big chimney, seventeen and a half
feet long at the base, had never been cut down. Its white-
oak sills were still sound. Of course the sag in the roof
was not an original feature, but it must date back quite a
while and certainly gives distinction. No two of the
windows are the same size, though most of them have
fifteen tiny panes. Once these windows had shutters, or
rather each one of them had a shutter, for the hinges are

left on one side of one of the windows, but the solid shutters themselves are long gone. What a wonderful greeny-blue they would be by this time!

It was originally a two-story half-house with a chimney at one end, but an early owner who wanted more room for his growing family built on an ell. Instead of the usual ell, or the lean-to continuing the roof down, as in the Hoxie house in Sandwich, he put a lean-to across the end of the house where the chimney was, adding a couple more fireplaces to heat the two new rooms. There are five fireplaces in that chimney now, for it is so big they can be side by side with the room partition between them. When I was there one of the fireplaces in the "new" part still served to heat the living room, though a range had been inserted in the kitchen one.

The house faced south, and I mean south. Experts can tell by the way a house like that faces the year it was built, the orienting was so true. It must have helped them to tell the time by the shadow on the window-sill, in the days before there were clocks.

Once the house was surrounded by pine woods, but they have long since been cut away and now it is rolling heath to the sea, with cranberry bogs and pasture for Steve's horse and cow. He named the deeply curving shore Pirate's Cove, probably out of whimsical regard for off-Cape taste. No doubt the realtors have improved it by this time to Mare Vista or Vikings Ho!

The Cove is a nice place to go swimming, and that is what the Halls used it for. On the sandy beach rests the hulk of a great ship cast ashore bottom up, its oaken timbers a foot or more through. You might see Cap'n Tucker tinkering away on his fishing boat there, and he was always good for a story. He could tell you about his three wrecks, and the South Sea maidens, or about that wonderful experience he—or it may have been Steve himself—had out fishing not long before right here close to home. Three blackfish, which are really small whales, came heading straight for his little boat, s-s-swis-s-shing through the water at a great rate. But when they were almost on him they plunged down under his boat and then cavorted up on the other side, leaping so high out of the water that he could see the sky under their shining bellies.

But to go back to the house: I never saw it all, but I did see the two most interesting rooms—the sitting room, and the kitchen in the old part of the house.

Like the Hoxie house, this has two fronts, and you can take your choice. From each front door a small entry takes you into the house, one into the old part and the other into the "new." Two families must have lived there at a time, no doubt parents and a married son, for there are two sitting rooms and two kitchens. The chimney, with its base eight feet by seventeen feet, six inches, takes up a lot of the room. Both kitchens have fireplaces and brick ovens, though as I said a range has been piped in under the mantel of the later kitchen.

The old kitchen had been closed up, but it was a high moment in my life when I was allowed to enter its shadowy precincts. There on the hearth stood the old utensils just as they had been left after the last meal had been cooked there. On the mantel shelf stood the candlesticks, ready to be lighted and taken up to bed. Odds and ends of furniture, long outworn but to any collector precious beyond rubies, just sat round. Nothing had been "fixed up"—things were just left natural as they always had been.

Two flights of stairs give access to the bedrooms, or chambers as they used to be called. The one off the front entry—we shall call it the front, to save argument—is far from modern but still fairly orthodox. But the back one, which goes up off a corner of this old kitchen, is a honey. You open what you think is a small cupboard door, or a broom closet, and there it is—all of it. Seventeen inches wide (how wide are you, if it isn't indelicate to ask?) and steep as it is narrow. But regular stairs, not chicken-ladder, with treads worn thin by generations of use. Only wide enough, though, for either your heels *or* your toes but not both at the same time if you're over, we'll say, six years old.

Under the main house was a small cellar with a stone-flagged floor. The beams and sills (white oak, as I mentioned before) were in plain sight, and the sills sounded like iron, but the cross beams of white pine were beginning to feel their age. There was a cool charm about that little cellar, with its tiny window looking out through the grass and the stems of the old-maid's pinks—you kept thinking what a ducky tea-room it would make.

There was no cellar at all under the later part of the house, and no doubt that accounts for the bulge in the sitting room floor. Steve was sure it was caused by the sand blowing in from outside and heaving up against the floor boards. Anyhow the effect was novel. If you sit in the rocker in the middle of the room it's four guesses for Sunday which corner you land up in. All the taller pieces of furniture round the edge of the room, like the secretary and so on, lean outboard like old-time sailors braced against the weather rail, as Lyman Armes expressed it. The wide old floor planks have been good sports and adapted themselves to the curves of the bulge without cracking or breaking away.

Round the room runs a two-plank wainscot forty inches high—they used to grow real trees when that addition was built on, maybe a hundred years ago. Butt-end posts, of course, in the corners, and over the broad mantel horizontal paneling to the ceiling. There was a summer-tree in the parlor but not, as I recall, in this more modern room.

Over the mantel was a panel of camphorwood with a full-rigged ship painted on it. Steve found it on the beach at Pirate's Cove. It was evidently the lid of some sailor's sea chest washed ashore from a wreck. He picked it up right after the *Portland* storm, but whether it came from the *Portland* herself or from some other luckless ship is anyone's guess. He thought the ship was the famous clipper *Red Jacket*. As she has a double or split top-s'l, it must have been painted after 1853, when that invention was introduced—to the joy of many a reefer. (It was invented by a Cape man, incidentally.) I learned my sails on her, some of them anyhow—mains'l, fores'l, t'gallant s'l, r'yal, skys'l, main jib, flying jib, jibber jib, fore jib . . . tapering gracefully into the blue sky.

It was from that sitting room with its fire smoldering on the hearth that Editor Armes came back triumphantly one early-fallish day bearing the tale of Deacon Uriah and the Sunday whale. Uriah Hall was Steve's great-grandfather and the man who built the old Lyceum Hall of Dennis—it used to be called the House Built by Uriah, in fact, but more of that later. This is the story of Uriah and his whale, as recorded by Lyman Armes.

Ever since the arrival of the Sunday whale there has been a minor moot point in the family traditions of the Halls of Dennis. It has to do with whether it was devout concern for the final decision of St. Peter or the daily judgments of his wife which transformed a hell-roaring Cape Cod harpooner into Deacon Uriah and made him banish the family rum barrel from the house.

This episode happened some three or four generations ago, and the descendants told it with what was either a twinkle in their eyes or else it was the reflection of the firelight as we sat in the old living room with the whale-back floor.

Uriah, it seems, was a whaler. What is more, he was a harpooner in his younger days before he quit whaling and became a deacon in the church—a regular daredevil on land or sea, with a fine collection of good old Cape cusswords. Cussing was more or less frowned upon in good church circles, but rum was a social amenity rather than a community evil. Uriah had a rum barrel right here in the front entry with a dipper hanging on the spigot handy for visiting friends.

Then all of a sudden Uriah calmed down and became Deacon Uriah. His language became almost ladylike, and he took the barrel—rum and all—down to the blacksmith shop and left it there. (Some of the less hallowed saw it there and bored a hole through the blacksmith's outer wall and into the barrel, inserted the hollow stem of a piece of kelp and applied suction with foreseeable results.)

In those days a black ball was raised on what is now called Black Ball Hill as a signal to the townspeople when

ships were coming in or leaving, when the Boston packet—
a two-masted schooner—arrived, or on those rare occasions
when there was a whale in the harbor. One Sunday morning a breathless man burst into Deacon Uriah's church
right in the middle of the sermon and yelled, "Black ball's
up—whale in the harbor!"

Led by the minister, who was more than willing to
preach some other time, the whole congregation headed
for the shore, the men organizing their boat crews as they
ran. In those days it was no light honor to be the first
boat to get an iron into a whale.

Deacon Uriah was to be the harpooner in one of the
boats that put off to tackle Leviathan. As his boat got
under way he stood up in the bow, harpoon in hand,
while the old thrills and the old cusswords boiled in his
veins. The race and the chase grew hotter as the boats drew
near the whale. Straining in every nerve, the Deacon was
transfigured. He ripped out the old war cry of the seas,
and with all the trimmings which an old harpooner could
muster to spur a whaleboat's crew to greater effort he
yelled:

"Wood to blubber, boys! Dammit, men, lay me to that
whale!"

And behold, the men "laid him to her" first of all. The
plunge of his good right arm sent the harpoon home. The
line whipped over the side, its snaky loops straightening
as the Sunday whale fluked and plunged below the surface.

When it was all over one of the men said, "Well,
Deacon, you fastened to her first, but you had to use some
downright shocking language to do it, didn't you?"

"I dunno, did I?" he asked.

When they told him all he had said, which is of course

more than has been reported here, he betrayed the fact that his getting religion had not been wholly because he feared for his immortal soul.

Alarmed, he cried, "Gracious, gracious! Don't tell Ma!"

But the hall which Uriah built to house the village lyceum meetings was a real contribution to local uplift. Schools to carry the young beyond the three R's were few and far between in those days—mostly private academies to fit seagoing lads with the lore of navigation so they could be captains some day, which apparently most of them were. But all up and down the hook there were village lyceums where both young and old of both sexes acquired something far better than our children or we ourselves have access to in our streamlined institutions. When Stephen Hall said it was the best thing in the way of village improvement and entertainment they ever had on the Cape he was understating it.

The lyceum was organized well over a century ago, and for more than half that time it was a flourishing local fixture. Every Wednesday evening, here in Dennis, the people gathered in the lyceum hall at seven o'clock—from the towns around as well as Dennis itself. There were no paid professional speakers or entertainers on the Dennis programs—the whole town attended, and those who wanted to take part did so. "Many a time I've stood up there quaking while I spoke my piece," a woman told me.

Each week the first hour was devoted to entertainment, in which children and grown-ups of all ages participated. Then came a short intermission during which everyone adjourned to the post office to get the mail. After that came the serious business of the evening—the debates.

All meetings and debates were held in accordance with

parliamentary rules, all questions discussed were voted upon and settled, then and there. "Many a question puzzling Congress was thrashed out and settled once and for all in the Dennis lyceum," the Halls assured us. It really was a mighty institution, a community school of statecraft and forceful expression, a source of information in never-ending variety.

But along in 1875 things began to go to the merry bowwows, and it grew so bad that there was serious talk of adjourning the old lyceum for good. The moment came when the fateful vote was to be taken.

This is the tale of how Freeman G. Hall, father of Stephen, wrote a rhyme of wrath which saved the day for the lyceum and kept it going a good forty years longer. He was a tall, well-built man, and a powerful speaker. Just as the members of the lyceum were going to cast their votes, he stepped up on the platform and addressed the meeting. Instead of making a formal speech he read his bucolic verses, which veiled a sting in good-humored vernacular. Lyman Armes copied it from the original yellowed, faded manuscript, and since its author gave it no title he named it himself:

WHEN FREEMAN G. BILED OVER

This feeble, sluggish, croaking wail
    Is creeping round the town:
"The Dennis Lyceum's sands are run—
    The good ship's going down."
I tell you what! Such talk as that
    Is most confounded rilin',
But I've held in—until tonight
    My blood has got to bilin'.

Ye people of Nobscussett town—
 Why ain't ye up and doin'?
If this here Lyceum goes to wrack
 The country goes to ruin!
'Tis time to blow the trumpet loud
 And raise one big Alarum!
What are you lazy whelps about
 Down on the Old Right Ar-um?

While you set countin' out your script
 A-readin', smokin', writin'—
A mighty airthen-quake down on
 Our commonwealth is lightin';
And here, you lubbers, sojournin'
 Right on the Right Arm's muscle,
Are goin' to yield your heritage
 Without the leastest tussle! . . .

You tell what gatherings you once had;
 The Lyceums—how invitin',
What glorious budgets and debates
 So lively and excitin'!
How them old fellers used to talk
 And get as high as ninety;
But you can't have such blessed times
 Because—you hain't a mind-ty.

Then he tells them plainly that the trouble is they are
sitting back and letting a few do the work, and concludes,

And where you see things standin' still
 All mixed up in confusion
You needn't ponder long before
 You'll come to this conclusion:

That folks are gettin' lazy, and
   All hands have been agreein'—
"Let others work—and we will do
   The hearin' and the seein'!"

What happened? Why, that night the Dennis Lyceum
was born again. The members agreed that so long as seven
men were at a meeting it would go on. And so it did, from
1875 to 1916. This time it was no doubt the rivalry of
movies and motors which brought its meetings to an end.
But the spirit of Freeman G. still carried on, and the
members would not vote to disband. In regular parliamentary order the men voted to adjourn *sine die* until such
time as another meeting is called by the president. And
that president at last accounts was Stephen Hall.

One of the men graduated from the Lyceum was a
young school teacher named Samuel McCall. It was there
he learned to talk on his feet and to debate, and later he
used this ability as governor of the state and in Congress.

It would seem as if Dennisers broke into rhyme whenever they were really roused about anything. There is the
long poem which Captain Marcus Hall wrote about Princess Scargo's having a fish pond dug for her, and not only
dug but named for her. If you don't believe this perfectly
good Indian legend, there is the pond right there before
your eyes—and more than that, the hill that used to be
in the pond before the squaws scooped it out with their
clamshells. The hill is pretty near a hundred and fifty feet
high, and it has a stone tower on top of it, and by the time
you've climbed the hill *and* the tower you are willing to
believe practically anything.

I was just too late to meet the author of this "poem,"

who must have been blessed with a nice twinkly sense of humor. He had got his last sailing orders and was casting loose from the old home dock. I don't know how much over ninety he was, but quite some. If you want all the verses they are in the magazine, August, 1926. It tells at some length how the chief of the Nobscussett tribe of Indians had a favorite child, daughter by his favorite squaw, named Scargo. Someone gave the little princess a hollowed pumpkin with some small fish in it. As they grew they needed more room, hence—to please the child—her doting father ordered the tribe to get busy and dig a pond for them. Of course this meant the women had to do the work—the men got them the clamshells. The story ends, on a human note:

> Where the shadows lie the deepest
>   Loving couples often pause,
> They are listening to the echoes—
>   'Tis the grumbling of the squaws.

Over by the edge of the pond, just off the Highway, is a modest quarter-acre of bayberry and cedar. The iron fence has no gate, and you have to crawl in between the rails. Here was buried the chief of the Nobscussetts, and this is all that remains of the tribe that once owned the whole countryside. Maybe little Scargo is there too, I'm not sure.

I climbed up to the top of the tower on Scargo Hill to see if I could locate a place I had heard of called Fun Town. Of course there are easier ways of locating it than this, even if it is the Cape version of a ghost town. But if you like poking round off the main roads looking for places that practically aren't there, like forgotten villages and so on, this way is as good as any. It can be done by going to Dennis and turning south by the church, but I recommend a combination of methods. Take the old country road where the stagecoach used to go hurtling along with the mail up to the top of the hill and look around, then when you've got your bearings go back to Dennis and take the road by the church over toward Punkhorn, and you come to four or five little houses grouped spaciously on a plain—and of course that's Fun Town.

No, the name doesn't mean what you think. It was never one of the local joy spots, quite the contrary. Just a place where they used to burn charcoal. There used to be some tall chimneys or funnels, called "funs" for short, so this was Fun Town. Punkhorn is something else, but I forget just what. There are a lot of forgotten spots on the Cape which would repay hunting down. For people who think they know their Cape it might add zest to a summer. Such places are Pucker Town, Hell Holler, and Weir Village. There were rumors of a sunken forest off the shore of Orleans that might be checked, not to mention a tale of a forest turned to stone over Corporation way, if you know where that is. It might be somewhere near Bass River, but I'm not at all sure.

If my directions are not perfectly clear in every case it is partly because my bump of direction is a cavity, and partly because I want you to have the fun of hunting round and getting lost as I did, and also partly because this is not a guidebook anyhow.

A newspaper clipping of the late 1920's tells of a dispute over the title to a ten-acre plot of land here in Dennis that indicates the difficulties which can come up in a place settled as long as this has been. Thomas Howes, first of the name to come to America, got the land in 1639, according to the clipping, and in addition to the 137 deeds which had to be reckoned with there were many and varied changes of topography. One of these is a river which used to connect a pond with the sea and was large enough so that small vessels sailed up it into the pond, but it has completely disappeared. I might add that the man, Gray, who wrote the book about the Norsemen landing at Chase Garden River, knew about all these changes and took them into his analysis of the situation.

The man who told me about the forest that turned to stone, or rather who started to tell me but something else came up and so my notes are sketchy, was Captain Preston Howes. On the Cape one yarn always leads to another, and this was specially true of this veteran of the seas. He knew a lot about the great October gale of 1841, one of the two most famous storms on this coast. (The other, of course, was the *Portland* storm in the late nineties.)

Captain Howes's father was out in that gale, one of the few men from Dennis who faced it and lived to get home. From that little village alone, he said, twenty-two men were lost, for the fishing fleets were all out on Georges Bank when the storm struck. They hit for home, but the wind tore off their sails and the seas swamped them.

The captain looked about sixty and had been out all day picking cranberries when I found him sitting in his warm, cosy kitchen reading the weekly paper. It seemed absurd to ask so young-looking a man anything about a storm that had happened eighty-five years ago, and indeed it turned out that his memories of it were not first-hand, because he was only three when it happened. It was vivid with him, though, from hearing about it from his father.

His seagoing career began at the ripe age of six when his father, Ansell Howes, who was captain of a fishing schooner, took him along for his first trip. They went out to the Georges. His outstanding memory of the trip was the finding of three barrels of rum on some shoals there. The men salvaged them and bored holes and struck straws in. . . . Little Preston stayed home a bit after that, to finish his schooling; but at nine he shipped as a regular hand and in due time became master of what we understood him to call the *Pink Pony*. This sounded so much more like the name of a tea-room than a vessel that I asked: "How come?"

"Oh, she was a pinkie and her name was the *Pony*," he explained. "They called her the pink *Pony* just as you'd say the clipper *Cloud*."

The year before I had been up the Maine coast in the Seacasot Mission boat, and we saw in the harbor at Jonesport the hull of what they claimed was the last of the pinkies. It is an obsolete type, deader even than the square-rigger. She was rigged fore-and-aft like a schooner. Her high, narrow stern, the taffrail with its chock for the boom, the rudder with its long tiller instead of a wheel, all belonged to a bygone age. But the captain could remember when there were four hundred of them afloat, and "folks went everywhere in them."

A high point in his career was being in San Francisco when the clipper *Flying Cloud* came in on her great record voyage—eighty-nine days out from New York. It must have been a stirring experience to see the famous ship come up the harbor in triumph that day!

One of my favorite blue-water men was Captain Daniel Robbins. He had just celebrated his ninetieth birthday the day I went to see him, and was jolly as a cricket. When he went out into the yard so that I might snap his picture he told his daughter he'd have to do something to get rid of the gal—she would make him talk! And I think he was the only victim of my kodak who did not make any remark about breaking it with his beauty, which shows both originality and a modest spirit.

For the past half-century, more or less, he had been a farmer, living contentedly on his thrifty acres here in Dennis. If it was all like his homestead lot there would not be a blade of grass out of place anywhere. His stone walls were straight, his fields clear, his trees well pruned and his building kept up to the minute. He could stand in his door and look out over his smooth fields and see not only them but the homes he had built for other people in the neighborhood. This year for the first time he had sold his cranberries on the vine. Up to then he had been out bossing his gang of men and taking active charge of the long process of getting the crop ready for shipping.

He was fourteen, he said, when he ran away to sea.

"I hove my pillowcase full of clothes out of the chamber window and clumb out after it. I was running away. Running away to sea. My folks didn't want me to go. All my brothers had gone to sea. I was the youngest, and they wanted to keep me home. So I had to go the best way I could," he explained simply.

This happened of course in the middle of the night. A friend of his, "a lot older man," was going to ship from Boston and had promised to pick Daniel up and take him along if he was out on the main road when he drove by.

Young Daniel was there, the pillowcase of clothes over his shoulder and love of the sea in every inch of him. They went off to Boston together, and he "didn't see home again for going on two years." The friend was only twenty, but of course that did seem "a lot older" to the fourteen-year-old.

The two lads shipped on a bark bound for N'Orleens. Daniel was rated as an ordinary seaman, thanks to experience on his brothers' boats where, among other useful accomplishments, he had learned to steer. His actual duties for most of this voyage were those of a cabin boy, serving the meals in the officers' cabin and helping out in the galley. But he was soon taking his trick at the wheel with the rest and lending a hand with the sails.

"I was light weight, so they used to send me up high. All the tops'ls were stationary, and you had to go aloft to set them."

"Did you carry t'gallants'ls?" I asked.

"T'gallants'ls? Yes, and r'yals, too. Yes— and skys'ls!"

It seems he had reason to remember that fact. It was on his last long voyage—but I'm getting ahead of the story. The bark lay over in New Orleans to refit. After two months the restless lad got tired of waiting for her and shipped in the square-rigger *Caroline and Mary Clark*, loaded with iron in her lower hold and with coke between-decks and bound for the far-away port of Archangel.

That was a trip for you! Rounding North Cape at latitude 72 north, icebergs in July and a sun that never sets, day or night. For the most venturesome tourists—in the days when there were tourists—the North Cape was the place where the fine big ships turned around and headed for home. But for the *Caroline and Mary Clark* and the little boy making sail on the skys'l yards it was a mere incident. Up and on and around they went, and left their load at Archangel and took on another quite different cargo—hemp and flaxseed—and for a place quite as different, New Orleans.

His pal had stayed behind, but when he got back he found him waiting. This older chap was, it seemed, homesick. He wanted to go back home to Cape Cod.

"I didn't know it at the time but what he really wanted," the captain confided, "was to get married. There was a girl he was engaged to, but he didn't dare go home without me for fear folks would think he had kidnaped me. So I had to go home with him."

"Stay long?"

"Three days," said the captain.

There was still a good bit of the world he hadn't seen, you understand. No time to settle down to fishing, not yet a while. His next voyage took him over to Rotterdam and then down through the Mediterranean to a place pronounced in old Cape fashion Try-eest.

"The captain had his wife and their little girl along. I was a regular seaman by this time. I used to like to steer because at dinnertime the little girl would come up the companionway from the cabin and give me a piece of cake. She and I were great chums, and she used to stay round and talk.

"Seems the captain's wife owned half the ship, and usually the captain and the mates owned shares in the vessels they sailed on. I heard a lot of talk about their interests and about how much the officers on other ships owned in them and all, and it made me want to work up to where I could own a ship. The captain said if I would stay by him he would make a man of me some day. But I figured it would be a long time before I got anywhere on a big vessel, because I didn't have anyone to push me. Seemed to me it would be better for me to start in small and work up, seeing I'd have to do it all myself."

The captain's wife fell ill, so the captain left the ship at one of the ports and took her back to the states. A young captain, the old one's brother-in-law, took nominal command but in reality the old mate "was a kind of a nurse for him" so they got along all right. But no cargo could be shipped at Try-eest because "England and Russia was at war." So back they came to Boston, and were three days beating back and forth off Boston Light trying to make the harbor.

"It was cold—awful cold. We were all iced up, rigging, spars, everything. I had a wooden club tied round my neck to break the ice off the sheets with so's we could tack ship. You couldn't handle the ropes till you'd smashed the ice off."

"Tell her," suggested the captain's daughter, "about the time you went aloft."

"That was the time," he said. "We'd just made the harbor, after all that tacking. Captain says to me, 'Boy, you climb up and run the pennant halliards and set the colors.' That meant going way up to the top of the mainmast, that was all ice, and the rigging iced up too. They sent me because I was light. That was seventy-five years ago, but I'll never forget it. Part of the way I had to shin up over the icy mast. A heavier man couldn't have done it.

"My hands lost all feeling. The only way I could tell I was holding on to anything was to look and see if I was. I couldn't feel a thing. Well, I got up there, way up to the top of the mast, and I got the halliards rove. Then I tied the ends to my hands so they wouldn't slip and all my work have to be done over again, and clumb down.

"Part ways down I fell. Easier to fall than climb any more. I let go and fell to the deck. No, it didn't kill me. I'm here yet," he pointed out.

Very much here was the captain. One glance at his straight, vigorous figure with the lively blue eyes twinkling in the ruddy face of him assured you of that. Those blue eyes seem to go with the business of being a sea captain on the Cape. As I've said before, all the deep-sea men I met had them—sea-blue eyes with the sparkle of sunlight and the keenness of a nor'east breeze.

There's a question I should like to have answered—do those wise blue optics come from much seafaring, from reflecting for years on end the color of deep water, the blue water of the Gulf Stream, or is it that men who are born with those eyes just naturally have to go to sea and become masters of their ships? There is bound to be some connection. Mind you, I'm not talking about inshore, shoal-water men. I mean your true deep-water sailors, the ones who've been off years at a time beyond "where the blue begins."

The captain was forty-four when he came ashore to live. He had worked up on the smaller vessels to be master. When he told about the gales he'd been out in I asked if he wasn't ever afraid.

"Afraid!" He was clearly scandalized at the idea. "Why, 'twouldn't do for a captain to be afraid! If he thinks there is danger, then is the time he puts on his nerve. He has to. There was one gale I didn't expect we'd last more'n two hours. Too much wind to carry sail, and we were being blown straight on shore. Water coming in, for we'd sprung a leak. Pumped all night. Took up a trap in the cabin floor and bailed, too.

"A Dennis man was with me, and his two boys. He wouldn't have minded if he hadn't had his boys along. We laid to the best we could and toward morning the wind moderated a mite, and we made sail enough to keep us off the coast. When he got to port the Dennis man said he was going to go ashore and take his boys, and I didn't blame him. But 'twouldn't do for a captain to get scared."

In the fall Lyman Armes quit the little magazine for a bigger job and went off to town, so I ran it alone through the winter and till it changed hands in the spring. I would drive down once or twice a month from Boston when the roads were open and make the rounds of my best friends and pick up what copy I could from the few who were writing.

One afternoon at the Halls' we were sitting in front of the fire (made Cape-fashion on a bed of ashes so thick they half buried the small andirons) and Steve got telling me a story he said was a real story and not a yarn. I'd have to believe it, because it was really true. He knew because he got it straight from one of the men it happened to, and he was a man you could rely on.

Two Dennis men were out in a fishing schooner. One was Captain Jonathan Ellis and the other was Bill Walker who was, if I remember rightly, a carpenter. She was an old vessel and far from seaworthy. Still they'd have got her back to port all right if the weather had stayed good. But it smeared up for a storm and the wind blew a gale, and the poor old thing couldn't take it. Cracks started in her deck, lengthwise ones of course. They kept getting wider and wider. The masts began working loose. She was starting to split in two, cracking wide open.

Captain Jonathan had four children at home; and he did some fast thinking. He yelled to his men to get out all the cable, and good stout rope it was. First they looped a length of it down under her bowsprit, which was jabbing every which way in the heavy seas, and worked it down under her bow; and then they winched the ends together at the capstan forrard, all the crew laboring with everything they had to get it taut. They took another cable aft and put it down under her stern and winched it up. In fact they just literally tied her up fore and aft so she held together. Then they worked her slowly back to port.

Of course she was days overdue and had long been given up for lost with all hands when she staggered up to her berth. Her owner met her there, with tears in his eyes.

"Are all the boys here?" he asked.

"Yes, but your vessel's done for."

"Never mind her, so long as the boys are all right!"

Another story concerned his great-uncle, Samuel Hall, wrecked at sea about the year 1812. Similar things must have happened or come terribly near happening during the war in the Pacific. It was not a story that had been much told, for it was one the family had tried to forget, and I appreciated the effort Steve made in telling it now. There was a quality of something like tenderness in the men concerned that we like to think of as Anglo-Saxon, though it may be more universal than we realize.

The crew was adrift without food or water, and the time came when the captain was faced with the grim necessity of drawing lots to see which one of them would give his life that the others might have food and live. The lots were drawn and the fearful fate befell great-uncle Samuel, then a cabin-boy only fifteen years old. But that gaunt crew of starving, desperate men refused to have it so. They demanded another draw among themselves, to save the boy. The lots were drawn again, and this time the cook drew the lot. He said a brief farewell, bent his head over a bucket and was killed.

This enabled the rest of the crew to survive for some days. "And just as they were going to draw lots again," Steve said, "they were rescued. Months later they came back home with one tale that they nor their sons nor their grandsons hardly ever told."

The Halls had a brother Frank who was principal of a school up in the city. He had a letter-perfect memory for all the stories he had ever heard, from boyhood up. I only met him once, and that is why I've only this one story of his, but it is a sample. It concerns Uncle Marshal Allen, an old Dennis chap with a circle of white whiskers round under his chin and a vivid way of talking that made pictures in words. When he was married he had only eighty cents. "But I bought a peck of meal and a piece of calliky, enough for Sally to make her a dress, and we went to housekeeping," he used to say. In spite of this modest beginning, he died quite well off.

But his description of a swordfishing experience, as remembered verbatim by Mr. Hall, is a fine example of the old forgotten folk speech of Cape Cod. Seems they got into a small boat to go swordfishing and had cast off when they saw a swordfish coming toward them. Said Uncle Marshal Allen:

And there he come, swinging along, curl, CURL, curl.
Went right under the bow of the boat.
I stud thar with the iron in my hand.
When he come under
I gin it to him.

Splash!
Away went Mr. Swordfish—
Curl, whirl, scurry, foam, zippery-ZEE!
Lather-buckle CRACK!!
   And off he went with forty fathom o' my best rope.

11. *Some Ha'wichers*

A MAN who made Harwich famous in his day and also
helped make American history was Captain Jonathan
Walker, "the man with the branded hand." His long-
forgotten story came to light while I was on the Cape,
among the papers of an East Harwich man, the late War-
ren G. Nickerson. The papers were turned over to the
Chatham town historian for his history, but I was allowed
to use the material in the magazine. It seems Mr. Nickerson
was a contemporary of the Branded Man and indeed knew
him well, so the story which he recorded briefly probably
came to him first-hand.

Seth and Nancy (Basset) Walker of East Harwich had
four sons, of whom the eldest was named David and the
youngest Jonathan. Young Jonathan went to sea when he
was seventeen; and by the time this story starts, July of
1844, he had already seen most of the world. A fuller
account than the Nickerson one was published the following year by the Boston Anti-Slavery society, embellished
with a woodcut of the branded hand and an engraved
portrait of Captain Walker. Then the poet Whittier wrote
an impassioned poem about him, and his fame was estab-
lished.

The engraving shows a face of the old Yankee type,
homely but "good," full of kindliness and simple honesty;
what we used to call the salt of the earth. One can be sure

that even if he could have known what he was letting himself in for he would have gone ahead just the same.

Captain Walker left Harwich in a sailing vessel for Mobile and went from there to Pensacola, where there was talk of raising a wreck and salvaging her cargo. He was there for some time, making friends and working—though not on the wreck, which proved to be too far gone to float. Along in June he found some Negroes who were trying to get away from a cruel master. They had got to Florida, but couldn't get off the shore. Florida was a perfect slave trap in those days, for it was nearly surrounded by water and few slaves knew anything about handling boats.

One of the slaves came to Captain Walker with his desperate story, and the captain was so touched by the plight of the runaways that of his own accord he offered to "share luck" with them and take a chance on getting them to the Bahamas, where they would be both free and safe. He understood there would be only three men, but seven turned up and he took them all. It was only an open boat with no cabin. For fourteen days they sailed when there was a wind and rowed when there was none—and there was a lot of rowing. Soon after they left shore Walker was taken ill, but he kept on going, for when he started anything he saw it through. So they kept on, under the broiling sun of a southern summer.

They had covered seven hundred terrible miles when a wrecking sloop hove in sight and hailed them. She offered them a tow to Key West, and when they refused the favor she took them along anyhow and turned them all over to the authorities—seven runaway slaves and their "stealer." From there a steamboat took them back to Pensacola—six days, Walker ill and in double irons in the stifling hold. The slaves were returned to their masters and Walker was sent to prison, one end of a log-chain on his ankle, the other linked to a shackle in the wall of his cell. His bail was placed at $10,000, a lot of money in those days.

All his former friends, even the northerner among them, deserted him. He was ill for several months but by November was well enough to stand trial. He was given a triple sentence—a heavy fine, with branding and pillory added.

The pillory is different from the stocks because the head is confined in the beam as well as the hands. Some merciful soul put a handkerchief over his head to protect it a little from the sun, but it was snatched away and the crowd was allowed to pelt him with rotten eggs.

The palm of his right hand was branded in court with the letters S S, supposed to stand for "slave stealer." But point of view makes a lot of difference—when at last he was free and able to return home to Harwich his friends and neighbors said the letters stood for Slave Salvation.

It is hard for us to realize after all these years the fierce wrath that blazed up in the north when the story became known. It fed the smoldering fires of the anti-slavery agitation and was one of the cumulative causes which led to the war and the final end of slavery in the south. Whittier's poem fanned the fury of passion to a white heat.

"Ho, men of Massachusetts, for the love of God, look there!" he cried, and adjured the Captain—

> Then lift that manly right hand,
> Bold ploughman of the wave!
> Its branded palm shall prophesy,
> Salvation to the Slave!

There are not as many Harwiches as there are Dennises. But there is Harwich, and North Harwich, and East Harwich, and South Harwich, and of course Harwich Port, not to mention Herring Brook, which used to be called Deerfield because there were so many deer running through the woods there. The waters of the little brook used to turn a millwheel; the original miller used the power for making coffins and, according to a tale sent in to the magazine, used to sleep in one of them himself. But after a while the herring took over. At first they were caught when the run was on and were used for eating or for fertilizer; then it was discovered their scales could be used for making artificial pearls.

The Port has a library and community house, new when I was there, a good if somewhat literal copy of a Cape-type house. A bit too symmetrical to be wholly convincing, and studying it makes you realize how practically impossible it is to reproduce these houses and get whatever it is that makes them so lovable. You can copy them shingle for shingle, and when you're through what you have is just another house. It isn't only the patina of age you miss, either—it must be something mental. Still this little library is a nice job, what with the fireplace in the children's room and the foxglove outside the windows and some really good detail.

But the main attraction in Harwich Port, to me at least, was the Allens. Captain Jairus Allen followed the sea for fifty years, and his wife went with him. He was master of every type of vessel, sail and steam, except the clipper. Now they were living in a trim and shipshape home on the main street of the village, and he was making ship models for the summer folks—models with rigging that "ran" and cabins furnished like those in which he and his wife had spent so many happy years.

Of the dozen or more vessels which the captain had commanded, Mrs. Allen's favorite was the *Henry Norwell*. They sailed on her eleven years and her cabin was "real homelike," Mrs. Allen said. The *Norwell* was named for a famous old Boston merchant who often came aboard to visit them. She started life as a three-masted schooner, but struck a gale in the English Channel which dismasted her—took her foremast and bowsprit and pretty well spoiled the rest of the rigging. Captain Allen took her into an island port and fixed up a jury rig and sailed her home to Boston, where they had been given up for lost. When she came out of repair dock the *Norwell* was a barkentine—and a graceful one, too. A painting of her called "Entrance to Mobile Bay" shows her with all sails set, a charming creature. At her wheel stand two figures, the captain and his wife.

"Of course the captain wouldn't ordinarily be at the wheel," Mrs. Allen explained, "it was just for the picture!"

Once they were out in the Bay of Mexico, loaded with lumber, when the vessel sprung a leak. They began throwing their deckload overboard, and this attracted the attention of a passing steamer. She came alongside and offered to take aboard anyone who wanted to come. The captain ordered his wife to go but she flatly refused to obey orders. She was going to stay with him and the boys, she was not going to desert them when they needed her most.

"For two weeks I didn't have my clothes off," she recalled.

One of the men was sick with chills and fever, but nobody could be spared, so he had to take his trick at the wheel like the others. She spent most of her time making hot tea for him and cold lemonade for the others. "When there wasn't anything else to do I sat and embroidered."

They took soundings in the hold, and Mrs. Allen made them show her the stick, though they didn't want to. Things looked bad. The cook was so scared he dared not stay in the galley. He had never been in a leaky vessel before, and he didn't like it. But when he came aft and saw Mrs. Allen sitting there so placidly embroidering pink roses on white linen he felt better.

"Well, ma'am," he said, "I guess if you can do that we aren't going to sink right off and I might as well go make the boys a pie."

The captain said the boys thought a lot of her after that little experience.

While they were in port at Mobile she used to go ashore for embroidery lessons, and everybody on board understood that she had to be rowed ashore when it came time for her lesson, whatever the weather, "even if the boat stood up on end most of the way."

Her home-staying sister complained, "You no sooner get your clothes shook out from one voyage than you're getting ready to leave on another."

But Mrs. Allen loved seeing the world, and she liked being able to make a home for the captain. Some of their vessels had "lovely cabins, all fixed up like your own home." On one, a new ship, she found the owners had provided china of the same pattern as that in her own cupboard back home on Cape Cod, and the rug on the cabin floor was the same as that in her parlor. With flowers and a canary, one could do wonders making a cabin like that look homelike.

One flaw in the life aboard ship—she got "so tired" of being the only woman round, and she used to long for another woman to talk with. The days in port were always a delight, because there was sure to be another ship in with a captain's wife aboard and while the vessel discharged her cargo and took on a new one they could visit together. (George Mathews of Yarmouth Port told me he remembered being in Calcutta as a child with his mother when there were ten captains' wives in port.)

Captain Allen began his career at the age of twelve. His father had died and left his mother with four small children, so he felt he had to do something to help support them. She was teaching in the village school but found time to teach him on the side the one craft which a small boy on Cape Cod was sure to find useful—she taught him to cook.

So at twelve he shipped as cook on a coasting schooner that was "corn-crackin'"—she carried corn from New York to Boston and fish from Gloucester to New York. He got $12 a month, which was good pay for a boy in those days, and they liked his cooking so well that on the second voyage they raised him fifty cents a month! But after this second voyage he got to be a sailor and that meant $14 a month. At eighteen he was second mate and at twenty he had become master of the *Norwell*. Between voyages he stayed home and studied navigation with his uncle, who had a school for seagoing lads in Harwich Port.

"You have to go to school to learn the theory," he explained, "but it's the practice that really counts, the years of experience under all sorts of conditions."

A white cat was held responsible for the loss of the only

ship he ever did lose—at least the sailors blamed it on her. But for a wreck it was an easy one. They were off Long Island in a snowstorm—an April snowstorm, of all things, that came up with a gale of wind blowing strong on shore. The vessel didn't have a chance to beat out against it, and that night at ten o'clock, in a heavy sea, she struck. Half an hour later the smother of snow vanished and left them with clear weather; but the gale was still raging and great seas were pounding the poor old vessel terribly. It was only a matter of a few hours before she would break up, for she was no longer young.

"If she was living yet she would be a hundred years old," the captain said.

But Luck was with them in spite of the white cat, for they had gone ashore "bang up against a Coast Guard station" and by midnight they had all been taken safely off. All, that is, except the white cat.

Next morning they rowed out to the wreck, of which only a topmast was showing above water. A rag of sail hung hammock-fashion from the spar and in this, curled up cosily, was the white cat, none the worse for having stood by the ship. They gave her to the wife of one of the Coast Guard men, who named her Miss Church after the vessel. But the boys always insisted she was a hoodoo.

One of the momentous experiences of the captain's life was being out in the *Portland* storm, off Cape Hatteras. That is a natural for wrecks, second only to Chatham. He had a broken rudderhead but managed somehow to rig a makeshift and with one small sail set up "forrard" was able to ride it out.

On the windowsill beside his workbench with the latest clipper model rested the captain's octant. That is an instrument whose subtle differences prevent it from being either a sextant or a quadrant. We took it out to the back yard, and he showed me how you shoot the sun to find out where you are at sea. It looked like a very intricate business, what with logarithms and all. But when you couldn't see the sun to shoot it, things were still more difficult, for then you had to go by dead reckoning, keeping track of every knot on every course with the log. Nowadays there is a lot of machinery that does such things more or less automatically, but in the days of sail it took very special brains to be a captain.

Newly finished on her cradle stood the model of the *James Baines*—fastest clipper ever built, she was—a Mackay masterpiece. The captain tells you with shining eyes (blue, of course) of her record, how she made 420 miles in twenty-four hours with all her skys'ls set and "everything drawing." It took him eight months to make this model of her. The tiny ropes were all spliced, and the rigging ran, and every last bit of hemp was in its right place. Only a sailor who knew where to put his hand in a black night with a gale blowing when ordered to take in a foresail could have made that model.

"You can't get it out of books," Captain Allen said, "you've got to know."

I imagine the Allen models have long since become collectible items.

Over in East Harwich, close to the Chatham line, I found another man who was also making collectible items, and they were already being collected so avidly that he was a year behind in his orders. Whether the garage was part of the workshop or the workshop part of the garage you couldn't tell for sure by merely looking at the outside of the small shingled building that housed both the car and the career of A. E. Crowell. Inside, the car had one end to itself and the career had the other end. It was a workshop like no other I have ever seen, and the chances are it was unique.

It was there that Mr. Crowell made birds. He made them out of wood, carved with a jackknife and painted. But wait —don't confuse him with the toy-makers of the shavings-shops that line the more populous roadsides with their crude output. He was a craftsman of a high order, an artist in his line. Some were calling him a genius, but one hates to use that much-abused word for so honest an ability as his.

When someone asked him why he did not move his shop over onto the main road his answer was character-istic both of him and of the Cape. He said there would be too many people round. So he stayed where he was, away off on a side road where you could find him if you knew the way or were willing to hunt. Through Harwich one went, turned right at the bank, followed the next left fork and turned left again on the first macadam crossroad, and there was his sign, "A. E. Crowell, maker of birds and decoys."

It was a bewildering place, that little shop. You seemed to have stepped into an aviary, but such a quiet aviary! Birds sitting around everywhere, perched on twigs or roost-ing on shelves or resting at ease on a box or a stove or practically anything. They were the livest looking things, with their heads cocked saucily on one side or held proudly up, their pert little eyes giving you the once-over as you came in. Only that strange, uncanny silence gave them away—there wasn't a twitter in them. So you discovered that they were just make-believe birds, all made out of wood by a cunning craftsman.

It was slow business making them, too. Each bird had to be carved carefully to scale with infinite patience in the matter of small feathers and still smaller toes, preceded by long study and careful observation of the living original.

On top of the cast-iron station stove stood a lovely little half-size mallard drake, his downy breast so softly modeled you couldn't believe it was wood. Most of the birds were small, but among them were the decoys. Such decoys they were as gunners rarely see, not the usual roughly chopped-out blocks painted black and white but beautifully proportioned birds, each one perfect to the last shining feather. Sheldrakes, goldeneyes, mallards, widgeons, pintails there were, and black ducks with a bright blue feather in each wing.

A bushel basket was half full of little miniature birds in the white, waiting to be painted. These came in sets, forty-eight to a set, all native Cape Cod birds. He was making them for schools and sending them all over the country.

There were many varieties of lifesize birds, too, to put in gardens—a lordly blue jay on a crooked stick was a thing of beauty and seemed to know it. Orioles, red-winged blackbirds, bluebirds, carved and painted so realistically that when you compared the oriole with the actual oriole skin that Mr. Crowell had there they were alike in everything but the texture.

His art training was limited to some lessons in oils that he took when a boy of fifteen "from a lady who came down from Middleboro in Plymouth county and had classes all over the Cape." The first picture he ever made, under her tutelage, was, oddly enough, of a duck.

But the boy had no thought of becoming an artist. He was, first and foremost, a gunner. That was at once his chosen sport and his profession. One time when he was connected with a private gunning camp there was trouble with the decoys. They simply did not decoy, the ducks would not take them seriously.

"I can make better decoys than those," he told his employers; and he did. They bought the birds he made, and told their friends; and soon his birds were everywhere. But he had about given up making decoys when I knew him, there was too much demand for the little birds, and more money in them.

He went out into the Cape woods for his models, and had stuffed birds sitting round his shop among the copies of them. Among them were some sea doves which he said were little auks, sitting up like small penguins.

The leisurely way things get done in these parts came out in the Harwich town meeting this year. A citizen took the floor to speak for an appropriation to plant new shade trees to replace those blown down by the second hurricane. "Now is the time—let's start this year," he urged. But the voters were not to be stampeded into any such rash action. Instead they decided, and so voted, to set aside $50 for a committee to investigate the matter. But this was wartime, and all the young of Harwich had gone into service; so it was an old-timers' meeting, and we can't take it as a sample of how things are today.

The citizens of Harwich ought to know how to run their town by this time, though, for this was their town meeting Number 251; and of course you understand that these meetings are held annually.

12. *Chatham and Her Deadly Sands*

OF ALL THE TOWNS, *Chatham* (and be sure you pronounce it right, with the *ham* as in "ham") is the most sea-conscious. This is quite natural. For her few square miles of territory she has forty-four miles of shore, and twenty of them are ocean beaches. Here on the Cape's sharp elbow nearly half the wrecks of the entire Atlantic and Gulf coasts of the United States have happened. There used to be a cemetery just for the bodies of sailors washed ashore after storms, but it has been closed. The *Portland* storm filled it up full. "Sand in your ears before morning" was the saying of many a sailor to his mate as he saw his ship being driven toward that treacherous lee shore.

The last I knew it took four life-saving stations of the Coast Guard to patrol the outer beaches, three lighthouses stood guard above the sandy bluffs, and four lightships kept watch in the tempestuous waters off the changing shores. Someone figured that if the wrecks of twenty years could be laid stem to stern they would build a bulwark from Chatham clear round to Provincetown. Captain George Crowell used to make a business of running his sloop from Boston Light down the Back Side, blowing up wrecks to get them out of the way.

It was a Coast Guard boast that up to 1896 no crew ever failed to reach its ship, even though it might be too late to do any good when it got there. Tough as the job was, it had its moments—as the time a French vessel with a cargo of champagne came ashore. The casks broke open and the wine gushed from the ship's scuppers. One old fellow on the rescuing crew thrust his sou'wester under a scupper, yelled—"God, boys, let's have a drink!"

What makes this shore so deadly is the constant shifting of the bars and shoals cornering out into the ocean. Charts are good only till the next storm, if then. Not only does the depth of the water change overnight but the shorelines romp around so you never can be sure just how far off you are. A point becomes an island or an island a peninsula, a new harbor is made or an old one is closed up, a lighthouse that should be on the shore is half a mile inland or slips off into the water. In one storm fifty-odd houses were washed away, a bar was thrown up in another place, the seas broke through the dunes, and the buildings back of them had to be moved in a hurry. So that is how it is, and there is nothing to do about it except keep as far offshore as you can—if you can.

Of course beachcombing was inevitable. No thrifty New Englander, on Cape or off, could bear to see anything wasted that could be salvaged. I never heard of moon-cussing there. They did not have to make wrecks, nature provided all they could use. Down Nauset way it was different.

As in Dennis everybody is a Hall or a Sears, so in Chatham they are more likely than not to be Nickersons. There was Captain Oscar Nickerson, for instance, who had a license for all crafts and all seas, and that is quite something. I was told that he knew who the man was who went from Chatham and married the Queen of the Sandwich Islands, but I never got round to asking him. It was

GRISTMILL, HARWICH

TWO-STORY HALF-HOUSE, WITH SALT-BOX ROOF, WEST BREWSTER

WATER MILL, BREWSTER

KENRICK HOUSE, SOUTH ORLEANS

like a Chathamite to do that sort of thing, all in his stride. The Queen's granddaughter, niece of Queen Liliuokalani, was brought home to Chatham by Captain Hiram Harding, according to my meager notes, and went to school in Chatham Port. Her name was Laura and she was very pretty, but she married an off-Caper—so that is the end of her so far as we are concerned. It would be a pretty story, the adjustments a part-Kanaka girl would have to make to Cape ways, wouldn't it?

When I went to Chatham I used to stay nights with dear Aunt Flora Nickerson. She wasn't really my aunt, of course—more likely a tenth cousin—but everyone in the village called her that. She taught a class of small children in Sunday school, and every time I went there she had a new tale for me. They were trying to translate New Testament stories into terms of everyday Chatham life. Aunt Flora said they preferred the lesson cards that had pictures of boats—salt-water pictures, she called them. But they were very critical. Gazing at a picture of Paul's shipwreck a small six-year-old said—as only a citizen of Chatham could say it—"Huh, I don't think that's much of a wreck!"

One day they were discussing the episode of the eunuch in the chariot (Acts 8:28). Aunt Flora asked, "Who was that fellow that was riding along in the team?"

A five-year-old answered eagerly, "Why, Aunt Flora, that was the eunuch—he was trying to read a leaf from out the Bible and he couldn't understand it."

"Well, who was that man that was coming along the street?"

"That was Philip, Aunt Flora—the man in the team wanted him to come aboard and tell him how to read the Bible!"

It must have been Aunt Flora who told me about the girl from New Bedford who wanted to teach school in Chatham. The chairman of the school committee was a retired shipmaster and he gave her a good quizzing to make sure she, a mainlander, was fitted to teach in his school.

"What's the latitude of the mouth of the Amazon?" he asked.

"Hasn't any," she answered smartly.

"How in heck did you know that?" he demanded, much taken aback.

"I went to sea five years in my father's ship," she explained.

He couldn't trip her in navigation, so he gave her the job.

Some of the older Chathamites, like Aunt Flora, could remember the Come-Outers, a vigorous religious group of half a century before. They had definite ideas of right and wrong, and dressed something like the Quakers in dull gray or brown clothes. The women wore bonnets and kerchiefs, plain and austere in every detail. They had seceded from the orthodox church because they did not believe in organization, and that is why they were called Come-Outers.

A Chatham woman went off to New York on a trip and brought home some very wordly new underwear. The Come-Outer woman who did her washing took one look at the frills and refused to touch them. "No," said she, "I won't wash anything so ungodly as lace-trimmed underwear!"

Quite a good bit of Chatham's shoreline is along inland waterways. Off Chatham Bay is Stage Harbor. From the old windmill there is a wide and wonderful view—180 degrees of living water. That, if you know your compass, is a whole half of the horizon. A lovely quiet unspoiled place as I knew it, with brown fish-nets drying on the coarse grass. In this part of the Cape walking is better than driving, you get to see so much more.

Take the flowers, for instance—they are specially lovely here in Chatham, I suppose because of the sea air or the soil or something. Just as the vegetables grown here have a sweeter flavor, from the sweet soil, so the flowers are more fragrant and more brightly colored than those on the mainland. The mayflowers in the April woods, the creamy-white clouds of shadbush along the roads, the blue flags in the swamps, and cardinal flowers and the swamp pinks, like azaleas but fragrant, old-maid's-pinks along the roadsides and in the dooryards, pink marsh mallow growing by the brackish pools on the marshes. In June the poverty grass spreads yellow over the moors. On the shores silvery clumps of dusty miller, and the tiny blossoms of the poorman's-weatherglass, and the gay beach peas, like sweet peas only smaller. The wild roses are deeper pink, and the climbers in the village gardens are specially luxuriant.

Speaking of Stage Harbor—as I was a while back—into it runs Oyster Pond River, from Oyster Pond just round the corner. Along in April I used to see the little schooner *Alice M. Wentworth* coming to anchor in the river with a load of oysters from Greenport, Long Island. A motorboat would tow a string of scows alongside and the oysters would be loaded over onto them. Then the motorboat towed the scows out round the pond while the crew shoveled the oysters overboard into the water. They call it planting oysters, and it is a simple form of agriculture—no plowing or spading or spraying or cultivation—just dump 'em over, and they do the rest. All they ask is a chance to rest on the creamy sands of Oyster Pond.

It seems oysters won't breed here—they prefer Long Island for that. But when they begin to grow there—well, they stop. They won't fatten. To be really lovable an oyster must be good and plump. There is practically no lure to a thin oyster. Here in the pond they put on plenty of good healthy flesh—by fall you wouldn't know those oysters. When the R months start, they are ready for market. Because the water is so clear and the sand so shining and the whole set-up so free from any sort of pollution folks say "clean as a Chatham oyster" when they really mean clean.

(Out in the far Northwest we raise oysters, too—bring the young uns from Japan, or did in the old days, and plant them here; and do they grow—two or three make a meal. But they taste different—sort of an iodine flavor or something. Good, but not the same.)

After the oyster season in Chatham along come the clams and quahaugs, to be packed for the New York market, where they are called fancy names like littlenecks and cherrystones, maybe because the benighted N'Yorkers don't know how to pronounce "quahaug." Delicious to eat raw right on the spot, dipped in the salt water for seasoning—unbelievably better than when dished up in a hotel dining room.

Down near the shore—which could be practically anywhere in Chatham, but I think it was over Chatham Port way—stood a tidy little house painted yellow with white trim. In it used to live Captain David Smith, a man who capitalized on his misfortunes in true Cape spirit. I was at Rose Hill one day—that is a summer place, and about the

best reproduction of a Cape house I have seen—and the
owner showed me a picture hanging on the parlor wall,
a painting of the bark *Maria J. Smith*. If you looked closely
you could see a place in the middle of the picture where
a hole had been carefully mended.

The *Maria* was the captain's ship, and the picture of
her belonged to his father. The old man made the hole in
a moment of rage when he heard the news that the ship had
been wrecked and was a total loss. He owned a lot of
stock in her—and so did his neighbors and friends, because
she was owned right here in Chatham. The reason he was
so upset was partly because his son was her master, and
also because the insurance had been allowed to lapse. In
those days there were no banks and you either invested
your savings in ships or put them under the bed. Remember Aunt Marthy Hoxie, back in Sandwich? The older
Smith went her one better—he used to keep $50,000 in gold
in a little horsehair trunk under his four-poster.

The *Maria* was being towed through the Strait of Juan
de Fuca, heading in toward Seattle, when her lines parted
and a southerly gale blew her onto the rugged shores of
Vancouver Island. The captain was so chagrined at the loss
of his ship that he could not bear to go home and face
his father and the other stockholders. He was a heavy
stockholder in her himself, but his sorrow was for them.
Anyway, it was not till fourteen years later that he went
home again.

But meanwhile he was making good in a big way.
This had been an unlucky voyage for him, for out in
India his wife, who sailed with him, caught the plague
and died. If he could have got ice he could have saved
her, he felt sure. But there was no ice. All the way across

the Pacific he was brooding over the problem of ice-making in the tropics. It had been done to some slight extent in other parts of the world, he knew. But he worked out his own plans for a machine, and got patents on them. The last I heard the models for it were at Rose Hill, the patent office having released them. For four years he worked on them, living in Honolulu. When he had the machine working the way he wanted it he went all over the world installing them; he devoted the rest of his life to the job.

Of all the captains who had gone out from Chatham I found only one blue-water man left, and that was Samuel G. Harding, as truly a man of the world as one might meet in a month's looking. He was a fine, upstanding old gentleman with a ruddy face and snowy sideburns and mustache, a heavy gold watch chain on his vest and a bluff dignity that made no show of itself but would stand no nonsense either. He did not look within twenty years of the eighty-five he claimed, and he had the vigor of a much younger man. He attributed his health to his coming back here to his native town when the doctors up in Boston told him he had only one more year to live. That was twenty-seven years before, and he was still going strong.

Once there was a small boy named Sammy Harding who lived in a farmhouse over near where the Chatham Bars Inn is now. This was in 1851, and he was ten years old. His father went to sea, but he didn't come home from his last voyage, and there was a widowed mother to be looked after. So little Sam asked if he might not leave school and go to sea. Being a wise mother she said no, he must wait a while longer. If he did his lessons well and did not miss a day at school for two years she would let him go then—sure, no doubt, that he would forget long before the time arrived.

But she didn't know the boy. Just two years to the day, she was surprised to see him come trudging home from school with all his books under his arm. He told her gravely that the time was up—he had kept his part of the bargain, had not missed a day for two years—now he was going to sea.

This was the start of his real education. As cabin boy on the bark *Rose Poole* he found life anything but rosy. "I got six dollars a month and a licking a day," was his description of it. But he looked back on the lickings as the more profitable part of his income. "It's the easiest way to learn," he said, "you don't have to be told twice."

He got a lesson in etiquette when the frigate *Constitution* hove in sight under full sail. It happened like this: It was a Sunday noon, and *Rose Poole* lay at anchor off the coast of Africa—the West Coast. Things were quiet outside, so quiet that if it hadn't been for the heat you might have supposed yourself anchored back home in some snug Cape Cod harbor.

The cabin boy was serving the captain's Sunday dinner down in the cabin. It was a serious business, and required the strictest attention. But Sam happened to glance out of a porthole, and there she was—a sight he was never to forget as long as he lived. Framed by the porthole was the grand old fighter, her clouds of white canvas tapering aloft to her skys'ls, her stately progress that of a great queen. The boy knew who she was—"Old Ironsides," venerable even then but still a thing of beauty.

Later when the captain went up onto the quarter-deck to watch her come about into the wind and drop anchor little Sam Harding went along too, almost jumping out of his skin with excitement.

"Oh, gorry," he gasped, first on one foot and then on the other, "gorry, ain't she BIG? Gorry, ain't she a BEAUTY? Gorry, she must have a thousand men on her! GORRY!"

The sailors in their Sunday white had manned the yards and were taking in sail with a precision that was unknown even on a well handled merchantman. It was unlike anything he had ever seen, and he became speechless with the wonder of it.

"Boy, get my spyglass!" barked the captain.

Sam made quick time to the cabin, so as not to miss anything. The captain took a long slow look through the glass. It seemed to the boy he would never put it down. He was beside himself with excitement. Finally when the captain had satisfied his curiosity little Sam piped up, "Please sir—oh, please, could I have just one look?"

Without a word the captain handed him the spyglass. He took a look at least as long as the captain's had been. When he passed it back, the captain said gruffly, "Come back if you want it again" and kicked him off the quarterdeck.

At thirteen young Harding felt himself a man grown. Not only had he been around the world but he had amassed a fortune. When he came home from that first voyage he had his whole year's pay, $72 in hard cash, in his pocket. He was not only a man, but a rich man. He hadn't known there was so much money in existence! It had to be spent wisely. He decided to give himself an education.

For a year he stayed home and went to an academy to

study navigation. A wise head that youngster had; he gave himself the kind of schooling he needed when he needed it. After that he went to sea again. At sixteen he was second mate on the bark *Seabird*. At eighteen he was first mate. At twenty-two he was captain of a beautiful bark named *Western Sea*.

For all he was so young he was a man of dignity and experience, with years of responsibility behind him. He was captain of his ship, king on his own quarter-deck. In his grand shoregoing clothes, with his high silk hat, his black broadcloth suit and his polished shoes, not to mention his flowing whiskers, he looked the part. But he was still a boy when he sailed out of Boston Harbor on that first voyage in command. He could chuckle about it as he told me how it felt, but it was not amusing at the time.

"When I dropped the pilot and took over the ship for the first time on my own responsibility," he told me, "a sort of stage fright seized me. I wanted to go overside with the pilot—wanted to run away and leave my ship! There I stood on my own quarter-deck, alone and friendless, for a captain must never be on intimate terms with even his first mate. I knew I had to get off by myself and face things. So I went to my cabin and sat down and put my feet on the table and had it out.

" 'See here,' I said to myself, 'you've got where you wanted to get, now buck up and be a captain!' "

Suddenly he felt himself strong enough to cope with anything or anybody. He went on deck, and from that minute he was in command, of himself as well as of his ship. Nobody on board ever had any doubts about that. Men twice his age called him the Old Man, but not to his face, and respectfully. But he always had to play a lone hand. It would never have done to ask questions of any of his officers. The chief mate would have told the second mate and he would have told the third, and pretty soon the cook in the galley would know the new captain was having to get advice from his subordinates.

He seemed to get along very well without their advice. Ten years he sailed the oceans of the world and most of their seas, and never lost a ship, was never in a wreck, had no hairbreadth escapes. He was gone for years at a stretch, trading with the natives in sunny Mediterranean ports, perhaps—he knew every harbor from the Rock of Gibraltar around the shores of "Mare Nostrum" and back along the gray African shores to the strait again. The west coast of Africa knew him well. Every little village heard the rattle of his anchor chains as he stopped in for a bit of trading. Keeping store for the natives on board ship, he called it— they would come swarming out from shore in their small boats. He had to have an expert knowledge of the habits and peculiarities of the different tribes as well as of their varying needs if he was to be a successful trader and earn good profits for his owners.

These owners were the Hardys of Boston—Alpheus and a brother. Captain Harding was master of one of their ships when at twenty-five years of age it occurred to him that if he was ever to get really acquainted with the wife he had married three years before he would have to take her to sea with him. So he went to Alpheus Hardy and asked permission to take her along on the next voyage. It was a common enough request to make—some owners even preferred to have their captains take their wives along with them. But Hardy did not.

"You won't carry sail as heavy, for one thing, if you

have your wife along," he objected, "you won't push her so hard."

The captain had to admit that this was true. He would not take so many chances.

"Besides that, you won't be on deck so much," pursued the owner. "You will be spending more time in the cabin."

"That is true, too," Harding agreed, "but there is another side to it, Mr. Hardy. When we are in port, waiting for a load, we captains get together on shore and go off for a good time—sometimes we don't go near our ships for three or four days at a stretch. Now if I had my wife along—"

"Take her—by all means take her!" cried the owner.

So he did, and she sailed with him for several voyages to different parts of the world. And if on her account he didn't crowd sail quite so hard, no one but himself knew the difference. At thirty-two they had both had enough, so he left the sea and came ashore for good.

Captain Harding was not the only Chathamite who knew about Old Ironsides. Lyman Armes went over to Chatham one day and came back with his hat full of yarns he got from Captain Oscar Nickerson, and one of them was about the old frigate.

"His grandfather had the story direct from Uncle Eben, who was right there in the thick of the powder smoke and flying splinters aboard the frigate *Constitution* when she won her famous victory over the *Guerrière* one August day in 1812." So he starts the story he wrote for the magazine. "And Uncle Eben explained that a barrel of British molasses was what helped the Yankee gunners most that day." He interpolates a bit of his own personal feeling here—"I want to stop and explain that this isn't fiction.

These little glints of eyewitness sidelights historians omit from textbooks in order to maintain the proper amount of dullness to make a boy's education an impressive and solemn task. They are history today, folklore to the next generation, and then they are forgotten. . . ."

It seems Uncle Eben Nickerson was brother of Captain Nickerson's great-grandfather. He was a fifer aboard the *Constitution* and author of a Chatham by-word familiar to this day among many of the older inhabitants of the town. It came out one day when Uncle Eben was living over his experiences in the war of 1812, trying to tell about the cold weather on a cruise into northern waters—"Cold?" he shivered, "Cold? Drummers with their mittens on and me with my damned old fife!"

He maintained that had it not been for that barrel of molasses the American ship might not have won the victory that day, for the odds were against her; and he may have been right.

Did you ever hear of switchel? It was an old-time soft drink, a mixture of molasses, ginger and water—purely a landlubber's tipple, pap for farmers' children. To make a jack tar drink switchel was to offer the supreme insult to his manhood. So when the crew of the mighty British fighting ship *Guerrière* spied Old Ironsides on the horizon and saw an engagement was imminent they made special preparations.

They were so sure of the outcome that before the battle started they got all ready to entertain their prisoners. Up from the hold they brought a big barrel of molasses and set it on the deck all ready for the switchel they intended to make those blank-blank Yankees drink. The barrel was there when the fight began.

Early in the engagement the good marksmanship of the American gunners raked the deck of the Britisher, and by good luck one of the shots smashed the barrel of molasses. The gooey mess ran out all over the deck and mixed with the blood of the wounded and dying. The combination made the deck so sticky it was almost impossible for the sailors to move fast enough to man the ropes for manoeuvring ship. In a sea battle this was a serious handicap, for you have to step lively on any sort of sailing craft. As a result the *Constitution* was able to outsail, outmanoeuvre and outfight its larger opponent—partly because of our better gunnery, Uncle Eben admitted, but partly also because of the barrel of molasses.

A generation down from Uncle Eben brings us to Grand Uncle Elnathan and the years just before the gold rush to Californy. Elnathan was a vigorous man, and independent. He had seven wives and thirty children, though not, I hasten to add, on the Cape. His folks here were "pretty strict religionists" and there was an open breach in the family when he decided to go west with some members of a new cult then active in Dennis Port, called Latter Day Saints.

First came the voyage to New York, then in a larger ship and with a greater company led by Brigham Young they sailed for New Orleans, thence up the Mississippi and from there overland to Salt Lake. Uncle Elnathan used to tell how many wooden axles were worn out on the long trek west. By the time the long wagon train reached Utah, Brigham Young was sick and riding in a litter. But one day he alighted and drove his staff into the ground and said, "Here will I build my city."

"We were a thousand miles from the nearest white settlement, Fort Laramie," Uncle Elnathan said, "and eleven hundred from the next nearest. There I helped drive the first stake in the building of Salt Lake City—the stake we hung our first camp kettle on."

He stayed there and married—and married—and married —and begot his share of the population, and prospered. Years later he returned to his old home on the Cape in a railroad train, and that is how we came to know about him.

One thing about the Cape, there's always something new and different turning up. That is because the people themselves are that way—born with copy in them. Nowhere else I've ever been compares with it. Getting out a magazine every fortnight as we did during the summer was no chore at all, there was always more to write about than we could write. Everywhere you went you found a story.

Poking round Stage Harbor one day I ran across a mild little man with a melancholy walrus mustache. He had a small shavings-shop back of his house, which was next-door-but-one to the old windmill, and puttered contentedly round making white-painted windmills and bird-houses to sell to the summer folks. Nobody would ever dream, to look at him, that he had played a part in the development of the airplane. But he had—a humble part but a useful one, and at times a pretty trying one. His life had not always been quiet like this, he had probably had about as much excitement packed into some of it as it is good for anybody to have. Being a pioneer aviator in the days before there was any aviation was not a tranquil life, nor a specially secure one.

Back in the late 1880's a wealthy Boston business man who came down-Cape summers got interested in flying.

When he was in Germany one year he watched the attempts the Germans were making to produce a heavier-than-air machine that would imitate bird flight and carry a man off the ground. He brought home patterns for what was then the most successful of these machines. His summer home was in Chatham, just across the Mill Pond from our friend's, so he got him to make a flying machine for him from the patterns.

"I was a regular Jack-of-all-trades," he explained modestly, "and he was real patient when I didn't get things just right."

Of course there were no motors then, and the planes had to depend on the wind for their power—wind and air currents. They were really gliders. Where you took off depended on how the wind was. If it was nor'east you carried the machine over to Morris Island and jumped from there. If it was sou'west, there was a hill overlooking the Mill Pond. If it wasn't either and you simply had to fly, you taxied off the barn roof. Many a time Jim or his employer flew off the barn roof. I asked him, stupidly, if he didn't get a lot of falls.

"Why, yes," he answered matter-of-factly, "it was all falls."

That was why they had to be so fussy about the direction of the wind, they had to be sure of falling into water, for water is a lot softer than land if you don't hit it from too far up. "We often came down up to our necks in the water," he explained, as if that was what you'd expect, of course.

Between taking off and coming down was the flight.

"If we went as much as fifty feet we thought it was a real good flight. Once in a while we'd go a little farther, but not often. Then, of course," he said, "we'd come down."

According to his description these early models must have been shaped a good deal like a bird. But the Boston man later worked out a more elaborate machine which eventually took on the appearance of a triplane. It even had rudders and propeller, though the latter was powered only by the wind. The framework was made of hollow hard-pine rods. The planes of the glider—or scaler, as they called it—were covered with Japanese silk. They were fifteen feet long and five feet wide.

Beneath the lower plane hung the flier's seat, if seat you could call it, for it was more like a child's swing, a thin rod suspended from two others. When the scaler took off for a flight two men ran with it, one at the tip of either wing, while the aviator ran in the middle, leaping onto the perch as the machine left the ground. Spry was the word for our flier in those days, and he must have had to develop an active mind as well as body, for besides keeping his balance on that slender rod he had to attend to the rudder ropes, which somewhat affected the course of the ride. As the entire flight lasted only a matter of seconds before the inevitable cold bath he had to work fast.

As part of his entertaining job he made kites and flew them, for his employer was making a study of air currents and sent up a lot of kites to find out the direction of the wind above the surface of the earth.

"Before we got through making them scalers," he told me proudly, "we got a machine that looked a lot like airplanes do today." He didn't have any of the models left for me to see. "A feller in Washington wanted my model, the last one I had, so I let him take it." Then he added,

"The patents were sold to a couple of brothers, lived out west somewheres. I forget their name."

He said he made toy airplanes sometimes, but folks didn't buy enough of them to make it pay. They'd rather have windmills and bird houses.

You have to look twice, but it's there—or was the last I knew, and things don't change much on the Cape except the shorelines. A fishing shanty on the beach, just beyond the Chatham Bars Inn. It is worth looking for, not for itself alone, but because it is the jumping-off place for Little Beach, and that is a government sanctuary for a big colony of terns. At low tide you can walk over to the beach, which is a low sandy island, if you have rubber boots or a bathing suit. Otherwise you row. Either way it is worth doing.

Maybe you know the terns as mackerel gulls. Smaller than ordinary gulls, very svelt and streamlined with their slim bodies and forked tails, pure white with a mantle of gray, a black cap and flame-red beak, and in flight lovely beyond words. But they are not at all hospitable. As you step onto the island they take to the air by the thousand, screaming at you shrilly, "Scoot! Scoot!"

They used to nest on North Beach, but when the skunks and rats bothered them they moved over here, bag and baggage. Their guardian, who was a fisherman named Howard Eldredge, guessed there might be 12,000 that year—double as many nests as the year before, anyhow. They need some sort of protection, for they are a natural temptation to boys. There is a ten-dollar fine for taking their eggs, and the guardian keeps a watchful eye on the nests. The birds let the sun hatch the eggs for them while they go fishing, a carefree arrangement surely. In the fall they take their young and fly south.

The picture stays with you vividly . . . shining blue sea, yellow sand, green marsh grass . . . a rush of white wings against the sky . . . thousands of white wings . . . and the air alive with the birds' cries . . .

13. *Turn of the Elbow*

As YOU DRIVE on along down, from Chatham to Orleans, you notice something odd about the town-line markers on the highway. The road follows the low-lying shores of Pleasant Bay, a safe landlocked harbor formerly much used by the fishing boats of the four towns abutting on it— Chatham, Harwich, Brewster and Orleans.

Chatham stops at Muddy Creek and then you are in Harwich, but pretty soon—perhaps a mile—you're out of Harwich and into Brewster. But Brewster stops almost before it starts—just a few rods, you can see one marker from the other, a sort of corridor to the beach, with Orleans from there on. My nose twitched the first time I saw it, and Aunt Flora told me the story.

Once on a time there was just one town where Brewster and Harwich are now, and it was Harwich. It crossed the Cape north and south, as Dennis does, but the Cape is a lot wider here. People lived along the two edges, either on the Bay side or on the Nantucket Sound side, with a spread of empty space in the middle and miles of hard going between the settlements. So it was decided after a good bit of feeling pro and con to split the town in two horizontally, the southern part keeping the old town name of Harwich while the new one named itself Brewster. This was for Elder William Brewster, the Pilgrims' minister, who had a lot to do with the early settling of this part of the Cape.

Harwich had some frontage on Pleasant Bay, and Brewster naturally wanted its share of the useful waterfront. Harwich was in no mood to be generous, but you can't go to war over your town boundaries in the Commonwealth of Massachusetts—it simply isn't done, and never was. They had to resort to arbitration. Each town sent one of its selectmen to meet with a third from either Chatham or Orleans (I forget which but I think it was Orleans), at a tavern on neutral soil. All would have gone well if they had not stayed for supper. The rum flowed freely, and the three men kept on splicing the main brace till one by one they went under the table. You can tell who went first by looking at the map or by driving along Route 28. Anyhow, that's the story as I heard it.

Feeling between the two towns was never too sweet. Apparently the children of North Dennis, next door, took sides, for Steve Hall said when he was a boy if you saw a Harwich boy you would yell, "Ha'wicher! Ha'wicher! Hairy-legger!" and then run, or else—for they were fighting words. And it seems as if the name must have been pronounced "Haywich" in those days, since he pronounced the epithet "Haywicher."

Brewster was one of the prosperous old towns, and many sea captains lived there. You can see their big four-square houses fronting on the King's Highway—different from those in Falmouth and Barnstable, though, for no town copied anything from its neighbors but each had plenty of ideas of its own and never hesitated to use them, architecturally or otherwise. Like town, like people.

Lizy Jane and I didn't go in strong for summer folks, but there was one man we wanted to meet because he was the author of the world's best-selling book next to the

Bible. He had a cottage in Brewster and his name was Brigham and the book was not Cape fiction nor indeed fiction at all but a textbook called "The Essentials of Geography."

There was a little road winding down to the sea from the Highway, and at its end was a gray-shingled cottage with windows facing the living opal-and-turquoise waters of the bay and the ocean beyond. Beneath the windows spread a white beach where the tide ran far out beyond the outer bar and left stretches of shimmering sand with shallow pools to catch the summer clouds. It was the only place I recall that was lovelier at low tide than at high.

The little cottage was one of a group, a small colony of professional people—doctors, lawyers, professors, clergymen—who made for themselves a highly congenial society. The Brighams' garden gate was so low I could really have stepped over it, but that did not seem a decorous way to enter the domain of a best-selling author, so I stooped down and unlatched it. A scrap of front yard with miracles of sweet alyssum and candytuft and gayer things blossoming from the sand, a Capy doorway and a welcome, and a chance to sit on the porch overlooking the beach while a child went to summon "Dody!" from the water. It was colorful down there, the children paddling about in their little scows of scarlet or green or orange, and the beach flowered with bright umbrellas.

Presently the professor arrived, wearing a black bathing suit and a gray goatee, and we started talking about geography. This, it seemed, had taken a turn for the worse since my school days with things like "statehood complexes" entering the picture. In fact the title of the book he was working on that summer was quite appalling—"The

United States of America—Studies in Physical, Regional, Industrial and Human Geography." But he had written a book about Cape geography, and I was delighted to find that in it he made a point of the difficulty you have finding your way round in a car. He said he had been coming here fifteen years and still got lost now and then. "You always think you're going in the opposite direction from where you want to go." When I told him about my system he thought I really had something.

Brewster was named, as I said, for William Brewster. Driving down from Boston one day I stopped off in Plymouth and met a descendant of his, also named William Brewster, treasurer of a local bank. He recognized my Cape name but said he didn't just place me.

"I shall know by the way you answer one question," he said, "whether you are a native of these parts. What," he asked, "is succotash?"

"Why—corn and beans," I answered innocently.

He shook his head. "You weren't raised around here. Succotash, the real genuine succotash, is altogether different from the stuff you buy in cans. If you want to know what the real thing is like you should be here on Forefathers' Day, the 21st of December. That is when it is always served by those who keep up the old traditions."

It seems you boil shell beans till they are almost a mush, and hulled corn—which should be the smoky white variety —and the broth of corned beef and of a fowl. It should be the consistency of a thick soup. But he warned me not to try making it till I had seen how it was done, which means being in Plymouth on or before Forefathers' Day.

Mr. Brewster put me another question—which I also muffed. "When," he asked, "is a twin not a twin?" He and his brother were born twins but when they grew up they were not, at least not exactly. This unusual circumstance is understandable if you know your world. Brother Isaac went to sea, and on one of his voyages he went round the world with the sun—*with* the sun, mind you. He lost a day when he crossed the date line in the Pacific, and never went back to pick it up, so it made him a day younger than William all the rest of his life.

What I had really stopped off in Plymouth for was to see the bones of the ancient vessel *Sparhawk*, or *Sparrowhawk*, in the museum there. She is the oldest ship in America, probably; and well worth seeing if one is interested in ship lore, but she really belongs in Orleans rather than Plymouth, for she was wrecked on the Orleans shore in 1626. The friendly Nauset Indians made the passengers and crew welcome and sent word to Plymouth, whither she was bound. Some men came from Plymouth by boat, landed at the little river which flows into the Bay between Orleans and Brewster, and crossed the couple of miles on foot to succor the shipwrecked party. They had patched up the boat and made her ready for reloading for the return voyage when another gale came up and drove her farther up the beach, wrecking her beyond repair.

Drifting sands soon covered her over, and she was completely lost to sight. In a few generations she was forgotten, too. The place where it happened was always called Old Ship Harbor, but no one remembered why. It was not till the time of the Civil War, 237 years after she was wrecked, that another storm washed the sand away and uncovered her ancient bones. An old cut shows a little high-pooped, sloop-rigged craft with a mast stepped well amidships, and for sails only a jib and a square-rigged mainsail. If you go to see her, consider seriously how you would have liked crossing the Atlantic in her. But it was to just such little vessels that our forefathers entrusted themselves, their wives and their children in their search for religious freedom.

Orleans is the next town beyond Brewster; and we shall go from Chatham across the Brewster corridor and so to South Orleans. A lot of Orleans is under water, what with the many inlets and marshes and branches of Pleasant Bay on the south and Town Cove and Nauset Harbor on the north. It is the first town we have come to that faces fully on the ocean, faces due east to the Old World of its origins. It has a short frontage on the Bay, but that is inside the crook of the elbow and of less importance than this, the beginning of the Cape's stormy Back Side, where it gets the full fury of the Atlantic.

Some six hundred years before the *Sparrowhawk* was wrecked here—the first of a long series of wrecks on Cape shores—another ship came along and made a little history. It is recorded in the Norse sagas that Leif Erikson and his crew landed here and drank honey-dew. Honey-dew? Oh, that is something that forms on the grass here in Orleans, a sweetish, honeylike liquid which made such an impression on the sweet-toothed explorers that they put it on record.

Here begin the long beaches reaching north for perhaps forty miles to the tip end of the Cape, the famous "wonder strand" with its magic of color and mirage and mystery and death.

During the 1920's, when I knew it, Orleans believed itself to be the healthiest town in the state, and the records for 1929, at least, give weight to the claim. The average

age of those deceasing was a little over 81 years. Average, mind you—with a girl of nineteen to be reckoned in, not to mention several chits in their early sixties. Three were over ninety, and most of the others in their high eighties. This is far enough down-Cape to get the full force of the winter storms, so the local saying seems good—"If you're tough enough to grow up on the Cape you're tough enough to live forever."

The last of the village smithies was still operating, and I got to know the blacksmith. For all I know he was the last on the Cape, and he certainly was the last in Orleans or its vicinity. Not long afterward he too sold out. Summer visitors used to bring their saddle horses from all over the Cape for him to shoe. I wonder how the horses get along nowadays.

He was shoeing a heavy-built cart horse whose heavy-built owner was looking on with professional interest because he had been a smith once himself. Outside a groom waited his turn at the heads of two restless little saddle horses. The smithy was straight out of a picture book with its dusky brown shadows, its blackened forge with the bit of charcoal fire smoldering on it and the row of horseshoes on the walls. The smith himself, peering shrewdly at you over his spectacles, might have stepped out of any one of several books which have been written about the Cape except for one thing—his limousine stood outside waiting for him!

They were discussing the color of one of the saddle horses.

"Huckleberry white, I'd say," drawled the smith.

"Huckleberry nothing," snorted the groom, "she's a discouraged gray."

"We used to call 'em huckleberry white," answered the shoer of horses pacifically, "but times has changed."

He buried a horseshoe in the coals and pumped the bellows till the fire glowed to a white heat. Then he pulled the shoe out with long tongs and hammered it into shape on his anvil, heated it again, hammered it again, clapped it smoking hot on the horse's horny hoof.

"Nothing's like it used to be," ruminated the blacksmith, holding the shoe back in the fire for a minute; "once there were eight of us blacksmiths here in Orleans, and all of us kept busy."

The heavy-built man said, "Well, in them days they used to have 256 horses in the town. Now I don't believe they's fifty."

"I doubt if there's that many, except maybe in summer. They bring me horses from all around, but still there's plenty of days I don't have enough to do to keep busy."

"Everything's automobiles now," contributed the groom.

"You've said it," agreed the smith, "they're driving out the horse, and the blacksmith's going with him."

"What's become of the other seven smiths here in Orleans?" I asked.

"Gone," said the smith lugubriously, "all gone."

"Oh, not all," put in the owner of the horse, cheerfully, "I'm still here, even if I have turned fisherman."

"He was one o' the seven," the smith explained. "That blue cart out there's his—he drives down to the beach at low tide and gets the fish out'n his traps."

"What fish there is," qualified the former smith, "but fishing's like smithing—it ain't what it used to be. They've got the bluefish all trapped off the shore—hardly ever get one nowadays. I remember the time we got so many I was tired hauling them out. Once I prayed I'd find my nets empty for a change—and what do you think?"

It was clearly an oratorical question, and none of us bothered to answer.

"Well, sir," said the fisherman, "I went down and there was a $3,000 catch of bluefish, just that one tide! And for once," he admitted, "I didn't complain about my prayers not being answered. But it's not like that now."

"There's still a living here for me," said the smith, "but there's more money fixing cars." He glanced complacently over at his own shining car and said, "I dunno as I'm sorry."

A fine double row of elms shaded the roadside post office of the village of South Orleans. The postmaster was John Kenrick, namesake and probably a collateral descendant of the John Kenrick whose ship *Columbia* (turned over to his lieutenant, Robert Gray) discovered the Columbia River and gave it her name. (We got around in those days.) The postmaster told me how those elms happened to get there. His father—also named John—was in Boston one autumn day in 1855 and strolling along the paths of the Common noticed the great elms were casting their seed. On the whim of the moment he gathered up a big bundle of them in the folds of the *Boston Herald* he was reading and brought them home to South Orleans. From the seedlings which sprouted from a generous planting came all the elms which became such stately trees by the Kenrick home and the little post office.

It was here that another Kenrick, cousin of the explorer, built a house about which I shall have more to say later—a true Cape-type house whose shingles are black with age.

Down on the South Orleans shore is a lovely little harbor called Kescayogansett Cove. It was named by the Nauset Indians who lived in Orleans and Eastham when the white men came. According to a contributor who sent us the information for the magazine, the name was packed with meaning. Its full interpretation sounds like a realtor's blurb, but there was a time when the description fitted many a place along these shores: "An abundance of bright sun and clear skies, and sweet soft air, and woods and fields, and the Red Man and red squirrels, and the red deer, and lakes, and ponds, and bay, and cove, with the broad ocean in the distance."

Looking off to sea along this coast on a warm summer afternoon you may sometimes see what is called locally the sea-glim. This is a strange unearthly light along the horizon between sea and sky—a white light said to presage a storm.

You have to be weatherwise in a place where weather means so vitally much, and most folks are. Every little farmhouse has its "glass" outside the back door, a good reliable barometer, and they rely on it as seafarers would, but they have other ways of forecasting that are just about as dependable. They know the difference between summer clouds that mean no harm and a sky that is "smurrin' up" for a storm. They know the portent of a backening wind—that's when the wind backs round by the north instead of coming round properly by the south, and you can look for trouble and not be disappointed.

Of course anyone can foretell a tempest, which is local for thundershower, by the look of the sky and the feel of the sultry air. But it takes a native-born Caper to foretell a storm from the way a rooster crows—if he crows up instead of down, you want to watch out. There might be something in that, too, for animals know more about changes in weather than we do.

All over the Cape, but especially from Orleans on down, it pays big interest to get off the main roads and either walk or (if you must drive) slow your car to its slowest and explore the little backroads which are still in the mood of the old Cape. With an eye for beauty, an inquiring mind and a loafing temperament you can make one of these little woodland roads, tufted with grass and covered with a husher-mat of pine needles, as full of sweet surprise as any Indian trail of Thoreau's day. Until you have loafed slow-footed along these roads you do not realize how much a tourist's vision is blurred by the speed of his motor. "Padding the road," they call this sort of walking, and the phrase surely fits.

You never know what is round the next corner. One day when I had completely lost my bearings on a woodland lane I came out at a deserted camp by the shore of a miniature lake in the wilderness. There in the twilight quiet, a doe and her fawn came daintily down to the water to drink, and a snatch of woodthrush song put it all to music. Another trail led to a clearing where two brothers were shingling their ancient house. It was filled with the litter of bachelor housekeeping, old books, old prints of ships, old sea chests and relics of whaling voyages and of heathen tribes in what were then the romantic South Sea Isles. We don't call them isles today, and they have lost their romance in grim reality.

In one woodshed I found an old oak chest used to store ancient magazines and such. Inside the lid an earlier owner had tacked its genealogy—it was brought over in the second voyage of the *Mayflower*. With that and its linen-fold paneling it later sold to a collector for big money.

From the people you meet on these back roads you pick up fragments of the old tongue, the lingua antiqua of the Cape. They themselves may bear the old names. It was deep in Harwich somewhere that I ran across an Emulous, and farther down the line lived another man named Abilene. On one back road I met Desire, and on another, some distance away, Virtue. Aunt Tempy's Pond was named for a woman named Temperance, a common name for women those days; but I never heard of a man being named that. I ran across a lot of very individual characteristic names. For women, Jemima, Jerusha, Sukey, Nabby, Pluma, Cynthia, Content, Chloe, Prudence, Love, Lovice (charming little name, that, isn't it?), Zemira, Bethany, and Bethia. Daty is short of Theodate, and Plina for Paulina. For men, besides Emulous and Abilene, were names like Jedediah, Abijah, Zenas, Zabina, Ziba, Jotham, Shubael—the *e* is silent—and Sylvanus. Of course such names would be found all over New England, but they have probably remained in use longer here.

When you hear a fragment of the old speech its rhythm and idiom suggest the shadowy whole, like reproducing a dinosaur from a couple of ancient bones. Such a fragment was that describing the swordfishing experience of Uncle Marshal Allen. Another was a chance remark—"I know he went by because I heard his feetnin' on the road." A woman apologized for the looks of her immaculate kitchen—"I just haven't had the sprawl to tackle my spring cleaning yet," she said. "Sprawl" is still common, and means ambition or git-up-and-git, or perhaps simply guts; it still carries a trace of its original meaning of struggle.

A woman telling of a disturbing experience said she was "all puckerstruck." That is a very intriguing word, for it harks back to the old English hobgoblin, that troublesome and mischief-making sprite, Puck. Another nice word, though with an un-nice meaning is "skinch," which means to cheat. A useful word, saying so much in so little.

"Feetnin'" may apply to the footprints made in the snow or the dust as well as the sound—you can say, "I followed his feetnin' in the snow." I've mentioned padding the road—of course that means to walk quietly, and harks back to the days of footpads.

A sad little phrase applied to a girl who was fading out from old-fashioned consumption. They said, "She's hiding away." Like "pining away," but says so much more, giving the feeling she was withdrawing from us, hiding herself already in her new home beyond our ken.

No doubt there are many other survivals of the speech of 1620, if one had the time to pad the roads looking for them.

14. *The Cape House As Is*

Up to now, you may have noticed, we have not had much to say about the "typical" old Cape Cod house. There have been saltbox-roof houses and rainbow-roof houses and houses with widows' walks or blue blinds or lean-to ells, there have been half-houses and two-to-one houses, but our old friend the Cape house has been missing.

For one thing I wanted to clear the decks for them, and for another I needed time to sort out my very mixed reactions to them—and that has now been achieved. I wonder how many Cape Cod people realize that to a large part of the country as a whole the name of their beloved Cape means a special kind of house and nothing else. Not very flattering, but surprisingly true. It has become practically an all-American style of small-house architecture, although in most places a Cape man would never recognize it. Recently a Seattle paper carried an advertisement of a "Spanish Cape Cod house"!

Of course the square story-and-a-half farmhouse with a chimney in the middle and a couple of windows each side of the front door is found all over New England—up and down the Maine coast, back among the Berkshires, and in Vermont and New Hampshire. But the Cape Cod builders of 1750 to 1820 or thereabouts took this boxlike house, which was an echo in wood of the thatched stone cottages of Old England, and adapted it to the needs and the conditions of their locality with honesty and sincerity and a fine sense of proportion. Because there was scarcity of materials they built it smaller, sometimes almost miniature, and they gave great attention to details.

Charming as this type of house is in the New England countryside with its setting of old stone walls and wine-glass elms and white birches, it is most at home in the open moorland country of the lower Cape. The old house sits low to the ground, and its great mothering spread of roof shields it from the sweep of the winds. At night the lights behind its tiny-paned windows shine far out over the dark rolling moors. It is one with its surroundings here, even to the weathering of its shingles.

But don't imagine I'm being romantic about it. To me it is the most absolutely lovable little house in the world, and yet I would never build one. My heart and my head would fight it out—and I think my head would win. This house was built to fit certain conditions, and it met them—and still meets them—beautifully. And "beautifully" is the word, too. But it is not adapted to modern living or to many climates. In fact it requires major changes right at the start to make it even buildable, let alone livable.

Who would, or could in most places, build a house without foundations, right smack on the ground? And who would want to devote fifty square feet of floor space to a chimney? Yet on these two features alone depends a good part of the little house's lure. Then its windows and doors are not standardized but have to be made by hand, taking time and skill as well as money.

The plan does not lend itself to the modern way of life, it lacks fluidity. The front entry is cramped and the living room at the rear can be reached only by going through one of the two front rooms, because the chimney is spang in the middle, or at least it is opposite the front door. The house belonged to a place and an era and a condition—large families plus scarcity of both money and materials. Because its builders had an instinct for design they gave it not only comfort and strength and honest functionalism but also beauty. More than all, it has the atmosphere of home practically built into it.

No one house on the Cape has all the features that go with the type, so we take a composite picture. Look at it from the road, first.

Maybe it is the formal kind, clapboarded and painted white, with green blinds and a white picket fence round the front dooryard. More likely it is shingled, left unpainted and weathered a light silvery gray, or, if it still has its original shingles, they are dark gray and when wet practically black, and with or without blinds. A third type combines the two finishes, with white clapboarded front and the rest of the house gray-shingled.

The house is nearly square, with an ell off to one side or the back, with a side door and sheltered dooryard in the angle. It sits flat on the ground, and the ridgepole of its plain sweeping roof is parallel to the road. Each side of the front door are two windows, but the door is not exactly in the middle nor are the windows likely to be the same distance from the ends. The roof comes down close to the top of the windows.

To one side of the flat boulder which forms the doorstone grows a lilac bush, maybe. There is not a vestige of landscaping but the little dooryard is crowded with flowers, the sorts which thrive in salt sea air. Under the window is a sweetbrier rose, an old cinnamon rose sprawls along the fence, growing as nature meant them, quite un-pruned and untended. Then the flowers in a hither-and-yon effect—old-maid's-pinks, nasturtiums, bachelor's but-tons and larkspurs and poppies, all more or less mixed in with the sparse wild grass that is never clipped but is forever blowing in the wind till the hay-makers get round to cutting it with a scythe, flowers and all.

Off to one side of the house or maybe back of it is likely to be a wind-riven orchard, the gnarly branches throwing shadows about on the soft grass beneath. These neglected orchards may not produce prize crops—as a matter of fact they do not—but they have a peace and love-liness no commercial orchard can touch. On a warm sum-mer day, with a hammock slung between a couple of aging apple trees and the air full of birds and bees and flitting fragrances of soil and sea—well, what I'm trying to say, as inoffensively as possible, is that the Cape house is not landscaped—and thank God for that.

Looking at our composite house again, the walls are low for two reasons: they are not raised up on foundations, and the rooms are low-posted, about seven feet, more or less. The roof is low-pitched too, though it allows for attic chambers if you want them. This house is definitely *not* a bungalow, it is a story-and-a-half house. The roof is a plain, unbroken sweep and there are *never*, NEVER any dormers in it. (If there are dormers, it is just another cottage, and probably a summer one.) It is a beautiful roof, and when it has its mossy old shingles rippling along over its warped planks it is one to get slightly lyrical over.

The windows are small and have small panes, not be-cause that is the fashion but because when they were made glass came small. The large pane is modern and much more functional. I have seen windows with twenty-four panes, but sixteen is common, eight in each sash, and so is fifteen, six below and nine above—uneven like that, and it adds a bit of interest. These tiny panes must be very difficult to keep as shining bright as the shipshape standards of the community require. Imagine sixty corners to be cleaned in a fifteen-pane window!

The typical house has two windows each side of the door, but many have only one, and they are not likely to be carefully placed. Each side of the gable window there may be a little four-paned cubby window. These cubbies under the eaves were where the children slept—on trundle beds, or feather beds, or maybe just straw on the floor.

The sash of the window is flush with the shingles, instead of being set in a couple of inches or more as in the modern house. But the window frames did not come ready made in those days, they had to be fashioned on the spot out of two-inch planks, set smack against the outer wall before the shingles were put on. You would suppose this would give the windows a bald look, like eyes without lashes, and so it would except for the artistry of the builders. They put a thicker plank across the top, projecting out beyond the sides and giving a good reveal, a sense of depth. That is one of the subtle refinements which make the Cape house what it is today.

Of course our house has blinds—not the solid shutters, which were on the oldest houses, but regulation ones with slats and inevitably painted green, a bright green which weathers and fades to subtle blue-green nuances. Exigent builders of today often drive their painters mad trying to imitate this color, for it is inimitable. These are practical blinds, not put on for show but meant to be used, and they have hinges and latches. They are decorative; but that is incidental to their pure functionalism.

Blinds help make the Uncle Barney house in Quivet one of the most crooned-over by lady tourists. This little white gem of a house has blinds each side of its 24-pane windows and also its door, and these latter have curved tops to fit the fanlight. This house was built about 1820, which explains why there is space between the door and the eaves, with their dainty dentilated trim, for the fanlight.

Quite unpremeditated is the color of the unpainted house. Probably they were left unpainted originally because paint cost too much, or because you did not paint shingles, only clapboards. They don't need the paint for a preservative, as many of the old ones have lasted literally for centuries without it. If they weather beautifully, a light silvery gray with a patina of lilac and green from the lichen which you do not notice till you get close, that is their good luck, and ours, not the result of any sort of "treatment."

What ornament there is centers about the front door. This seldom-used "company" entrance was the one deliberate attempt at effect. It is always a Huguenot-cross door, the double cross that gives six panels, two small ones at the top and four longer ones below, with a thumb-latch and knocker of brass or other metal. Sometimes the square upper panels are replaced with glass to light the entry, but this is when the roof comes down too low for even the strip of small panes so often found. If the roof is high enough there may be a fanlight, but this is likely to belong to a later period. You can generally guess the age of a house by the distance between the tops of the windows or door and the roof. The older ones are so close there is barely room for a gutter.

Either side of the door there may—or may not—be side lights, a single vertical row of small panes set into the door-frame and not coming clear to the floor, sometimes only half way.

The wide doorstone is flat and irregular, never shaped or hewn but left as it was found, probably on a beach somewhere. The path to the road may be strewn with broken clamshells, but more likely it is just a path.

Like most front doors in New England, this one was used only on special occasions and was otherwise kept tight shut, like the fore room or parlor whose door was close behind it. It has been regarded as a symbol of the Puritan nature. But just as symbolical is the side door, with its hospitality and easy warm-hearted friendliness— and just as easy if not always as warm-hearted gossip. There, if you were rattling home in the democrat wagon, you would stop and light for a bit of talk with the good-wife while your men dickered over a brood sow or maybe a bar'l of sweet cider. Both doors have their part in our heritage, if you want to go symbolical. The symbol is a bit sour, for the Cape was not settled by Puritans anyhow, but by Pilgrims, who were different.

Maybe the chimney ought to have been mentioned along with the roof, for it really is a part of it, so far as looks go, rising solidly and squarely from it, sharing its fine propor-tions and giving the whole house its sense of substance and permanence. Fortunate are the houses which have kept their chimneys intact through the rise and fall of the Stove Age. It must indeed have been a temptation to tear down that great bulky mass of masonry and clear the center of the house for a passageway and stairs and closets. Many a house-owner succumbed, and you really can't blame them, in spite of the pitiful brick toothpicks that stick up from the old roofs. When they did not tear them out it was probably because they were hard up. The most interesting houses, from an architectural standpoint, are likely to be those whose folks were poor in the Victorian era. God help the houses that were built or remodeled during those years —say after the 1820's. For once poverty was a blessing.

The chimneys had to be large in a house which was heated wholly by fireplaces. The three main rooms at least must have them, and they had to be large enough to take four-foot or five-foot logs. That meant the chimney must be wide enough to accommodate them, and as a result it was often the size of a young room.

There is one detail of the outside of the house which I have neglected to mention, and you might not notice it if I don't—I didn't till an architect called it to my attention. That is the way the vergeboards are tapered. They edge the gable, close against the roof, and ordinarily they are straight boards. In these old houses, however, they taper ever so little toward the ridgepole. It is an unexpected touch of the Greek in these simple builders—you remember a secret of the grace of the Greek column was its almost imperceptible tapering toward the top, accentuating the effect of perspective. These tapering vergeboards are rarely noticed, but they subtly enhance the effect of the whole.

You will have noticed that none of the houses built in the 1600's were this type of house. The so-called Cape house is not really Early American, although it developed before the Revolution. Witness the Hoxie house in Sandwich, the Bowerman house in Falmouth, and the Howes-Hall house in North Dennis. No, these little houses were all built, so far as I could discover, during the 1700's, and most of them well along in the century, say the latter half of it. The type was an evolvement, the result of several generations of experience with Cape weather, Cape soil and Cape materials.

Most of its attractiveness comes from its sincerity—functionalism, if you prefer. It was not trying to copy or reproduce anybody else's house, and it was not aiming to conform to any orthodox style of architecture. Its builders may have had the English cottage in the back of their head, and that may be why they built so solidly, but they were not tied to it or any other type. There was no self-consciousness about them, no effort to establish a new mode for others to follow. Each house was planned and built to meet its owner's needs, and if it did not he changed it till it did, and his sons and sons' sons after him did the same.

One does not realize just what adaptability to environment means until an effort is made to transplant this Cape-type house to another part of the country and make it livable. It is a very popular style in Seattle, for instance, and although it is still called a Cape Cod house it has become unrecognizable. The climate requires large window-space, so the windows have been much enlarged, and the blinds left off, or a vestigial remain nailed on flat against the siding—they don't call it clapboarding—for a "color note." Then the low effect is altogether lost because of the building laws, which require eight-foot ceilings, not to mention sills eighteen inches above the ground. Because westerners like bungalows, the house is considered one, with a low ranch roof and practically no attic, and often no basement—they don't even call it a cellar. About all that remains of the original type is a door in the middle and one or two windows each side of it—an exactness rarely found in the original, where off-centering was carried to a fine art. The result is a small white box, "four rooms, bath and utility," which does have one point in common with its model—and that is a sad lack of closet-room.

In time, I am sure, each part of the country will evolve its own small-house or farmhouse type. Outside of New England I have found only one state which has done this and done it well, and that is Utah. There I saw farmhouses built of a combination of logs and a native salmon-pink stone which was quite lovely, in that rich green setting. It just needs native materials to do it anywhere, and a simple honesty—oh yes, and of course a good sense of proportion, with which man is either born or not born, unfortunately.

One thing about the Cape houses has puzzled me, and that is, why they were built so solidly. It did not strike me till I saw how the pioneers who came to the Northwest less than a century ago built their houses. These men were of the same sturdy stock as the Pilgrims and had the same savvy about doing things, even if they did not have the same good taste in architecture, which they didn't. They had everything in their favor—an abundance of heavy timber standing right on the house lot, easily worked fir, with a steam sawmill within reach for cutting it up any way they wanted it. What they did was to work it up into two-by-fours and build flimsy houses that looked decrepit before their builders were through with them.

Yet our forefathers, with their hard, difficult woods, none too plentiful even at first and often having to be hauled from some distance, and then worked up by hand—sawed and hewn, hour upon patient back-breaking hour, beams and planks and boards and all, with smaller trees—with all these handicaps they used their wood lavishly. Beams and sills and corner posts a foot or more through, put together so solidly that after two or three hundred years they stand as sound as ever. Climate and soil helped, but they had something to work on.

All of this brings us to the Little Gray House on the road from Chatham to Orleans. Almost everybody who goes by stops to look at it, and when they have gone on they don't forget it, though they can hardly tell you why. Probably because, while it hasn't all the classic features of the Cape house, it has enough of them to give it that quality for which "charm" is a poor and much overworked word.

The old homestead of the Kenrick family, it sits there in the bright sunshine, flanked on one side by a huge old lilac bush and on the other by a massive spruce tree, and it has "home" written large all over it. When I knew it, it had been bought by a Cambridge family and was being well handled—made livable without undue changes.

This present house was built in 1792, the same year the Columbia River was discovered. Captain John Kenrick of Orleans and Captain Robert Gray of Boston reached the far northwest that year. While Gray stayed behind to discover the river he named Columbia for his ship, Kenrick took his 90-ton *Lady Washington* and went on to the west.

According to local tradition he went on around the world and was the first American skipper to do so. He was born in an earlier house on this site. If or when he came back from the northwest no doubt he visited his kinsfolk in this present house.

Its spruce tree came from away—spruces do not grow on the Cape except when brought here. Fishermen on the Grand Banks used to go ashore now and then on the Labrador just for "a smell o' the earth," and often they took up a spruce seedling and brought it home to be set out beside the door. Whenever you see spruces in a Cape dooryard, that is likely to be how they came here.

Three things about this house remind one of ships. One is the way the roof is built inside—wide planks rabbeted together run from ridge to eaves. That is the way such roofs are usually built, instead of being boarded horizontally as we do nowadays. An old carpenter told me that kind of rabbeting used to be done in the decks of ships to save oakum in calking. More unusual were the corner posts in the rooms downstairs, for they curved out at the top like the knees of a ship and gave extra strength to the support of the roof.

I suspect there was a wreck involved in the finish of the best room—a whole wall of lovely paneling about the fireplace. Orleans is right next door to Chatham, and had plenty of wrecks on her own shore besides. The paneled wall in the best room slopes ever so little downward at the top, as if it had been made to fit the curved ceiling of a ship's cabin.

The sills of this house rest directly on the sand. Its very

typical cellar is a round brick-walled pit reached by a trap door in the floor of one of the small rooms off the old kitchen. In the fall houses like this are banked up all around with seaweed from the beaches, which provides excellent insulation.

This house has the typical layout, too. The chimney is the heart of the house, and it sure is big-hearted. Five feet across the front end and seven across the back, and about eleven feet deep, it holds three fireplaces, not to mention a brick oven and cubbies galore. A tiny front entry gives right and left into the square front rooms. The back of the house is cut up into five rooms—the big kitchen, now used as a living room (which it always was, really), flanked at each end by two small rooms. These were originally chambers—barely large enough to hold a bed—and butteries. The smaller of the two front rooms was of course the family chamber, with the big tester bed and the dresser of mahogany or cherry or pine. The wide board floors in all the rooms were worn with long use and were, if I remember rightly, spatter painted.

By the way, spatter painting makes a practical finish for any floor and I wonder it isn't more often used—perhaps because it is a lengthy process. First come the base coats of a dark color—say blue or green or black—then when they are dry a stiff brush or whisk broom is dipped into a light contrasting color like ivory or yellow or red and this is spattered all over it. When this dries another color is spattered on, and maybe a third after that. Finally, it should be varnished for durability.

Between two of the small rooms off the kitchen a door opened onto the steep little attic stairs. The attic, dimly lit by its two small windows, with its huge chimney rising into the shadows, was dark and spooky. You could just make out the heavy beams and rafters, and see the construction of the roof. All the timbers were dark with age. These roofs certainly shed the rain, even when by every law of God and man they ought to leak like a sieve. I was up in the attic of another such house one day during a tempest, and the rain was coming down solid. It was an older house than the Kenrick one, or else it had not been so well looked after—anyhow, the roof boards had warped and pulled apart so that there were cracks between them— wide enough to permit one to look out and see the sky. But not a drop of rain came into that attic, and the owner told me proudly that it never leaked. He did not know why, and I'm sure I do not, but that is the fact.

In most of the old houses which have been "restored" the interior woodwork has been painted white. There seems to be a general impression that white was the only color our forebears ever used inside their houses. But I saw one specially lovable little house whose woodwork had been scraped down through many coats of paint to its original honey-colored pine. And the many coats were of many colors, including turquoise blue and a soft yellow. I've often seen old chairs painted Chinese red or bright yellow or green and decorated with black or gold. Those Pilgrim ancestors of ours may have gone in a bit heavily for theology, but they liked color as much as anyone. They were a pretty human lot anyhow, when you come to know them, and on the Cape you do come to know them.

15. *The Spunk of Eastham*

THINGS BEGIN to look different the minute you turn the elbow at Orleans and start heading north on the 25-mile stretch to Provincetown.

Behind you now are the shady-laned villages with their romantic old houses and their graceful white-spired churches and all the intimate, sheltered beauty of the Upper and the Middle Cape. You may be heading north—in fact, you are—but you are definitely down-Cape.

A wide level country opens before you, with frequent glimpses of the sea now on one side and then on the other. On the ocean side the moors blend into the green salt marshes and beyond them is a scalloping of creamy dunes with V's of bright blue sea let in between the scallops. Sometimes the moors are bare and brown, sometimes they are lush green with spreads of yellow gorse or patches of purple vetch—depending on the time of year. A small shallow bay makes in to the marshes from an inlet to the sea with many spidery arms and branches that all reflect the sky among the marsh grass. On the Bay side the shore is low and sedgy. The beaches run out a long way and are covered with sedge grass. Here the campmeeting crowds used to land, but more of them later. On one of the roads to the Bay is the Eastham post office, and from its front steps you can count five ponds.

Between the ponds and the marshes and the little inland

sea, a good part of the town of Eastham is under water, but of the portion which remains dry only about two per cent is regarded as fit for general agriculture, although about fifteen per cent of it is actually under cultivation.

When you look at the worn-out old fields with their bald spots of sandy yellow soil showing through the sparse grass it is hard to realize that this was once the garden spot of the Cape and on up to Plymouth. Champlain noticed the cornfields of the Indians when he came along here in 1605. The Pilgrims found them when they were exploring from their first landing in Provincetown. They sailed on to Plymouth and settled there, but later they had serious thoughts of moving their colony back here to Eastham, because of its fertility. Instead of doing that they came here by boat to trade with the Indians for their corn. On these same poor barren fields the first white settlers cut hay that was twelve feet tall. It is a dramatic illustration of what happens when you take from the soil and put nothing back—an old New England custom seen here at its peak.

As you drive along the flat fields remind you of Kansas, with a touch of Holland in the windmills. But there are clumps of stunted pines to tie you to the Cape, and if you listen sharply there is the low, dull roar of the rote on the outer beaches. It is too windy for shade trees, and the boxy little white houses along the Highway stand out bare in the sunshine. There are none of the conventional charms. The Highway is a straight flat black ribbon. Its chief attraction is the occasional side road which might get you away from it toward bay or ocean. Most of these roads are neat black ribbons, too, only less wide and straight than the parent Highway. But don't let it fool you.

Nowhere did I find appearances more deceitful, even in Dennis. There is plenty to see and to hear if one will take time to stop, look, and listen.

Eastham is the first town below Orleans, and remember to give the "ham" its full due. Not "Eastham" but "East-ham." It has a couple of villages on the Highway, and you can drive through them both without noticing either. The entire population of the township today is less than 600, and the villages consist of a country store and a slight thickening of the houses along the road. In one of those neat little white houses I used to sit and listen for hours while George and Susan Wiley told me stories, but you won't find those stories here. They were so good I forgot to take notes.

I liked Eastham.

The forebear to whom I owe my Cape name and kin-ship was a lay preacher in Eastham in its early days. His little church, built about 1646, a couple of years after the place was settled, was twenty feet square and had a thatched roof. No doubt the Reverend was a farmer and a fisherman during the week when he wasn't working on his hour-long sermons for the Sabbath day. Most of the Crosbys of Massachusetts are of Irish descent, but those of English ancestry are likely to stem from Thomas of Eastham or his brothers. He is the nearest approach to a clergyman in my whole family tree and gives it a faint sweet odor of sanctity. However, he is mentioned in early Plymouth records as being fined for "breaking the peace with Peregrine White" and what with one thing and an-other he must have been a pretty vital sort of person, I should say.

Not much of that early settlement is left. In a letter

written me in 1926 Mr. Frederick Snow, a descendant of
those first settlers, wrote that he had just been in one of
the old houses. "It stands on the main road in the Pilgrim
Settlement, opposite the Governor Thomas Prince house,
recently destroyed. The Doane house contains two paneled
doors from the Prince house, and these must be of the
earliest period. It also contains a door from Minot's Ledge
Lighthouse that was washed away in the great storm of
the early 1850's. The door was picked up on the beach.
Anything useful was picked up and put to service. I have
no doubt that much paneling was salvaged from the many
fine ships that were cast ashore on the back side of the
Cape."

Comparatively modern—mid-Victorian, I'd say—but
packed with interest is the mansard-roofed white house
which sits on a knoll above the Highway as the explorer
comes driving in from Orleans. It may be identified by the
gateway made of the jawbones of a humpbacked whale,
with the skull and tusks of an Arctic walrus on the wall
close by. The man who built the snug little house and put
up the gateway was of course a whaler, and his name was
Captain Edward Penniman. The Gothic arch of bleached
white bones against the summer sky, with a bit of view
framed between them of green meadows and blue bay, always intrigued me; and one day I stopped Lizy Jane alongside the turnstile and went in to see if there might be a
story.

The house turned out to be practically a museum, for it
was filled with trophies of the great days of polar whaling.
Captain Penniman was known throughout his profession
as the Luckiest Whaler, and that meant the luckiest one
who ever went out of New Bedford, the great whaling

center of those days. Hearing his story led to the conclusion that his biggest stroke of luck was his wife, for she was certainly responsible for a lot of his good fortune. They had both sailed away long since on their final voyage, but their son and daughter were living there and graciously showed me their treasures and told me some of their experiences.

Edward Penniman's mother had taught him to cook when he was still a small boy, so he was ready to ship as cook when he was only eleven years old. He had to do all the cooking for captain and the mate and the crew, and if anyone went hungry it was his hard luck. The galley was his, and his alone.

Every day the captain, who in his world was second only to the Almighty, told him what to cook and he cooked it, to the best of his knowledge and ability.

"This day," finished the captain, after listing the main dishes of the meal, "we will have rice."

"How much, sir?" asked the little cook.

"A mug to a man," said the Captain.

"Yes, sir," said the cook dutifully.

The mugs were deep and big and yellow, and they held a lot. The lad had never cooked rice before. He knew it had to be boiled with a proper amount of salt, but of its expansive properties he knew nothing. Naturally he thought the captain's orders involved a mug of raw rice to a man, and he acted accordingly. When he got it cooked the galley looked as if a snowstorm had hit it. The captain, being a good soul, said the joke was on him. The youthful chef did not think there was any joke. He had to clean up the galley.

But that was the way the Luckiest Whaler got his start.

Master of his ship at twenty-seven, he used to sail on long whaling voyages that kept him away from Eastham four years at a time, and took him three times around the world. With him, for twenty years, sailed his wife. Such a wife she was as few men have today—a helpmate in more ways than one.

On a small table in a corner of the parlor of the Penniman home a bit of embroidered net, neatly folded, lies on top of a group of scrimshaw ivory and other handiwork. This tidy was netted by hand, and then a pattern was darned onto it. Not a stitch was awry or out of place. An off-Cape visitor would have supposed of course it was done by some lady sitting at a tranquil fireside with nothing more on her mind than thoughts of the morrow's meals. But a note penned in faded ink says that it was made on shipboard in 1865 while the ship was being chased through the Arctic ocean by the British privateer, the dreaded *Shenandoah*.

A French captain warned them he had seen six Yankee whaling vessels burning at sea, so Captain Penniman called in his whaleboats out among the ice floes by firing an old cannon that he found between-decks. They put too much powder in the first charge, and the recoil sent the rusty gun smashing down through the deck. The captain heard screams from the cabin and rushed down to find blood and broken glass everywhere. His wife and small son were both badly scared and somewhat scratched by the glass, but otherwise unhurt. He quieted them with the assurance that it was their own gun and not that of the enemy which had caused the trouble, and went back on deck to fire again, this time with a lighter charge.

It took three shots to bring in the boats, some of which

were several miles away. Eventually they got under way and just in time, for they saw the *Shenandoah's* sails on the horizon. A fog helped them get away. They nearly ran on a reef but finally got clear of danger, after a long chase through the ice-strewn water. If they had been captured the presence of the captain's wife would have prevented the British from burning the ship, they learned afterward, but the vessel would have been bonded and sent with prisoners to Honolulu, which was also something to be avoided.

We must admire the nerve of the little woman down in the cabin netting away at her tidy as they fled along the Arctic Circle.

The owners of the barks in which the Pennimans shipped always used to write and ask Mrs. Penniman if she was ready to go on a voyage before they broached the subject to the captain himself. This was because they knew he would not go until she could go too.

Sometimes they left three children at home, sometimes they took one of them along. Both the son and the daughter who now lived in the house in Eastham went on a four-year voyage with their parents when they were small, and they have vivid memories of the great ships with their decks scoured white, and their crews of bearded men who manned the whaleboats, and the excitement of whaling.

Once the boats were all out looking for whales. The first mate had been drowned, so the captain had to go out in command of one of the whaleboats in his place. Only Mrs. Penniman and the ship's carpenter were left on board with a few of the crew. The boats were five miles off when the skipper's wife sighted a big sperm whale close alongside.

Eager to get the men back, she told the carpenter to hoist a flag to bring them in. In his excitement he bettered his instructions and hoisted it union-down.

The captain saw what he supposed was a signal of distress, and thinking his small son must have fallen overboard, he drove his crew for the ship, five miles away, as fast as they could make it. They got there exhausted, to find all safe.

The captain's wrath at the false signal was mollified by the size of the whale, for it gave them $10,000 worth of oil. They got thirty barrels of oil from the head alone. When they got into port the ship had the most valuable cargo ever brought into New Bedford. Her owners gave Mrs. Penniman $600 as a token of their appreciation for her help. With this money from her whale she bought herself a sealskin coat.

But the lady's greatest feat came one time when they were lying off the coast of Patagonia. It was a fine bright day and the captain, who was fond of gunning, took a party ashore to get some ducks. Mrs. Penniman was left on board with only the cook and two or three green men. Up came one of the sudden hurricanes of the tropics and drove the bark far out to sea.

With consternation and dismay the captain saw her go. Not only did he fear, with good reason, the loss of his ship and his wife, but the plight of himself and his crew on that hostile shore was serious in the extreme. With no supplies and with the danger of attack from the natives, it meant certain death for them all.

However, the captain had reckoned without his wife. Two days later back came the *Europa* with all sails set, came up smartly into the wind and dropped her anchor.

Mrs. Penniman was a good navigator. She had taken the latitude and longitude as they left, and although they were blown a hundred miles out to sea, and in spite of the short-handed crew, she was able to work the ship back to her husband.

This was the same bark, *Europa*, which brought in the valuable cargo already mentioned. She was off the Patagonian shores for three years on that cruise. The captain had a lot of spare time on his hands, and he used much of it making fancy and useful articles for his wife out of the ivory of the whales' teeth. Some of the things he trimmed with shell from the tortoises they found in southern seas. Canes and piecrust wheels, rolling pins with ivory handles, puzzles and trick boxes, all elaborately and beautifully designed, show many hours of patient and skillful craftsmanship.

Whales' teeth engraved with elaborate designs adorn the mantelpiece of the house in Eastham. The captain was an artist in scrimshaw work, and it is hard to realize the fine clear lines were pricked and etched with the point of a fine cambric needle.

On the walls hang rare old prints of whaling scenes, showing the different stages of the long process, from the first sighting to the trying out with its clouds of black smoke. They are signed by Benjamin Russell of New Bedford, and the artist apparently knew the business to the last detail. One of the prints showed "Right Whaling in the Bering Straits and Arctic Ocean," while another claimed to depict "Sperm Whaling in All Its Varieties."

The house was built by Captain Penniman when he retired, along in the 1880's, and in its day was a model of elegance. From it one gets probably the finest view in town, for it looks out over the moors and dunes and bay to the ocean.

Back in Revolutionary days Eastham had thrice her present population, and there were other villages back along the side roads. One such was Thumper Town—and when you are counting ponds from the post office is a good time to start looking for it. Just keep on going down across the railroad, then down the Kingsbury road; and when you get there ask someone's advice about where to look next—it was in that general neighborhood. But to find Hell's Kitchen, turn left off from the Highway at the store beyond Eastham and go to the shore, then take a road to the right and follow it. It is now a summer colony, though. I think it was the keeper of this store who was looked up to as one of the fine honest men of his day. They said he trusted everyone, and took it for granted they were as honest as he was. As a result, if they were not they would be ashamed to let him know it, and he always got his money. There was a story about his overcharging a man ten cents once and scouring the whole lower Cape looking for him, in order to return the dime. Speaking of Hell's Kitchen, there was also Hell Holler, reached by a sandy old road.

The back roads lead to the quiet forgotten places, out to where the beach plums grow in season. They wander along through clumps of scrub pines or between the fields of one-time farms. If the visitor knows where to look there are traces of the old villages, some of them hardly even a name any more. These are likely to be on the Bay side. The roads on the Back Side lead out over the moors or down to the ocean.

This moorland waste, beautiful as it is in some of its

moods, is an object lesson in what happens when two major errors are made in succession. It would be fatal anywhere else and the Cape, stripped of its woods, might have gone back into the sea. Fortunately it is a durable old spit, and whatever it uses for backbone in place of rock can take it.

White folks were not to blame for the first error, for the Indians must have started cutting down the forests, but we finished the job. They must have been sizable trees, too, judging from the trunk of one I saw at Nauset, sticking out half way down the sandy bluff. A storm a few days before had left it exposed after perhaps centuries in hiding there. It was the trunk of a big tree; as I recall, two or three feet in diameter. Don't chortle, you west-coasters, that is big for New England and very big for Eastham today where their best timber would be regarded as underbrush in the Far Northwest. If there was one such tree there must have been others, for they have to grow in stands to grow at all in the high winds.

For the second error our folks were wholly to blame—forever taking and never giving back. The Indians planted fish and perhaps seaweed with their seed, and their crops flourished. The fertility may have begun to coast when they turned their garden lands over to us, but it certainly took a nose dive afterward.

As a result, and not so long ago either, the wolf howled loud and long down many a sandy lane and living was lean indeed. A farmer was lucky if he had a second shirt to change into on washdays. If the wolf no longer howled in my day it was thanks not to the Founding Fathers but to the county farm bureau combined with a streak of sand in the native character. Nearly every farmhouse had at least one car parked in the barn between the haymows, and some of them had bathrooms and sun porches. It was done with asparagus, plus the aforementioned human assistance.

The story of asparagus in Eastham is a miniature of the story of farming in America. When the farmer worked under intelligent guidance, and cooperated with his neighbors, and when his family worked with him, he flourished. That is, he did if the market was right, and prices were up—and if another part of the state nearer Boston, seeing him doing well, did not cut in with competition—and if there was no drought or blight or hurricane. There was a time during those boom twenties when the asparagus growers of Eastham were doing extremely well. A man with a ten-acre patch—about as much as he could work himself without hiring labor—could clear $200 an acre, and get his winter money from turnips planted between the rows.

To a Cape man who owns his place and has a cow and hens and a garden, not to mention a thrifty wife, an income of $1,000 a year is affluence. He earns most of it in about three months of active work for the whole family in the field or the bunching-shed, and the rest of the time when the chores are done he can go fishing or haying or maybe shingle the barn or sit round the cracker bar'l in Brackett's store.

Things looked good for a while. The boys stayed home on the farms instead of going off to the city to work. There was plenty for them to do, and money for doing it. They planted their own beds and worked on the older ones of their neighbors till their own came in. It looked like a foolproof business, for an asparagus bed lasts fifteen or twenty years. The crops were pretty sure fire, and folks up in Boston liked the good Cape "grass." But by now everyone was in the game or getting into it, and going strong. There was still market enough for them if it hadn't been for outsiders waking up to the possibilities and starting to pour their "grass" into the Boston market too. Prices began to take a slide—today one of the few crops that do well on this sandy soil is almost extinct. Where once there were scores of asparagus beds there are hardly ten acres of it in the whole township.

This was the town's second try with asparagus. Whether it is to be the last remains to be seen, but it might have to wait for a different sort of set-up. They tried it once before, some years ago. With the land all run out as it was it looked promising, for it is one thing that likes sandy soil with a tang of salt in it. Everybody who was not cultivating summer boarders took to raising it—plain old-fashioned "grass," with its blights and its cutworms and all. First the competition brought prices down, and then the blight took the crops three years running. "Eastham was so down and out they had to take her clean off the map," one of the farmers told me.

The farm bureau stepped in and showed them how to raise a blightproof root and how to spray for cutworms, and how to build up their markets. "Cooperate!" they said—to the most individualistic farmer on God's green earth. Get together, organize, grade your product, adopt a brand to advertise your quality and ship to Boston as a unit. They did all those little things, bought their own truck and sent a five-ton load off on its hundred-mile run up to Boston every night during the cutting season.

One thing they had not done was to change the distribution system, which needed something more than spraying with Paris green to make it work. Funny thing I've noticed about farming—the minute you get too good at it, it backfires. The grower really must be poor enough to keep production down if he is to make a living—with plenty of people going hungry for what he has. Of course the end-trouble in Eastham was the depression on top of everything. I do not pretend to know anything about economics and such, but I think it's a safe guess the farmers on the lower Cape won't be too hot for the next boom in asparagus-growing under the present system.

But they were riding high during the 1920's. What I liked best about the eager young Yankee farmers there was their wives. They were quite different from the farmers' wives of fact and fiction—most fact, and practically all fiction. No worn and patient drudges with sad sweet eyes and hands roughened by toil. They had charm and poise, and they knew how to wear their pretty clothes. They read new books and talked about them. They had a sense of humor that bubbled over into their conversation —those I met, anyhow—and they loved their life.

Oh, of course they worked—did their own housework and brought up their babies and helped out in the bunching sheds during the season—but they liked it. For duration at least it was an old folks' town, like a lot of others. Now that the war is over—we shall see. The farm bureau talks of cultivating the wild beach plums. There should not be much competition in them. Eastham would have to have a future, it has so much sand—the kind that beach plums and asparagus grow in, and the kind that grows in characters.

It has been said—whether by me or by someone else I

don't remember, but anyhow I believe it to be true—that the Yankee pioneer of the future will be the man who comes back from the West to reclaim the sterile acres of old New England. He'll be something of a hero when he comes ridin' round the mountain.

An experiment in farming was being got under way by a tall, blond, slow-spoken young westerner that intrigued my imagination. A wealthy Boston man had bought a couple of hundred acres of barren heath and salt marsh for an experimental farm. In charge of it he put an ex-cowboy named Charlie Gunn, with a local wife—she was one of us Crosbys, great-granddaughter of the Joshua Crosby who was gunner aboard Old Ironsides in the War of 1812. The neighbors—which means the townsfolk at large—were viewing the project with the natural pessimism for any off-Cape effort. They pointed out that as a starter the experimenters had planted 2,400 young pines, of which only twelve survived. Not twelve hundred, notice, but twelve.

Of course the land was not promising—sandy, covered with sparse grass, bayberry bushes, sweetfern, wild blackberry vines, gorse and the other small flowers of the heath country. Still Mr. Gunn hoped for the best, and he tried everything—here five acres of asparagus, a three-acre patch of Soudan grass, a nine-acre field of corn, fifteen acres of hay, plots of rye, oats, mangels and other vegetables. For stock he began with half a dozen pedigreed Guernseys and some pigs—the belted sort with the white towel of their breed over their shoulders. Down back of the great red barn with its silo he had a thousand Rhode Island reds with some noisy guinea hens to scare away the hawks, and a pool for the Muscovy ducks. Down in a clump of pines were a family of turkeys, and over on the marsh some geese. He was quite literally trying everything in samples, and was on the eve of what looked like success when the owner died and the farm was broken up.

The Gunns bought a dairy farm in one of the few really fertile spots in town. Mrs. Gunn wrote me the other day that they had dug down eight feet without reaching any bottom to the fine rich loam which a glacier once left there. They were retailing their milk and doing well.

In a little old-fashioned farm over on the other side of town I ran across a story with true heart interest. Nobody thought she was anything very special, just a little old grade hen, sort of gray and yellow and pindlin'. But she had won the love and filial devotion of four of the hugest geese I ever saw. The farmer gave them to her still in the egg, and she hatched them out and watched them anxiously through a puzzling infancy to an alarming adolescence. Up to the minute they discovered the pool down back of the barn they were well-behaved goslings, but from then on the little yaller hen spent her days frantically trotting back and forth along the edge of the water trying her darnedest to be maternal. After a while she made up her mind it was no use, they didn't seem to be drowning, so she returned to the normal life of the hen-yard.

But here is the interesting point. The four huge geese I saw parading round the dooryard that summer afternoon had their little mother with them. They never forgot her. Every evening when they came home to be fed they would cut her out from the other hens—driving them away with lordly flappings of their wings—and get her off in a corner by herself. Then they would start telling her everything that had happened all the day long, with many loud quack-quackings. She would listen, and answer with quick little cluck-clucks of understanding. Their owner said this was a daily routine with them, and he wasn't going to do anything to break it up. The family was not going to be separated so long as its members felt like this about one another.

The house where this happened is over on the Bay side, and I think you can see it from the Highway. You'll know it if you do, for it is a fine example of Cape-mobile architecture. Some people call it the "telescope house" and some call it the "after-thought house." Anyhow it was evidently assembled from various parts of the town, or even the county (there is a house in Orleans brought up from Truro) and some of it is much older than the rest. Clearly the final ell is the earliest, but whether they brought up the rest of the house and attached it, one time and another, or whether it was an afterthought I never knew.

Somebody had just found an old account book in the attic of the Atwood house on the Highway, and it certainly gave a glimpse of life in that neighborhood around 1823, when its records were kept. The ell of this house was then the village store, and all the town evidently came trading. The shopkeeper, Joshua Atwood, was fortunate in having a star customer right from the start. He must have helped keep things moving, judging from the pages of closely written entries. Whatever else he bought, and he was a liberal buyer, the Star Customer always went home with a gallon of rum. He drank a gallon a week, apparently. About every fourth line on the page is rum. It did not run him down much financially, for it was only ten cents a quart or thirty-eight cents by the gallon. There was gin, too—a pint and a quarter of it plus a pint of brandy for thirty-nine cents all told. Hyson tea was thirty cents a quarter-pound. So why drink tea? Tobacco was cheap, too, the kind meant to be whittled off and chewed of course—twenty cents a pound. A pound should last quite a while.

The Star Customer did a lot of shopping for his women-folk. He paid $2.33 for seven yards of bombazet, smooth worsted dress goods. That was pretty high, considering his next purchase, brown linen, cost only four cents a yard. He bought his wife a pair of kid shoes, a pair of kid gloves and a ruffle—and paid $2.24 for the lot. To light his house he got an oil lamp and some sperm oil to fill it—the lamp was fifteen cents, but the oil cost twenty cents a quart. Potatoes were forty-two cents a bushel, four and three-quarter cents a pound, but sugar twelve and one-half cents. Sometimes the bills were paid in cash, often they were worked out. Haying was a lucrative occupation. It brought more than other jobs. If a man worked all day—and no doubt that meant ALL day—he got a whole dollar for it. One customer—not the Star—ran an account for three years, and then paid it all off by one day's mowing.

Across the road from the store in North Eastham was a ten-acre space known as Millennial Grove. A few years after our Star Customer started his account the Grove was in full swing, beginning in 1828 and running on for thirty years or more. The camp meetings held there every summer drew great crowds, sometimes 5,000 people coming what were then great distances to attend them. They made the town famous far and wide.

An Orleans woman wrote the magazine about the Grove and told us something of its story besides enclosing a yellowed, tattered page from *Gleason's Pictorial Companion*, published in 1852, with an account of the doings there illustrated by woodcuts. She got her story from an elderly woman who used to go to the revivals.

The Grove was well located, not only because it was on the main road but because it was not far from the Bay shore. This was important, for so many of the people came by water from Boston and other faraway places. When their packet or steamer, whichever it might be, reached shoal water it would still be a long way from shore, so a series of transfers would begin. First small boats came and took the passengers aboard and as far inshore as they could go. When they grounded, all sorts of horse-drawn carts and wagons and carry-alls splashed up alongside and were filled up with passengers—whole families of men, women and children crowding into them—and dragged onto the beach. From there they could walk up to the Grove.

Visitors from different towns and cities and the different churches in the larger cities had their own tents set up in cleared spaces in the Grove. The ground was covered with straw, and at night the campers spread their bedding on it. In each tent a curtain divided the men from the women sleepers. Back of the tents was a sort of kitchen with long tables where everyone ate together. Out front was the speaker's stand with rows of wooden benches for the audience and of course a mourners' bench for penitent sinners. Besides the regular services, prayer meetings were often held in the tents. The early meetings were a great success and many converts were made, but later on "the picnic spirit became more prevalent and the meetings were finally discontinued."

I quote the language of *Gleason's Pictorial Drawing Room Companion* just as it comes: "We are in the steamer *Naushon* for the purpose of attending the Methodist Camp Meeting at Eastham, but unluckily a long, low swamp of level land and shallow water intervenes between us and the shore and we have, consequently, to embark in a boat whose sails are flapping against their masts, at the side of the steamer. We descend into it. It is large enough on ordinary occasions to carry twenty passengers without discomfort. But what is the matter? We have already forty in it at the least. 'You do not mean to take any more?' The boatman answers, 'O yes, we carried seventy yesterday and we can manage to do as much today.' And accordingly more and more are squeezed into it until, at length, sixty-seven in all, we quit the side of the *Naushon*. Away we run, heeling over with the wind and occasionally taking the salt spray of an impudent wave in our faces, as we peer curiously over its side at several square-looking pill-boxes—for so they seem—drawn, some by one, some by two horses, which are struggling with the waves nearer in to the shore. Yet what is our astonishment, as we come up to the first of these, to see the anchor let go, and as the boat swings round with the tide, to hear the voice of a jolly-looking driver, in brown Holland coat, and cloth cap, emerge from the front of what we supposed a pillbox but is a vehicle, asking who wanted to go ashore first. We spring in, to find eight more individuals stowed alongside of us like bales of cotton, and off we are driven, helter-skelter, the horses stumbling, and the water plashing round us, some quarter of a mile through the receding tide.

'Plague take it!' shouts an unphilosophical fellow-adventurer, as he is jerked from a place in the corner of the cart onto our hat, which is flattened, while we feel a rush of cold water from the other side, drenching the nether portion of our persons. This for the moment completes our misery.

"We repair to Millennial Grove, where the Camp Meeting is held. The hour for evening exercise is now gradually approaching, and nothing can be more gratifying to the chance observer than the order and regularity which marks those who attend it, while nothing will be gayer and more agreeable than the aspect of the whole scene. Scores of lamps spot the trees which grow among the benches arranged before the long and narrow stage from which the exhortation is to be delivered, and which is now filled with clergymen, and a congregation of considerably more than a thousand. In the morning we return in time to attend the ten o'clock prayer meeting; but let us advise any of our friends who have an inclination to attend a camp meeting at Eastham, to inspect the weather-glass before they take their place in the steamer—for scarcely do we leave the ground, and the congregation assembles, than the rain begins, and drives them within their tents. Very perseveringly did it pour down until four o'clock, when wet and weary we repair to a boat, and cruise about the coast in the fog which is settling down upon the waters, until the steamer's paddle-wheels are heard."

16. *Wonder Strand*

WHEN Henry David Thoreau started his famous walk down-Cape he started it at Eastham. He had seen a long stretch of beach on the map, and it looked like a nice walk. So he took the train from Boston to its Cape railhead, which a century ago was Sandwich, and there boarded a stagecoach. He was traveling the hard way. Most travelers came by packet in those days, comfortable little craft sailing every day, weather permitting, from Boston. Maybe he wanted to see the scenery, or maybe he was afraid of being seasick.

He left the stage at Orleans, and spent the night there. If he expected to get to the beach from Orleans he was disappointed, for he had to detour round the inlets and marshes to Eastham before he could find a side road to the ocean. It must have been the road to the lighthouse—lighthouses they were then, three of them he noted with disapproval, for his landlubberly soul was shocked at such extravagance. He was sure one would have served the purpose. It does today; but times have changed. Those three have long since washed away. The lighthouse I knew was the seventh.

Theoretically the long beach begins at the southern end of Monomoy and runs along up the outer edge of the Cape's forearm, around the elegantly curving wrist and to the tip of the tapered forefinger, which is Race Point.

All told that is about fifty miles. Most of it is north-westerly, but more north than west, and all of it is down-Cape—one place where north is "down."

But actually the beach begins at Eastham, beyond Ton-set. From there it is one fine unbroken stretch of perhaps thirty miles. I have never walked the whole of it, just sampled it in half a dozen places from the Nauset life-saving station and the lighthouse several miles beyond, and Cahoon's Hollow and Pamet River life-saving stations, and Highland Light, and Peakéd Hill Bar and Race Point life-saving stations. It is a lot of beach, and it gives on more water than a person could believe if he had never seen it.

It was at the Tonset end of the beach that the one and only shot to reach our shores in the First World War was fired—it was not aimed at the beach, but it fell there. The target was a barge being towed along. The German sub must have had a Dummkopf of a captain to shoot at such a thing, and a nervous gunner to miss it. Besides the shot which landed on shore another—at least one other—fell into the water, for some ten years later a fisherman on T Wharf showed me a German shell he had picked up in his nets off Nauset.

Along here on top of the dune Henry Beston built himself a cabin and spent a year getting material for his book, *The Outermost House* (published in 1928). Driving along through Eastham after dark I have often seen the tiny glimmer of his light out across the moors and the marshes. It was a couple of miles south of the life-saving station, and his only visitors were the men of the patrol. There was no road, so he had to pack everything on his back. In such a setting he produced what seems to me to be the outstanding book on the Cape. Certainly it reflects the changing seasons of the Nauset world with imagination and fidelity.

Those who know the long beach well understand why the much-traveled Norsemen remembered it as the Wonder Strand. But they say to get its full magic it is necessary to see it from the water as they did. Sometimes it is lifted by mirages or changed and magnified with veils of shifting mists or reflected lighting. Sometimes it is spotlighted by the sun through a hole in the clouds, sometimes it is hidden by a sudden thick blanket of gray fog. It may be a thing of wonder and mystery or it may be savage and cruel and beastly, a lee shore with shoals and shallows and the mad ocean clawing at its sliding sands.

The best way for landlubbering transients like you and me to get the feel of the beach is to go down alone—and that means alone—at sunset and stroll slowly northward. The tide should be on the ebb, for that leaves room to walk where it is easiest going, on sand that has been packed by the water.

A modern hiker has his choice of several roads from the Highway. My favorite was the one to the life-saving station at Nauset, which turns off at Eastham village. Besides the human interest at the station, and a breeches-buoy drill, there is a path down to the beach.

The sea runs along at the right—coming in from half a world away to crash in white water at the wayfarer's feet. The sandy, irregular bluff runs along at the left, its crest of coarse grass printed sharp against the clear pale green of the western sky. Under foot is the beach, soft and creamy where it is dry up near the foot of the bluff, but firm and yellow where it is still damp from the retreating tide. Not all the thirty miles of beach ahead can be seen, partly because it takes a turn at Truro and partly because—well, it can not, that's all. It isn't that kind of a beach. But the footfarer thinks he can see it—he thinks he can see very much farther, oh, very much—away off into some strange, distant, unreal world that never comes any nearer or becomes any more real when one tries to walk toward it.

The color begins to get you. Beyond the white surf the green combers pounding out their eternal rote, the green blending out into the water, the blue sparkling away into silver as it makes for Spain. Perhaps a pinpoint of white sail or a wisp of distant smoke accents the immensity of the sea. The bluffs or sandy dunes are creamy-buff, with patches on their tawny sides of gray-green beach grass of the darker scrub pine or oak. Far in the distance the three lines of bluff and sand and sea appear to meet—but if they don't, you can't prove it.

The bluff is not a straight line, it has shallow points and bays to catch the fancy. From behind any one of them something strange and unlikely might come cavorting forth upon the beach to chase its long shadow into the white ruching of the summer surf. It might be a black-bearded pirate or a moon-cusser with his lantern, it might be a yellow-haired Viking or a red-haired rumrunner, it might be a shipwrecked sailor with a parrot on his fist—it might be a witch screaming for her cat, it would more probably be a Coast Guard patrol—and he wouldn't be frisking with his shadow.

One certainly gets looking for something to happen as he walks along—the stage is all set for action, and any minute it should get going. But the lurking ghosts of

Nauset stay hidden from most of us, and perhaps it is just as well. What with the twilight coming on, they might make us puckerstruck.

At first, with the sun not yet down, the colors are the usual blue and green and yellow that might be expected. Then it goes, and instantly everything is changed. The world becomes opalescent, translucent, faery. Veils of illusion blur the lines of surf and sea and sand, so that now they sweep away softly into nowhere. The sky turns unimaginable colors and the sea picks them up. The blades of grass that fringe the bluff become sharp little black swords against the fiery west.

Unless the ears are keen enough to catch the shifting of the sand or the brushing of the sedge grass, the only sound is the soft sh-shing of the surf on the sand. To be sure there is always the dull roar of the waves as they comb and break, but that has long since become unheard, it is a part of what seems to be the silence.

The afterglow fades and the colors grow subtler and fade into nuances of gray, and the tramper finds sand in his shoes and it's time for him to turn back—and he finds he has not come very far after all. But he is never quite the same afterward. It's twenty years since I walked on Nauset at sunset—and it is still with me. Wonder Strand indeed.

It was somewhere along this southern end of Nauset that the first Cape Cod canal was cut through. That was Jeremiah's Gutter, and it was cut through from Rock Harbor on the Bay side of Orleans to the Town Cove, following pretty close, I judge, to the Eastham line. No man-made canal was this, but dug by one of the masterful storms which are forever changing the face of things in

Barnstable county. It happened right in the nick of time, too—in fact, it might be said the timing was perfect.

I mentioned pirates a while back. They beset these shores a couple of hundred years ago, and many of them came to grief on them like their betters. One such was Black Sam Bellamy, whose ship the *Whidah* was wrecked in 1717 in a gale that came to be named for him, the Bellamy storm. The wreck was on the Back Side, down along the beach near Cahoon's Hollow, just beyond Eastham. The *Whidah* had half a dozen prizes along; some of the other vessels got away, but she piled up on the outer bar and all but two of her men drowned.

Now it was this same gale, the Bellamy storm, which cut the Gutter through from the Bay to the Back Side, so the authorities from Boston were able to save a lot of time. Instead of having to sail away out around Provincetown they landed at Rock Harbor and sent their whaleboat through the new short cut to Nauset. They buried a hundred dead pirates and took the two survivors back to Boston to hang.

All they were in time to salvage—in spite of the short cut—was the *Whidah*'s chains and anchor. The rest of Black Sam's booty and personal property had been taken care of already by enterprising neighbors. There was a good deal of velvet in this sort of beachcombing, from Chatham on down to Race Point. It was salvage of a sort, and the spoils of the sea were put to good use. Nobody seems to have had any special scruples about it except the authorities. They made quite a fuss about the *Whidah*'s cargo.

Carried farther, and quite different, was moon-cussing.

That really was in bad repute. Anybody who did it kept still about it. Today most people will tell you it never happened, really it never did, not on Cape Cod. Maybe not. It is supposed to have been common enough down round New Jersey, where they had wrecks too, though not so many as up here.

This is the how of moon-cussing: It is a dark stormy night, and a ship is known to be in the offing. Down to the beach goes a moon-cusser, stealthily. Sheltered from sight of those on shore by the dunes he shows a light—maybe a lantern or perhaps he builds a driftwood fire on the beach. The ship's captain thinks he is nearing port at last, and heads in. She hits the bar, and that is that. No Coast Guard in those days, just a gentleman waiting on the beach for morning when the ship would be broken up and her stuff washed ashore. Sinister business, and no wonder nobody claims it!

Moon-cussing? Oh, the moon might chance to come out behind a cloud rack in time for the skipper to see the line of surf on the bar and veer off. That left the gentleman in waiting nothing to do but cuss out the moon and go home.

Scattered all along the Back Side, six or eight miles apart, are the life-saving stations of the Coast Guard. Half way between each two is a small shelter where their patrols meet and swap tickets and can report back by phone if anything is doing. Summer days it is a pleasant walk along the little path that meanders over the edge of the heath on the crest of the bluff or over the dunes by the sea. The sun is warm and the sea air is fresh and sweet, and the world is altogether good. There are likely to be a lot of summer folks around and girls in one-piecers on the beach and youngsters playing in the sand, and anything but lonesome.

But winter nights, even the usual ones when there isn't any wreck, it is different. Maybe the tide is half way up the dunes and the hollows between them are aflood—then the patrol has to stumble back among the underbrush and bushes farther in from shore, and that makes more distance as well as rougher going. The icy spray is thrown over the dunes and stings him like shot. The snow is driving down from the north, and the mercury breaks zero. But it's like the army—you're in, and you stick.

When there's a wreck—well, they have to get out the boat and go out to it, unless it happens far enough inshore so they can reach it with the breeches buoy.

Summer folks like to stroll down to the station on Thursdays—I think that was the day—to watch the drill. A mast has been set up on the moors, and the men practice shooting the breeches buoy at it—an odd sort of target practice, but vitally important, for good marksmanship may be the difference between life and death.

When a vessel goes aground offshore far enough in to reach, the cart containing the buoy and its intricate rigging is rushed down to the edge of the beach and the rope is shot out to it from a gun. If it reaches the ship the sailors grab it and pull it in and make it fast. Hanging from the rope is a pair of canvas shorts, and one of the men climbs into these and slides ashore or is pulled along by the lifeguards. He climbs out, and the buoy is pulled back to the ship for the next passengers. Sure they get a ducking, maybe it is practically all one ducking till they get ashore; but at that it is better than being washed overboard. The men are brought off one at a time, and it is slow work—especially when a man can feel his ship breaking up under him.

The station where the men live as well as make their headquarters is close to the shore, as near the beach as it can be without getting within reach of the winter seas. I remember a story-and-a-half white-shingled building with a big cheerful room where they sat and ate, with red-checked tablecloths and sunny windows looking out to sea, and a dormitory room above.

In summer it is a quiet life, with only a routine of patrol and looking after the gear. If a person goes down to the beach for a dip in the sweet-looking ocean, he soon notices that a man has strolled up to the lookout-stand on the bluff and is keeping an eye on him. That is because of the undertow. The bather does not see it, but he feels it when it gets him, and then is when he needs a friend. That guard is the friend.

As I said, a fairly easy life in summer, and not unpleasant if one does not mind living away from home without much shore leave. Also if one does not mind low pay. I forget how much the men got back there in the twenties—seems to me it was $15 a week and board. In the winter they sure earn it, and then some. Quiet chaps, like most men who have to do with the sea, and not long on talking. But they have stories if you can get them, and these are likely to be heroic stuff.

We were lucky in getting for the magazine a first-hand account of a rescue by the Nauset crew. It is a human document worth preserving. The event had happened a couple of years before, but it had been repeated with variations several times since. The writer was Captain

Henry O. Daniels, who at the time we knew him was in charge of the Cahoon's Hollow station but had formerly been at Nauset.

"At 2.30 A.M., January 13, I came off watch and turned in." (So begins the Captain's explicit narrative.) "The storm had begun to clear at this time, wind shifting from E.N.E. to S.E. Rain had stopped and thick fog had taken its place.

"At 5.30 A.M. Boatswain (L) Abbot H. Walker, officer in charge of the Nauset station, called all hands. As we came into the messroom I asked Mr. Walker where the trouble was. He said he had got word from the Chatham Wireless Station that the S. 19 was ashore five miles north of Nauset Light, and he had sent Surfman Z. A. Adams out there.

"About this time we got another message saying the sub was five miles south of the light. Mr. Walker immediately called Boatswain (L) Clark, officer in charge of the Orleans Coast Guard Station, who at once left the station and went to the harbor and reported over the telephone that he could see something on the outer bar, but the sea was breaking over it so that he could not tell what it was.

"Surfman Wilbur C. Chase of Nauset had gone south; he was at the telephone while Mr. Walker and Mr. Clark were talking. Chase said from where he was he could make her out, and it was a submarine.

"We then started, taking surfboat and beach gear. As we got near her we could see that she was offshore too far to use the gun and breeches buoy, so we left that and kept on going with the surfboat until we were abreast of her. [Note: this would be hauled along the beach on wheels.]

"The sea was breaking clean over her and nothing

showed but the conning tower, with one seaman tied on top of that semaphoring to us. The spray going over him made it impossible for us to get his message and, the sea getting rougher all the time, we decided to try and get to her with the surfboat without losing any time.

"Mr. Walker and myself thought there might be a chance to make it, although it looked bad. We launched the surfboat, surfmen William Eldridge, Kenneth Young, Russell Taylor, Wilbur Chase, and Boatswain's Mate Henry O. Daniels rowing; Mr. Walker, the Boatswain (L), was in charge of the boat.

"We worked boat out over the inner bars with great difficulty, shipping water from most every sea. When we had pulled to about seventy-five yards from the submarine, three seas swept over her and as we met the first sea our boat started to climb over it, but the sea was too steep and we turned completely over, boat landing bottom up.

"Before leaving the beach Mr. Walker had told all hands to watch him, not to look over their backs to see what was coming. As the boat tipped I saw surfmen Eldridge and Young thrown overboard and Mr. Walker pitched over the stern. As I was rowing stroke oar I had no chance to get clear, and when I came to the top I found myself under the boat and my face covered with blood, caused from the gunwale of the boat hitting me across my face. As the boat lifted on a sea, I hauled myself from under the boat and swam to her and crawled on top, where I saw Surfman Chase, between surfmen Taylor and Young. Chase was in a bad way, the water shocking him so he could not help himself. Taylor and Young were trying to get him to the boat. I got Chase by the collar of his coat and with the help of Taylor and Young got him on top of the boat, where we all hung on. Mr. Walker was astern, swimming for the boat, Surfman Eldridge just ahead of him. Eldridge reached the boat and passed an oar to Mr. Walker, who then pulled himself to the boat, this making all hands clinging to her still bottom up.

"We were drifting in with the tide toward the shore, about a quarter of a mile away from us, every sea burying boat and men. As we came in over one bar, we took a sea that drove the boat to the bottom, washing all hands away from her and taking five feet of her bow out and turning her right side up. We hung on again till we drifted to the shore, where the Cahoon's Hollow crew pulled us out of the surf and got us to a gunning blind about one mile up the beach.

"Frank Freeman and his wife had seen us when we turned over and had watched us being dragged from the surf. They immediately filled a large thermos jug with hot coffee and rowed more than a mile, getting to this camp shortly after we got there, and believe me, I never can show my appreciation to them for what they did for us that day. I honestly believe Mrs. Freeman saved Surfman Chase, as she worked over him one hour and a half, wrapping hot blankets around him as fast as I could pass them to her.

"Forty-five minutes overboard in the middle of January does a lot of things to a man. I saw each man as he came from the surf, and his face was as black as a Negro. and it was all he could do to stand on his feet.

"After getting warm and feeling better, we walked back to the station, got something to eat, took our other boat, and got on board the submarine about nine o'clock that night."

So that story ends. Lyman Armes tried to get Captain Daniels to enlarge on the last sentence, which was the biggest part of the story, but he wouldn't—he said that didn't matter, they just went out and did it.

A mile or so north—down-Cape—from the Coast Guard station is Nauset Light.

Like most buildings on the Cape this steel structure is peripatetic. It used to be one of twins over in Chatham, but they moved it down here to take the place of the last of three wooden towers. These had succeeded in turn the three brick ones which Thoreau eyed with disapproval because he did not know Nauset. One day at a low run of tide I spied a few bricks far out from shore, nearly covered with sand. They were all that remained of the second brick tower. Far out beyond that, under water, were the remains of the first one. On the top of the seventy-foot cliff where I stood were a few bricks left from the most landward of the three; and no doubt by now those are gone overboard too.

The three white-shingled wooden towers were built in 1892 to replace them, and were set farther back from the edge of the sandy cliff. But the sea came creeping toward them, undercutting the cliff and threatening with every storm to finish the job. So the government auctioned them off, and eager summer folks bought them in at anywhere from $12.50 to $50 apiece and made them into cottages—anybody can see them on Nauset Moors without half looking.

The lighthouse keeper told me that what Nauset loses "makes Monomoy," the long sandspit that dangles down from Chatham. As you look at the map it does not look probable, but he must have known. Monomoy was certainly being made from somewhere. Its lighthouse, which used to be on the tip of the point, was a mile or more inland at last accounts.

This seventh lighthouse at Nauset is on a concrete base but can be moved back when—not if—the time comes.

17. *Wellfleet for Her Pride*

In her heyday Wellfleet was a whaling town, and a prideful one. When the children of Provincetown chanted their jeering little song about Truro, which supplied them with milk because there wasn't any grass for cows down their way, they put her down like that—

> Provincetown for beauty,
>   Wellfleet for her pride—
> If it hadn't been for milk-carts
>   Truro would've died!

Even in my day there was still an air of old-fashioned gentility, of elegance even, about her that was quite foreign to the rest of the lower Cape. A sort of Sunday-afternoon repose, too, reminiscent of Sandwich and suggesting a storied past. I don't recall getting to know anyone there, but the village lingers in my memory as a blur of dignified white houses with elms to shadow them, and a white church of the better period.

According to the *American Guide* the elevation of the village is five feet; but a hill rises back of it, pleasantly green, and in front is the sheltered harbor. That harbor used to be deep enough for whaling vessels to lie comfortably at anchor in it, but now like most of the bay harbors it is silted up. Just why I didn't get better acquainted with the village is a mystery to me now. Probably because it—or the bulk of it—lay a bit to one side of the main highway, but more likely because I was putting for Provincetown for a first-night at the Wharf or a one-man show at the art gallery or on the trail of a nice hot story with a nice hot creamy-buttery lobster chowder at the end of it.

Propped up on my desk is the Wellfleet sheet of the United States Geological Survey map. The layout of the town fascinates me, for while I did neglect the village I put in a lot of time and mileage exploring the back roads of the township, which are the wildest and most bewildering of any I found. Many of the five-thousand miles we put on Lizy Jane's speedometer that season were scored over or through or hunting for those roads.

The township is long and narrow and presents a long straight back to the ocean some seven miles from Eastham to the Truro line. Its Bay side is as crooked and convoluted and contorted as the Back Side is simple. Up through the middle and slopping over the line into Truro are half a dozen ponds with such nice prosy everyday names as Gull Pond, and Herring, and Slough, and Horseleech, and Higgins. There was a road around these ponds on the map, and I spent a lot of time looking for it, but I never did find it, for it had vanished completely, just gone back into the landscape.

Back here among the ponds, and not down by the water, the first settlers built their village. The ponds gave them fresh water. Water can be had almost anywhere on the Cape by going down twenty-five feet for it, but the colonists were doubtless too busy getting themselves housed and provided for to dig if they didn't have to. Anyhow here is where they built their first houses, and here other settlers on outlying farms used to come from miles around to wash their clothes in the ponds. They made a picnic of it, their men turning up promptly for their "'leven o'clock," which of course was a drink of rum. This was all right in summer, but it is a puzzle how they did in winter—probably they broke holes in the ice, or simply waited for spring.

Here among the scrub pines stood a stone tablet marking the site of the first schoolhouse of Wellfleet. One or two of the original houses still remained, but the rest were piles of brick from their great chimneys, or small overgrown cellar holes, or maybe an old stone doorstep with a run-out lilac still guarding it. Groves of locust trees were rapidly taking over what was left of the village—it may have been they who stole the lost road.

Part of what was left of the deserted village was burned over by a forest fire that spring. The Cape was the worst fire hazard east of Idaho, because of its combination of pitch pines and high winds. The fire got started in the woods around the ponds, and threatened the present village of Wellfleet itself. Over in Eastham the party-line phones rang all night long getting out the fire-fighters. Out on the highway cars filled with relays of men headed for the fire streamed past night and day, meeting cars bringing back loads of exhausted men for a few hours of rest. At that the village would have gone, had it not been for a shift of wind which turned the fire on its tracks and headed it back toward where it started.

One of the roads back in here among the ponds was the original King's Highway for which the entire main Cape highway is named. This followed the main north-and-south trail of the Pamet Indians. It was on one of these back roads that I ran across a selectman of the town who showed me the house where his great-grandfather was living that memorable night when Thoreau stopped by and asked for a bed. He could not tell me much about his famous visitor, but he did mention that his great-grand-father was—or had been—a pirate. I wonder if Thoreau knew that!

Most of these roads followed the old trails which the Indians had made for themselves in the happy days before the white men took over, and this accounts for their irre-sponsible grades and curves—it would always be easier to walk round a tree than to cut it down, and so they walked and so we drive. Also if there is a hill they climb it instead of staying in the valleys. J. G. Peters, Jr., wrote an article for the magazine about the Indians of this region, and he explained that "like all wild creatures, the Indians traveled mostly along the ridges."

Herring Pond is the source of Herring River, which flows into Wellfleet harbor, and all north of this river, clear out to Race Point, once lived the tribe known as Pamets—pronounced *pammet*. The Nausets lived to the south, the Pamets to the north. Mr. Peters made a study of their ways and collected many of their artifacts—bits of pottery, arrowheads, spears, tomahawks, and so on. From what he found out about them they must have been more all-round craftsmen than the Indians of the west coast. They were good farmers, expert fishermen and hunters, and their womenfolk had most of the primitive arts—they made baskets, pottery, mats. Their pottery, Mr. Peters said, was of clay from the clay-pounds at North Truro mixed with lime and tiny bits of quartz and gravel and baked in a slow fire. They had a good sense of form, and decorated their bowls when the clay was still wet and plastic by binding it with braided ropes of rush and grasses.

The Pamets lived in huts which sound like those long-houses which the Indians of Puget Sound were building for themselves at the same time some 3,500 miles away. According to the way the Pilgrims described what they found, the long huts had walls and arched roofs covered with several thicknesses of woven mats. The smoke went out through a hole in the roof. They were built in the forests which covered the lower Cape in those days, and Peters thinks they must have been "quite snug and homey"; but they sound pretty chilly to me, come winter.

He mentions their building good canoes, but questions whether they were birch bark or dugouts. Out around Cape Flattery the Indians still make dugout canoes for their pelagic sealing, and I know it requires a fine big cedar tree with plenty of clear wood in it to make a fair-sized canoe. There were cedars on the Cape in early days, but I doubt if they ever raised much of that sort of tree which grows in the rain-forests of the Puget Sound country. It would seem more likely they made them of birch bark, as they did elsewhere along the New England coast. The bark canoes I have seen were not so finely streamlined as the dugouts, but they were much steadier in the water, more like the flat-bottomed ones of Greenland. Dugouts, I'm guessing, resemble those of the South Seas. It occurs to me that canoes would make a swell hobby for someone; they would take one into the depths of ethnology, I imagine.

Today about all that remains of the Pamet Indians, besides Mr. Peter's collection, is a couple of names. Their name clings to the little river which bisects the Cape at

Truro and to the life-saving station at one end of it. Their word for high land, Tashmuit, is still to be seen, says Mr. Peters, on an old house near Highland Light.

One of my exploring trips led off through the village to where Route 6 turned off, but instead of turning off, the explorer kept on going and bore across the railroad tracks—and I find an urgent memo to say something about Cape Cod railroad crossings, probably because I had narrowly missed meeting something on one. They are many and blind, and even if there are few trains they offer a hazard. A driver is much more likely to run into the trains than they are to run into him, but it would be rough on the paint job either way.

This road took me into the most desolate part of the Cape—wild moors and hills, great bare hills covered with coarse grass—winding sandy roads that were often mere tracks. For one five-mile stretch there was not a house; and that is a long way in Barnstable county. Open treeless country. The little river widens to a pond, separated from the Bay by a ridge. A fine view of Wellfleet harbor. A road out to the beach, probably used for hauling seaweed for fertilizer or banking houses in winter. But all very lonely.

The population of the whole township is well under a thousand, and Wellfleet today is a small village. Once it was famous as a whaling center. This was back in Revolutionary times, when it was the home port of some thirty whaling vessels, putting out from here on their four-year-long voyages to all parts of the world. It's said the name of the town is a contraction of Whale Fleet, but it isn't—it is just another English place-name.

One of their famous captains was Jesse Holbrook. He killed fifty-two whales, and "sparms at that," on one voyage, according to Swift, and this desirable record got him a fine job with a London whaling company teaching their men how he did it.

The first whaling done by our ancestors was well inshore—in fact, really on shore. Big fellows used to get stranded, to run aground on the flats at low tide, and then everyone would turn to and make hay—or blubber—as fast as possible. When this happened less and less frequently they began venturing out farther from shore till they were wandering all over the world and were soon teaching the game to Nantucketmen and others. Whaling reached its prime during the century around 1800—say from the Revolution to the Civil War.

After the decline set in, Wellfleet's fortunes began to wane. During the middle part of the nineteenth century it came back for a while as a fishing port—was second only to Gloucester. Later one of its captains went cruising down the coast in his own vessel and brought home a bunch of bananas. This led to the founding of the United Fruit Company with him as one of its officials—Captain Baker was distinctly a home-town boy who made good.

But whaling was its big heartbeat, and the town was never quite the same again. It meant a lot to most of the towns on the Cape, but probably most of all to Wellfleet.

I ran across a whaler's logbook which gave a better picture of what the job was like than anything else I have read. It was handwritten, of course, and what with the combination of faded ink, pitching ship and reluctant penman, plus strange and unknown words, it took imagination to read some of it. At that I missed out on a lot of rigging, not to mention latitude.

Whaling must have been the huskiest, most all-round unbeatable sport the world has yet devised for red-blooded men. Oil has always been a hazardous game. It still is, even when it is played on the rolling plains of Texas instead of on the rolling seas of the South Atlantic. Wildcatting for oil, on land or sea, is played in the open with old Dame Nature holding most of the cards and playing them close to her chest with plenty of extras up her sleeves. But crude petroleum doesn't begin to take the daring and skill that striking whale oil on the hoof required. There is a difference between taking your roll and a few months of your time boring for a duster and staking your life near the business end of a whale.

We landlubbers don't realize about whales—we can't. It is not natural we should. We never see them, even in aquariums. How should we know that a grown-up whale is fifty to a hundred feet long, and when it is floating on the surface it is high as the top of a one-story house? When it opens its mouth a whaleboat with half a dozen men could row in quite easily if they wanted to—which they would not.

If the monster is angered, as he is more than likely to be, he can charge the parent ship and wreck her, and when he gets through with a mere whaleboat it looks like the remains of a box of toothpicks.

If he is harpooned and heads for the open with the boat in tow, the crew keeps going. There is no gentle riding of the waves, either—the boat cuts them like a knife. It is speed, brothers. Boats caught like this have been known to lose their mother ship during the course of such a wild ride and never find her again. A Captain Sparks of Provincetown and his crew went riding with a whale back in the 1880's, and lost sight of their ship. They cut loose from their "horse" and set out to row themselves ashore, the nearest point of which they knew was a thousand miles away. They managed to kill another whale for fresh meat, and were finally picked up.

This logbook I mentioned was kept for the *John and Elizabeth* by her mate, one A. G. Parker, during a whaling voyage to the South Atlantic. He illustrated it with drawings of whales—sometimes whole whales, sometimes their heads, or the flukes of their tails. He had a nice feeling for curves, and some of them were quite Mae-Westy. A few of them looked upside down but they were not, they were "R." whales, which means right ones, and I judge a right whale was the right kind for them to chase as it was the kind which had whalebone.

The log begins in July, 1832. Sunday, July 29, he records: "This day commences with Baffling winds from S by E or SSE. Squally. Steering SE by S sharp on the wind —middle and latter great calm with light showers of rain. Saw two ships Employed in Reading. So Ends this sacred Day." The reader can do his own punctuating.

A few days later things got interesting. "Aug. 10—Spoke ship *Eagle* of New Bedford. Informed us there was a Pirat to leward had been chasing him all day." Next day there was more excitement but not all of it was legible: "Capt. Hgiht [?] of Ship *Eagle* informed us of this Brig Pirat. She sent up her Pirats in order to catch him but did not the Brig was 6 miles to Leward of us, had bin standing on the same tack with us all day. The Information we got from the *Eagle* rather alarmed us, we set fore and main [stuns'ls?] fly of it now to company with the *Eagle*, the Pirat to chase of us Boath. 6 P.M. Boath of us tacked Ship, stood from Lee [?] so as to Deceive her, crowded all the sail we could in order to git out of his site. Next morning no Brig to be seene, the *Eagle* was 4 miles to Leward."

Late that fall comes a different sort of entry: "Saw a whale to windward near by, lowered our Boats, Struck. After being fast for an hour or more the whale came up near Mr. Bennet's Boat, run his head in to the Boat, turned it over, killed one man instantly. Broke his neck and one of his Legs. We cut our Line from the whale, went to their rescue, took the remainds of the Crew into our Boat, came on Board, Dressed the Body, Sewed it up in canvas Bedd for Burial. 6 o'clock P.M. the Capt. read a chapter in the Bible, likewise a prayer, we then Lowered the Body to the Deep."

The usual entries ran more like this: "Dec. 15, 1838—Saw 8 R. whales and two or three Shoals of Sperm." Or, a month later—"Saturday commences with rugged weather ... saw whales near by, chased, did not stick, came near it, came on board. Saw as many as 30 R. whales, got one, cut it in, took us till 2 o'clock A.M. Sunday morning. Weather by this time raining. So ends this day." The last entry on another page chronicles the long process of "boiling down" a couple of whales they had taken, and ends laconically, "Saw 10 or 12 whales got one took Long Side. Lay By." Considering he has already mentioned it is "rugged weather" there was probably more to the story than the weary mate felt like telling.

Such was the life of the men who went out of Wellfleet during her big days.

As in Eastham, there were long periods of poverty and stagnation. The wolf howled plenty back among the forgotten villages of the Wellfleet hinterland. The old folks died off, and no new ones came into the town. One generation followed another in the old houses, living in the old ways.

An elderly friend of mine went down to Wellfleet to teach in a country school when she was a girl—it must have been around 1900. No new house had been built there since anyone could remember. When the word "lath" came up in the reading lesson none of her pupils knew the meaning of the word. She had to take the class to see an old house that was falling down to show them some laths exposed by broken plaster.

Nowadays things of course are different. Fishing is the main business, next to tourists, but in peace times there are plenty of those. During the war an encampment back on the Wellfleet plains helped keep things moving. But it is not like what it used to be when there was a village over on Bound Brook Island, and fifty children went to the village school.

18. *Truro Gets the Ocean*

OF ALL THE CAPE, not even excepting Chatham, it is at Truro one gets the feeling of the ocean most strongly. It lies there in all its nakedness with nothing to soften or mitigate it, nothing to break the shock of its appalling force. Back from the beach is a sweep of windy moors, and to the east the ground falls away abruptly to the ocean a hundred and forty feet below.

The tall coarse grass that covers the moors is forever swept by the wind. One day it marches it relentlessly toward the sea, but the next day, perhaps, it changes its mind and marches it back again. The few trees are small and stunted and twisted into queer shapes.

A boy whose family took summer boarders was asked by one of them how he came back from Sunday school—by the road?

"Oh, no," he said, "we have a short cut through the woods."

"What woods?" she asked, surprised.

"Why, the woods just this side of town."

"Where I come from," the lady corrected him severely, "we don't call anything a woods unless it is taller than your head!"

The small boy said, "Well, it is taller than my head, anyhow, and it's the woods."

Out on top of the cliffs stands Cape Cod Light, the lighthouse known all up and down as High Land Light— and it is pronounced as two words, not slurred into "high-l'nd" as landlubbers from the mainland often do. For it is high land, as is realized after a climb up to the top of the cliff from a swim. Though anyone rash enough to go swimming there is lucky to be on hand for the climb afterward. Farther up the beach is a Coast Guard station—in fact they come regularly along the Back Side— Nauset, Cahoon's Hollow, Pamet River, High Land Light, High Head, Peakéd Hill, Race Point.

One of the Coast Guard men told me that with the passing of sail there were few wrecks along the Back Side now because a ship with power could stand off a lee shore where a sailing vessel was literally powerless and could not save herself. But that very next winter came storms that brought back the old days with wrecks a plenty. Just along here seven vessels were driven ashore and a total of thirty-seven men were lost in spite of all the Coast Guard crews could do to save them. The weather was mild as far as temperature and snowfall went—only touched zero once, and the snow melted off in a day or two, even though inland the cities were still blanketed with it. But there were some terrific gales, and the outer beaches got the full force of them.

Wrecks are nothing a bystander is likely to write about. For one thing of course there are no bystanders. A person is either being wrecked himself, or else he is trying to get help to those who are. But it is like the war, you have to be in action to know how it feels. It is not anything you can conjure up in smoke-wreaths. Coast Guardsmen would be the logical historians, but they are not likely to be talkative. They are the strong, quiet sort —and I suspect that those who like to laugh at strong quiet men are themselves neither strong nor quiet.

However Mr. Peters, who wrote about the Indians, found an old-timer who was willing to tell him about a wreck he was in once, along here at High Land. I shall let the old Coast Guardsman tell the story his own way, just as Mr. Peters did. References to walking on the beach will be noticed. There is a broad beach some years, other years the seas crash up against the foot of the cliff, or even undercut it, or eat the beach out in scallops with points of sand running out with deep water dark between them.

Mr. Peters called his story "When Men Were Deep-anchored," and that is a title that fits the Cape character of the past few generations—they were anchored deep and sure to their homes, and their families, and their moral and religious convictions, as a few still are today.

The author says the Old-Timer settled himself into a more comfortable position in his old armchair and puffed slowly on his battered corncob pipe, the silence in the room unbroken except for the ticking of the clock on the mantel and the snapping of the fire in the parlor stove. Then he started talking:

"Those were great days, young man, great days. Men were deep-anchored, and they lived hard and died hard, too, in the Service. When you've spent eighteen years a-walking the beach in fair weather and foul—pulled off to all kinds of wrecks and salvaged vessels—like as not you'll find it pretty hard to pick out the one time that stands out highest and dryest in your mind. But there's one night I'll never forget, as long as I live.

"One winter, a number of years before you were born, I had the morning watch north from High Land. We'd had a northeaster the day before, and that night the wind had backened round to the nor'west and it blowed like fury, with now and then a snow-squall, and cold as all get-out. What with the easter and the shift of wind the cross-seas were frothing and boiling right up the bank in places.

"Well, as I was saying, I had the 'daylight' north from the station. That night all the boys had been on the lookout for wrecks, but had seen nothing.

"After muggin' up on steaming hot coffee I started north along the beach. Things were lightening up a mite as the scudding black clouds were breaking up in places and the moon was beginning to shine through. In places I had to take to the bank to get out of the reach of the big rollers. Whenever I could I went down to follow the wash along, lookin' for drift and wreckage. There was plenty of old stuff. In those days there were so many ships lost all winter that there was always plenty of old drift on the beach. I've seen the beach lined with slathers of it.

"When I got to the Half-way House I was pretty tuckered, I can tell you it's no fun walking along the beach with heavy rubber boots, with a freezin' wind a-drivin' the stingin' sand in your face and eyes, but the watch before me had left a good warm fire and it didn't take me very long to get warm.

"It seemed as if I waited for nigh a year, and still the watch from the High Head station showed no signs of comin'. So I decided to walk up to meet him. I had a funny kind of feeling that something was wrong to the nor'ard.

"Those days there weren't any telephones strung up between stations. If the man you were supposed to meet didn't show up after a reasonable time we had to go along his beat till we met him or found out what was wrong.

"So I started along the beach toward High Head. The weather was still pretty wild, but the tide was ebbing and I followed the beach all the way. The seas had washed up a lot of stuff and 'twan't long before I began to see drift that told me there had been a wreck up north. I started poking over some wreckage that was all wound and snarled with kelp and seaweed, and found a bucket.

"Now a dozen buckets on the beach might not mean anything, but this one did. It belonged to a station lifeboat. I carried it along with me—and by this time I was feeling pretty nervous. Then I found an oar from a lifeboat, and I was pretty sartin that something had happened to one of the crews north of us.

"I turned right around and started back to the station as fast as a fair wind and rubber boots would let me. On my way back I stumbled across a lifebelt marked 'U.S.L.-SS.' and seems as if my heart sank way down in my boot soles when I picked it up.

"The Old Man was eatin' breakfast when I walked into the station. When he looked at the lifebelt in my hand he had a pretty good idea what was comin'. I told him what I'd seen, and that there was a vessel wrecked to the nor'ard of us, too. He jumped up from the table and began snapping out orders.

" 'Number 2 and Number 4 start to the south'ard as fast as you can hipper.' Then to me, 'You get some coffee while me and Number 5 are gettin' ready, and come to the nor'ard with us.'

"We felt pretty jumpy as we plowed through the sand north. We were used to pickin' up bodies, but it makes a big difference whether you expect to find a stranger's body or that of a fellow surfman. Quarter of a mile beyond the Half-way House, half way down the rising, laying where the ebbing tide had left it, was the body of Captain Atkins of the Peakéd Hill station. I wisht I could tell you how we felt as we stood there with uncovered heads lookin' down at the body of the man we all knew and thought a heap of. For a minute we stood in that gray morning, too full for words, with the ocean thundering and grumbling and hissing at our feet. We lifted the remains and carried it up to the bank and put it in the shelter of some drift. You know, the captain was the father of young Atkins of our crew.

"A little farther on we spied another body just outside the smother and drifting to the south'ard. The Old Man left Number 5 to follow the body alongshore and him and me started back to the station at a dog trot. Never a word did we say to each other all the way back. Young Atkins had just come in from the south'ard and was sittin' near the stove when we come in. The Old Man went over to him and laying a hand on his shoulder, sez in a voice gentle as a woman's, 'Atkins, my boy, go upstairs and stay till I call you. We have just picked up your father's body on the beach.'

"Young feller, did you ever wound a rabbit and go up to finish him and be gripped by the pitiful, stricken look in his big eyes? Well, sir, that's just the way that poor chap looked at us. Then he got up without a word and clumped slowlike up the steps, like a man walkin' in his sleep.

"The Old Man turns to me and says in a husky voice, 'Skuppy, you and the rest of the crew take the wagon and get the bodies. I'm going up to the Light to telegrapn the superintendent.'

"Near the station we met Number 5, who had been follerin' the other body along. It was almost in the wash. One of our crew, a big strapper named McKinnon, tied a rope about his waist for us to hold onto so the undertow couldn't get him, and after a tussle he dragged it ashore. The two men who had gone to the south'ard brought in another body. We had found that morning the bodies of three of the Peakéd Hill men—Atkins, Taylor and Maho.

"They had lost their lives that night fightin' in the cold and dark to save the crew of the wrecked sloop *C. M. Trumbull*—you've heard that story a good many times.

"Well, sir, how we hated to walk the beach the next night! When it came time for the sunset watch the Old Man saw how we felt. 'Boys,' he says, 'for the next few nights we'll double on each watch.' And for the next week you can imagine our feelings as the two of us, side by side, mighty thankful of each other's company, where before we had never felt lonely, walked the moonlit beach."

Of course the big story at High Land and along there is the wreck of the steamer in the storm that was given her name—the *Portland*. People still remembered it vividly, for it happened in the autumn of 1898. I heard the story from Isaac Morton Small and his wife. Their house was near the edge of the cliff, and they got the full force of the hundred-mile gale. In fact all the windows on the windward side of the house were blown in. They tried stuffing pillows in the first window that went, but the pillows were snatched out and whirled away and never found. A mattress was jammed into the opening, but it went the way of the pillows, so they gave up and took refuge in the lee side of the house. Just before it grew too dark to see they looked out and saw a sight they had never seen before—the ocean white. Foam covered it completely, with no patches of dark water between. Next morning patches of foam lay on the grass, 140 feet above the surface of the water.

Nothing could have lived in a sea like that. The *Portland*, which had the Boston-to-Portland run, had been warned by the weather bureau but sailed as usual that gray November afternoon. Blown far out of her course, she kept afloat that night and all next day. At four in the afternoon the Coast Guard at Race Point heard two sharp blasts of her whistle, as they suppose. That night at ten o'clock the patrolmen from that station south came on her wreckage and some bodies. Of course no one knows just where she went down, but the ship-wise and storm-wise men of Truro think it must have been ten or twelve miles north of High Land Light.

A man in Centerville, Charles L. Ayling, had a room in his basement fixed up as a ship's cabin and in it stood a ship's steering wheel with the name PORTLAND painted on it. The wheel was picked up on this outer shore.

Mr. Small, whom I mentioned above, was born here on the highlands of North Truro, and when I first met him he had just celebrated his eightieth birthday by making a hole-in-one on his golf links near the lighthouse. These links have the most original and characteristic clubhouse of all the many on the Cape, for it is the cabin of a wrecked ship brought up from the beach below. It sits there complete, with pilot house, bridge and steering wheel, with a ship's ladder from the deck. Inside the cabin, used for lounge and lockers, the beams were still marked "certified to the use of steering gear" or "certified to sleeping quarters for 4 seamen," and so on. Her name board hangs above the bridge—*Coleraine*. She had been wrecked on the beach, and the owners told Mr. Small he could have her cabin if he could get it. So he got it. When I asked him, marveling, how he managed to get it up the cliff, he said airily, "Oh, we cut it in two and ran it up on skids."

There is a small country store near the lighthouse for the convenience of the summer boarders. Its windows are all frosted glass. This is not an attempt at fancy decor, but the result of the sand blown up from the beach far below and ground on the window panes. Every so often they have to take the glass out and put new panes in. One pane is hinged so it can be opened for the telescope to poke out.

A woman had the rather lonely job of reporting ships to towboat companies in Boston. She was on duty all day long, every day in the year, and little of a nautical nature escaped her bright sea-wise eyes. Many of the freighters and liners and tankers she knew by sight. If she could not read the name with her powerful long spy-glass, about as long as she was tall, she looked for something distinctive in the stacks or upperworks.

You spy a black speck away out on the still blue summer ocean, and you ask uncertainly if that is a ship? Or just a bit of driftwood? Miss Williams would raise her glass and take a hasty squint at it. "Yes, the *Scythia*," she would say, "red funnel with black top." And she'd turn to her telegraph key and send the information clicking up to Boston.

Whenever there was a high wind she was kept busy

sending the news of its speed to the Boston weather bureau, for they get all the wind there is at High Land and they get it from every direction. The anemometer box on the windowsill gave her the speed—it was only three miles, that midsummer day, but she watched it go to 100 the night of the *Portland* storm.

Back in the days when Truro had a harbor it had a couple of thousand people and was a thriving town. But that was a century ago, and since then the harbor has filled up and the population has dwindled to about five hundred, many of them artists and writers who have bought some of the old homesteads and settled down in the contented Cape way.

Some of those left in the town are not even old-line Americans, but they seem to have taken on something of the old-line character and guts. I met a man with a Portuguese name who was pioneering in fruit. He was out to prove you could make a living growing fruit in sand. An experienced orchardist, he stuck to his thesis and proved it to the hilt. Not only did he raise enough apples and peaches to market profitably at retail but he won prizes for them at county fairs—not just Barnstable Fair, either.

At the start people warned him he might raise a few apples, but no use trying to raise peaches. "You might have thought, to hear them talk," he said, "that there was a law against peaches in this county."

When he had shown them, he turned to town affairs. With so small a population an able-minded man has to do his part. He was town treasurer and town clerk and tax collector at that time, and dear knows what by now. It gave him so much to do that he was limiting himself to three hundred trees, what he called a man-and-a-half size orchard—his time and part of another's. Of course he had small fruits besides, not to mention a cow and poultry and a garden.

Growing fruit anywhere down-Cape, you are up against two things. One is the sand, the other is the wind. He got round the sand by putting in plenty of fertilizer and doing a lot of cultivating, which he considered necessary to hold what moisture there was. As for the wind—the lay of the land in Truro, with its hills and valleys, is a help. He planted his trees on the sheltered slopes and set out a wind-break of pines above them. As a result, when you drove along the main highway you could see his trim little white house with its neat outbuildings and white picket fences, but the orchard was out of sight behind a hill. He told me how beautiful it was in springtime, and showed me pictures he had taken when it was in full bloom which certainly bore out his words.

There was a pear tree on the place which showed what fruit could do in Truro. The original sapling had been washed ashore from a wreck a hundred years before. Some-one picked it up and planted it here on this farm. Its fruit was poor—a little button pear that was mealy rather than juicy, so the orchardist's father grafted Clapp's Favorite on all its branches. When I saw it, it was still bearing about half a peck of the old kind, but that fall it had produced a good bushel of excellent pears. All around the tree the soil was like snow—white sand!

At one period of her long history it may have been true, as the children's jingle says, that if it hadn't been for her milk-carts Truro would have died. But she did have them, and the cows to back them, so she came through. Today she has the artists.

It is a perfect place for them—its own natural and paintable beauty, its lovely little old farmhouses to be had for a price, its simple and unexacting way of life. It is only five or ten miles from Provincetown, too, which is near enough when it is wanted, and far enough when it is not. Some go up to town for the winter, others stay down and see it through. There is nothing dull about a normal winter.

Somebody showed me a picture of a Truro artist dressed up for the annual Beachcombers' ball in Provincetown, and that is how I came to meet Gerrit Beneker. In the picture he was a sailor of 1812 with white bell trousers, a short jacket with brass buttons and a black sailor hat, and half-moon whiskers. In his hand he carried a parrot cage complete with parrot. In fact, Beneker had made the parrot himself out of a crookneck squash with tail and wings of corn husks. A fine spunky bird it was, too.

His eye for the decorative had already made him famous. He had discovered the artistic possibilities of the American working man and immortalized them in a prize-winning poster for The Other War. Those who can remember back that far will remember that man, for he looked out from three million posters all over the land—a husky bronzed giant in old felt hat and blue overalls plastered with war-drive buttons who proclaimed "We'll finish the job!" A man in Provincetown posed for it.

I found the Benekers—three children besides father and mother—living a nice normal American life in their old Cape house with its white paint and blue blinds and its glimpse of the Bay through a cleft in the dunes. The living room had the usual white wainscot and paneled mantel above the plain brick fireplace, and the usual comfortable furniture to go with it—nothing in the least arty or exotic. But it had a rich glow of color from the paintings on the walls—Beneker's own pictures, their colors heavy-larded on the canvas with a magic that made them light and dancing to the eye. He had just finished a portrait of MacMillan, who was a down-Cape hero since he had been lucky enough to be born in Provincetown.

Presently we all piled into their car and headed for their pet bathing beach. It was off the beaten track, up a hill and off into a winding lane and across a sunny tarn where tall rushes and cattails grew so thick they looked like an etching. The little road skirted the shoulders of sand hills where pines and poplars and huckleberry bushes grew, and paused in the shadow of Corn Hill before running out onto the beach—a good beach it was, too, on the Bay Side, but Corn Hill was the big item for me right then.

Yes—the one and only Corn Hill. There sixteen of the Pilgrim Fathers, led as a tablet states by Myles Standish and William Bradford, on November 16, 1620—this number 16 seems to turn up—discovered a cache of corn buried by the Indians for their winter food. With what searchings of heart and soul we can never know but only hope, they took ten bushels of it, paying it back the following year. They named it Corn Hill.

One day I set out by myself to go to the top of the hill, but the road ended in a barnyard and there was only a footpath to the summit. My notes mention a sawtooth row of old gray summer cottages against the sky "like comb of underbred rooster."

But the view comes back without the help of notes. It was May—late May. The moors were in full blow with yellow gorse and purple vetch and the creamy foam of beach plums and the fragrant green of sweetfern and bay. Far

apart on their winding lanes little white houses with flow-
ering lilacs in their dooryards. Meandering through its
marshes wandered the Pamet river, a small tidewater stream
crossing nearly to the ocean.

Surely some day God will let me go back to Truro in
the spring.

19. *Provincetown for Beauty*

PERHAPS by this time the state has caught up with it, but when I knew the Cape it had the best roads in Massachusetts. However, this was a modern development. There was a time, and not so long ago, when it had the worst. Positively the worst. For this I had the word of a man who should know, Charles L. Ayling of Centerville. He drove the first automobile to enter Provincetown—drove it all the way from Centerville, a good round fifty miles of misery. He found out about the roads, and he never forgot.

It happened in 1901, and Mr. Ayling was the proud owner of a Stanley Steamer. If you are that old you remember the little red devils with their bicycle tires and their guest seat up front over the engine. I had my first auto ride in such a car and on such a guest seat, and there is no thrill in the world of transportation to compare with it. I rode in the open cockpit of a seaplane before the days of windshields, so I know.

Mr. Ayling had already driven his little contraption as far as Eastham, and that is half way to Provincetown. It had not been any picnic, but he made it. Easthamites used to consider it all a horse could do in a day to go over to Orleans—three miles—and back. If you had a real good horse he might make it in half a day, but he had to have a good long rest before being used again.

For one thing the roads were not graded—they followed,

as I have said before, old Indian trails, using whatever contours nature provided and detouring any rock or stump or barn they might encounter. If the hill was steep, why, the road was steep, too, as a matter of course. The roads themselves, outside the villages, consisted of two ruts. The grading would not have mattered if the roads had been reasonable.

The ruts were the unfortunate feature. If they had been the same distance apart as the Stanley's wheels, they would have been all right, for the little car had clearance enough. But they were not. Most of us have forgotten a detail of the not-so-distant past, but it was still fresh in Mr. Ayling's memory when he told me about it—Cape carts and wagons and buggies had to be specially built for sandy roads, a wider gauge than those of the rest of the civilized world. Those old blue beach wagons of theirs, and all their other rolling stock, had wheels with a good six inches wider spread than mainland vehicles. So naturally the ruts they made in the sand were six inches wider, too. No car or cart brought in from "away" could possibly track in them. If the wheels on one side were in, as they were sure to be, the wheels on the other side were out, and out meant up—scrabbling along on the sand several inches higher.

In the villages you might find good shell roads, or anyhow gravel, but not between them. Just long stretches of sand.

"Dead sand," said Mr. Ayling, "without any bottom to it."

That was why everybody said the trip couldn't be made. Nobody ever had driven an auto through to Provincetown, and nobody ever would. Period. There must have been moments—plural number—when he agreed with them.

One bright summer morning, just after daylight, he and a friend climbed aboard with a box of lunch and an extra can of gasoline and chuffed boldly out of the Ayling stable. They had to take the gasoline because in those days there were no gas stations on the King's Highway—and in fact no King's Highway worth mentioning.

The first little steamers burned kerosene to heat the water to produce the steam to furnish the power to get her there and get her back, in theory anyhow. But later models used gasoline. They were pretty smooth propositions once they got going, though that took time because the water had to be heated till it boiled, to get up steam enough for pressure. Once that was done, off the car went with a whoosh, and ran along gently and quietly—I always regretted the steamers, they were so much softer going than even the modern combustion-engine cars.

This car could make thirty-five miles with a tail wind, if she could be kept on the road while she was making it. On a hill she had plenty of power, too, for a short spurt, but she tired easily. On this trip she never had a chance to show her speed. It ranged from o to 15 m.p.h. with the emphasis on o.

They were thirsty little brutes, those steamers, but luckily every village had its watering trough for horses, and so at every village the Stanley stopped for a drink. How the news of its coming got round is a mystery, for there were no phones in those days, not to speak of. But everywhere the entire population of the place turned out to have a look at the car. Sea captains, fishermen, farmers, women with their aprons thrown over their heads or with calico sunbonnets, children of all ages and sizes, they flocked to the watering trough to see this red monster

BEACH GRASS, NAUSET

AN ELABORATE DEVELOPMENT OF THE CAPE HOUSE, WELLFLEET

STUDIO QUARTER, PROVINCETOWN

OUT BACK, PROVINCETOWN

with its steaming breath. A more daring youngster would venture to lay a timid hand on the car, but his mother would snatch him back—no knowing what minute it might blow up.

Men and women all told Mr. Ayling the same thing— he'd never in the Lord's world make Provincetown in a contraption like that. If it didn't blow up it would certainly bog down.

Stops for water were few compared with stops for other reasons, most of them tires. Tires weren't what they are today, they were smooth-treaded, fragile things, practically bicycle tires. Punctures and blow-outs were almost hourly occurrences, and the driver took along a repair kit and plugged the holes as they happened. The idea of spares had not percolated, but it would have taken a lot, and the operator would have to do his own repairing anyhow, sooner or later, for there were no repairmen anywhere.

Horses slowed things up, too. It was years before they got used to motor cars, and this first one was specially terrifying. The two pioneers had a regular routine—the friend got out and held the horse's head while Ayling stuck to the tiller. If the horse was reasonable he was led past the car, but if he balked his head was held while the car was driven past him.

Getting stuck in the sand was what slowed them most. It happened more and more frequently beyond the East-hams. They averaged about a stop a mile, all told, on the trip, and they never stopped unless they had to.

Getting stuck meant going into the woods and cutting branches of scrub pine to put under the wheels to give them traction. The men could not stop to pick up the branches to take along to use next time, because if they once got going they wouldn't want to stop. It was easier to cut a fresh supply each time.

But where there were hills, as in Truro, they needed more than pine boughs, they had to get out and push. And the passenger and driver had to do some fancy stepping to get aboard again when the car started. One such stop was in front of Truro's hilltop cemetery—and Mr. Ayling said to his friend, "I see your finish, Bill!"

Riding along—when they did ride—was not too comfortable, because one side of the car was so much higher than the other from being up out of the rut. It also complicated the steering. You had to fight the tiller all the way.

At dusk they came to the beginning of the long main street in Provincetown. Little Stan was fresh as a daisy, showed no sign of strain at all, but the two men were weary and exhausted and wanted nothing so much as something to eat and a bed to tumble into. But the news of their approach had grapevined ahead of them, so they were met in state by the Town Crier with his clanging bell. He stalked before them into town ringing his bell and calling out the townspeople to see this strange ungodly sight. That was not his main purpose, though; he felt the need of keeping the street clear of horses and teams so no damage would be done—he was without a doubt the Cape's first traffic officer.

A crowd gathered and fell in behind the car, awestruck and docile. They were indeed afraid to venture too near, and kept a respectful distance between themselves and the little red demon, but they followed along to see what the end of this strange business might be.

The pioneers were eager to reach the shelter of the old

Gifford House on the upper street. Now the town's lay-out is, as always, that of a ladder which parallels the water-front for three or four miles—two long streets connected at intervals by steep little lanes or cross-roads. They are steep because the upper street is much higher than the lower street—the ladder rests on edge.

When the Stanley came to the lane which led up to Bradford Street, where the hotel was, she paused, and her owner took an appraising look at the grade. The crowd closed in about them and began telling them they couldn't possibly make it, not in that contraption—better get a couple of good horses and hitch onto it, the hill was so steep they wouldn't get half way up.

But little Stanley showed them. She was, as I said, good for a spurt and she spurted—headed round into the lane and whoosh! up she went in a red flash and a cloud of steam, like the demon she resembled. The folks stared after her open-mouthed and open-eyed.

But her troubles were not over when she got to the hotel. The proprietor refused point blank to let them park the car anywhere near his place. The goldurned thing might blow up in the middle of the night, and then where would his hotel be? He was taking no chances. Owners of near-by barns felt the same way. They did not want their barns exploding, especially in the middle of the night. After some hunting the two weary men located an old barn away out in the middle of a field back of the town and put the car up there. They knew nobody would monkey with it, the folks would be afraid of its blowing up.

Next morning Ayling and his passenger set out on a search for gasoline. They had a little left, but not enough to get them home. This was their sole chance to tank up.

First they went to the drugstore. The druggist gave them all he had, which was a gallon. He suggested the paint shop, and they bought out the painter's entire stock, three gallons. He told them they now had all there was in town. They paid seventy-five cents a gallon for what they got.

The trip back to Centerville was the same as the trip down, only in reverse. Same stops, same crowds, same experiences except for one thing—nobody told them now that it couldn't be done. It had been done. But I may add it was a whole year before anyone else did it.

Provincetown still had a town crier in those days—in fact the last of the famous line did not retire until the year I was on the Cape. They did not replace him, but they surely will when the local chamber of commerce wakes up to his value as atmosphere.

The criers kept the town informed of what was going on in town as well as in the world outside. One of the earlier criers gave a momentous story to the world—nothing less than the arrival in town of the "great red dragon" of Revelation—he saw it with his own eyes. He was sober too—he made solemn affidavy that he was not "unduly excited by liquor or otherwise."

First he saw a great commotion half a mile out from shore off Herring Cove, a whirlpool it was, twenty feet across. Out of it poked a great head "big as a 200-gallon cask" with six eyes the size of dinner plates, three red and three light green. The crier hid himself and watched. The creature surfaced and swam toward shore, came within thirty feet of where he was hidden. Its body was three hundred feet long and covered with fish scales the size of a barrel-head. The open mouth showed four rows of teeth, each of them a couple of feet long. Whether it was a bad breath or b.o. we shall never know, but he smelled strongly of sulphur, and he was so hot he scorched the beach grass when he came ashore. He put off cross-lots for Pasture Pond and disappeared, taking the water down with him into a hole which has proved to be bottomless—all this according to the crier's sworn affidavit.

But the last of the criers, Walter Smith, never had the luck to break so remarkable a story. His had been the usual tales of storm and stress and lost and found and fishing boats in and their hauls—routine stuff. He was seventy-eight when he retired, and had only held the job for twenty-seven years—that is, legally. But he began when he was five, really, trudging along at the heels of the crier of that day, Ambrose Hill. There had been many between Hill and himself, including Briggs, Howard, Coleman, Atwood, MacCurdy, Turner and the man who saw the sarpint. Each of them was a character in his own right.

The earliest known inhabitant of Provincetown was like the dragon in one respect—she left no descendants. This was the mermaid whom Hendrik Hudson's men reported seeing when they went ashore looking for water and found wild grapes. The Pilgrims did not mention her when they came along ten years later, so she must have died, perhaps of old age—or are mermaids forever young and fair? I wouldn't know. It may simply have been that the wild grapes were out of season when they landed.

Compared with most of the Cape villages Provincetown looks like a city. It has indeed four thousand people the year round, a fourth of whom are native Yankees and the rest Portuguese. In summer it crams in several thousand more, mostly devotees of the three arts. Many of these are the arty sort, hangers-on of the arts rather than true artists, but amongst them are some of the great names in American painting and drama and letters. Although the Cape Cod element has lost hold of the town politically, it has kept it looking much the same as it always has. It still looks essentially like Provincetown, and that is unlike any other town or village on this green earth.

Cupped in the curving hand of the Cape's end it runs east and west along the shore of the sheltered harbor. Once this beach was the only highway and all the houses fronted on it as on a street, facing south. Then the county ran a street along behind them and some of their owners turned them round to face the street and others moved theirs bodily back across it, keeping them still with their faces to the south. Provincetown folks make a point of doing that when they can. There is not much room between the street and the beach, and most of it is jammed with small shops and sheds and dock-houses and so on. On the landward side are still many of the cottage houses with their scraps of white-picketed, gay-flowered dooryards, and a few—mercifully few—of a later Victorian vintage. In summer these small old houses are more than likely to be shops of one sort or another—antiques, local curios, rugs. When fall comes the owners pull in their signs and their window-shows and return to the business of living—on the hay they have made during the two or three months of financial sunshine. I always hoped for a chance to spend a winter in Provincetown, for that is when you really get the feeling of the place. The people have the clubs and church socials and friendly get-togethers for which they have no time in summer.

The town has a double life, in fact I suspect there is a lot of color and interest in its third, or Portuguese, phase, only it seems to have been generally overlooked, by others as well as by me. But in spite of its multiple aspects the town retains its unity, still can call its soul its own. What sort of fight this has involved, what courage and persistence and gritting of Yankee teeth, no outsider can ever know. We can only hope that some day the inside story of Provincetown may be written—by an insider.

Commercial street was not meant for automobiles, it was laid out for democrat wagons and beach wagons and buggies. Two cars can pass all right, but not three. The sidewalks are the same way—good for two but not three. If the street were straight it would be easier navigating, but it follows faithfully the meander-line of the beach. When the tourist traffic is at its height in summer and the Boston boat disgorges its daily hordes of picnickers, the congestion really is something. A Provincetown traffic cop can give points to anyone in the business.

It is a jolly good-natured mob, and what with the clean salt air blowing freshly through and the bright sun laughing down and the colorful art students and flowers and all —nobody minds.

Next to the lobster stew in an upstairs eatery the thing I remember most vividly about that street is the smell of a couple of salt cod drying on the door of a weathered old fish-house on the water side. A whiff of air brought the smell across the narrow sidewalk. You know what a smell can do to you, when it comes straight out of your past? Removes you instantly from where you are to where you were last time you smelled it. I was a small girl down in Maine in my grandmother's back shed where she kept, as every orderly housewife did, a stack of strip-fish.

Strip-fish was the greatest delicacy of my childhood.

Cod, hake or haddock split wide open and flattened to the size and shape of a boy's kite, its backbone and innards removed, flesh soaked in brine and spread out on flakes— wooden racks—to dry in the sun. In that Maine village the fishermen used an island in the cove for the drying be- cause it was free from dust and interference. The result was entirely different from the flabby white stuff sold in the stores to be made into codfish balls. That had to be cooked, and even then it didn't taste natural. Strip-fish was firm and solid and tanned a deep ivory or golden brown by the honest sunshine instead of bleached God- knows-how. You gripped the fish firmly with one hand and stripped the strips off with the other. Then, if you were piecening, as I generally was, you ate it straight. Oh, man, it was good! My mouth waters for it now. Many a supper we had of it in the big old farmhouse kitchen— strip-fish 'n' baked potatoes dripping with butter just out of the churn, and all the milk you could drink still warm from the little Jersey cow out in the barn. No doubt many a Cape Cod child grew up on meals like that, too.

The fish which I saw and smelled was probably caught and cured by a Portuguese fisherman, and might not have tasted the same. The *American Guide* says it is called skully-jo—and the kids carry it around in their pockets like candy, which well they might. I would. It should be incorporated into the summer "atmosphere" along with the town crier, for it belongs to the town's past as well as its present.

Most of the atmosphere of the town is honestly come by, like the figurehead of the lovely lady perched on the front-porch roof of one of the houses. Her head and shoulders were carved of wood and set up beneath the bowsprit of some elegant and spirited ship. I met a woman who saw her picked up, for when the woman was a little girl she sailed with her mother on the vessel of which her father was captain. It was back in 1866, and the vessel was a whaling schooner out of Provincetown. Out in mid-ocean the lookout spied what he thought at first was the body of a woman floating face up in the water. A boat put out to her and picked her up. Nobody knows who she was or the name of her ship, or can guess how she became separated from it. Just another little mystery of the sea.

A Provincetown woman—Nancy Smith, who wrote *The Provincetown Book*—did an article for the magazine on the fanlighted doorways of the town. "Houses here have never been pretentious," she says. "This was the richest town in the state, per capita, in 1850, but it was not the fashion to build any but the one-story Cape house with small windows and simple doors. Both our doors and our windows were made to shut out the cold wind from houses that faced the storms."

Under one house in Provincetown is a strange stone wall, found when the builder was excavating for his cellar, about 1850. It was thirty feet below the original level of the ground there, and was of rocks laid in mortar, but the rocks were like none to be found anywhere around. At the base of the wall they found the remains of a cleverly packed floor, and of a fireplace. It is called the Norse Wall House, and people believe it is the remains of a Norse dwelling. Students say that the Viking ships carried such rocks as ballast.

Here near Provincetown is supposed to be the site of the Keelness mentioned in the sagas—one of their boats was wrecked there and they had to repair it. They named it for the new keel they put in—Cape Keel. If Nauset was their Wonder Strand and Chase Garden River their Crossness, it is logical to regard this as their Keelness. "Ness" means cape or headland.

There have been many wrecks around the tip end of the Cape since the days of the Norsemen. Even the harbor, sheltered as it is, feels the force of a southerly gale. I happened along shortly after such a storm and saw the effects of it. The Coast Guard cutter *Morrill* had been moored there when the wind came, and she broke away from her moorings and set out to make an impression on the immediate waterfront. While it lasted it must have been wild for all concerned.

The storm came up from the s'uth'ard and gathered speed till by nine o'clock that night it was coming in at eighty miles an hour. It got by the tip of Wood End Point and focused on the cutter. The crashing and the crunching of her steel bow as she rammed into whatever got in her way resounded over a good part of Provincetown. Her lights and her wildly playing searchlight plunged and swung with her through the stormy dark as she reeled broadside in the rollers piled in by the wind, or staggered forward head on, or swung back in a lull and started in all over again.

The wharves and piers were crowded with sightseers, including the young bride of the *Morrill's* captain, till someone on the cutter roared out through a megaphone, "Everybody get off the wharves!" That order probably saved lives, for the wharves were pretty well wrecked.

One long wharf was a stump at the shore or landward end, and an island farther out. The cutter had cavorted into it head on and annihilated its middle reaches. A pier had completely disappeared except at low tide when a few snags could still be seen sticking up through the sand. The scanty remains of what had been the white casino buildings on the end of this pier sat drunkenly upon the beach.

The *Morrill* herself took it all in her stride. She went back to Boston a few days later under her own steam, little the worse for wear.

It was the Provincetown Players who put the place on the American map, though the native population is inclined to lay it to the Pilgrims. But the Players took their company and their name to Broadway and showed the world how plays should be acted—revolutionized the cut-and-dried hamming of the ancients, which has never been the same since.

After them came several companies. The Wharf Players had a jolly little theater out on a wharf. It was fun listening to the water swishing around the pilings in the dark away down under. In fact I liked it so much that after I went back to Boston I took a loft on T Wharf and spent five happy years there. Wharves are, I think, the best of all places to work and to live—and to play.

The Winston-Moore Players had a little theater in a barn just off the waterfront. It was there I saw for the first time a production of Eugene O'Neill's famous play, *Anna Christie*. It was written in Provincetown, if I remember rightly. Anyhow the scene is laid on a barge. It was foggy that night in Provincetown and the foghorn was blowing and the fog sifted in with the smell of the sea through the open door, and audience and actors were one in it. The curtain was rung up by a ship's bell, and the exit was marked by the larboard light of a ship. The audience was completely aboard that barge.

That company was specially respected in town, I heard. "No funnydiddles," the townspeople said. They had a cook they adored. She mothered and chaperoned and cooked for them. Her offer, early in the season, to wait for her pay till it came handy to give it to her went to their hearts. So far she had not had to wait, and from the looks of the house that foggy evening she would not have to. There had been a moment near the start of the venture when the business manager had to borrow a postage stamp, but now they were square with the world and going strong.

In summer the cultural life of the town is exceptional for anywhere. Nobody goes there merely to rest and enjoy himself, he goes to find some sort of intellectual release— maybe emotional too—to get some of the work done that he feels he can not do anywhere else. There are of course a lot of dilettanti, but enough first-rate work has been done to justify the place. The art museum is open, the art classes in full swing and the studio life going handsome—not to mention the little theaters and the writers and musicians. Several times during the summer I took Lizy Jane down the fifty miles from Centerville for a first night or a one-man show at the gallery. She was not much larger or spunkier than the Stanley, but things had changed a lot in twenty-five years. I did not have to stop for water or fixing flats or dead sand, and we did not have to ride high on one side because of ruts, for there were no ruts any longer, just smooth black highways a driver could forget about.

But life really begins, as I intimated, in the fall when the outsiders depart and the place is left to its normal quiet little self. Don't imagine the cultural life of the community is over, either, when the sight-seeing bus stops running. You don't know the New England woman and especially the Cape Cod woman if you suppose that. They would find something worth doing anywhere.

One of their liveliest interests is the Historical Museum. At that time it was an active and going concern, managed by sixty ladies, all of whom were descended from the same *Mayflower* ancestor, Samuel Hopkins. A highly successful progenitor, I should say. There were not sixty to begin with, only six, and it was thirty or forty years ago when they woke up to the fact that Provincetown was rapidly losing its precious store of historical possessions. Not only were people selling them off to collectors at ridiculously low prices but many, in their ignorance of what was of value and what was not, were actually throwing them away on the town dump! (Whence they were being salvaged by impecunious artists to feather their fish-house studios.)

The women did what we women always do, they had them a club. Just a small study club at first—but not the usual kind. They studied their own families and collected old stories and legends and folklore and put it in papers to read at their meetings. On the side they began a humble collection of "old things," till they had a small showcaseful. This emboldened them to consider buying a small cottage for a museum—some quaint picturesque little place. By now they had increased their membership to twenty-four and started an earnest drive to stop the exodus of antiques and get them together for exhibition.

The kind of house they wanted was fortunately not to be had, for it would soon have been too small. Instead they had to take what they could get, an ugly Victorian mansion with a mansard roof, painted brown as such a house deserved to be, but very—oh, very—dignified. It was none too large, for the contributions came pouring in; and by now it must be stuffed to overflowing. The club enlarged itself to sixty, all as I have said granddaughters many times great of one *Mayflower* ancestor—and, no doubt, of most of the other Pilgrims as well. But these ladies, flower of New England aristocracy though they were, were no more afraid of hard work than their illustrious foremothers. They got brooms and mops and pails and went to work to clean that big house from roof to cellar, scrubbing the big high-posted rooms till they shone. Cleverly they divided their membership into committees, gave each committee a room to clean, garnish and—fill.

I judge the filling was the easiest part. One room was turned over to Donald MacMillan for his Arctic trophies. Another is devoted to whaling implements. In the book room I was specially interested in a Bible dated 1690 that was rescued from the British warship *Somerset* when she came ashore on Peakéd Hill Bar while chasing full tilt after a Frenchman. The seas lifted her over and threw her up on the beach, and the thrifty townsfolk took care of whatever was of value to them. That was in 1778—remember the lines in "Paul Revere's Ride"—

> Where swinging wide at her moorings lay
> The *Somerset*, British man-of-war.

To get the quality which makes this museum different one should prowl through it at the heels of a local Yankee. You come to the picture of a girl of long ago and he says, "Yes, I remember seeing her when I was a child, but she was an old lady then." You look at the portrait of Jonathan Cook, and you hear that he was the richest man in town in his day—why, he had silver spoons on his table! The guide knows, because his grandmother told him. He keeps recognizing family dishes and furniture and remembering stories about them. A museum is fun when you go through it like that.

In Truro I mentioned Beneker's going to the Beachcombers' Ball in Provincetown. This is an annual affair and combines the entrancements of a mardi-gras, a barndance and a Fourth-of-July parade. Everybody takes some part. The affair begins with a parade through the streets to the Town Hall. There the spectators line up to form an aisle for the paraders to pass through, only it is really a gauntlet. The costumes receive a lot of free and fearless criticism before their wearers get them safely into the hall. There they are judged and prizes awarded—sometimes pictures by local artists. The ball gives scope for the sort of originality in which this colony delights; and it is certainly colorful.

Just why artists are so keen about Provincetown is a subject much discussed. It may be the lighting. Whether or not one is conscious of it, it's there—comes down and hits the water all around and then reflects onto the land and diffuses—something like that. Any time of day and any kind of weather the lighting is what might be called atmospheric if you can forgive the word. Just a matter of vibrations, maybe . . . Sunrises and sunsets are both over the water—out of the sea in the morning, into the sea at night.

But say you are not an artist, and have driven down from Boston today. Only 125 miles—but there was so much to see along the route that you have taken all day for it, and are jaded. So you look up a room for the night in one of the little old houses where they rent the front chamber to tourists—I wonder if it still has a washstand in the corner with a bowl and jug?—and you feed yourself a good meal at one of the many tea rooms or restaurants.

Then what to do with the evening? Something restful and easy on the nerves. No more old houses or early-Americana, no more summer theaters or water sports. Somebody asks, "Why don't you drive Out Back and see the sunset?"

I have forgotten just where the road takes off, but it heads for the Race Point life-saving station and makes a loop round the end of the Cape. It takes you onto the beach and you drive over the *Somerset* buried dear knows how far below you in the sand. But mostly it takes you over the dunes—golden sand with coarse beach grass vivid green in the slanting sunlight, black clumps of scrub pines planted to hold the sand there for you, mats of scented bayberry on the sand—but forever dunes, dunes, dunes. On the beaches beyond them the ocean is breaking softly. The light is changing all the time and land and sea and sky change with it, and you yourself are changing.

A breath of evening wind comes playing about you and turns the grass now this way, now that.

It is a wide and magic world, and all your own. Cape Cod—and you love it, too.